Up Against Foucault

This book introduces key aspects of Foucault's work to feminists in ways which are less intimidating and abstracted than much of the existing literature in this area. It includes an introduction to Foucault's terms and fills a gap in the literature by clarifying the links between the everyday realities of women's lives and Foucault's work on sexuality and power. The contributors explore the implications of including gender in analyses of power relations, sexuality and the body. They bring their expertise from different locations in social theory and philosophy to bear on some core issues: the ways in which Foucault provokes feminists into questioning their grasp of power relations and the implications of the absence of gender in his work.

They show that in spite of his own lack of interest in gender, Foucault does appear to have much to offer feminism. He proposes new ways of understanding the control of women and especially the control of sexuality and bodies. In addition the contributors cover new ground in relating Foucault's challenge to feminism to feminism's challenge to Foucault. Feminists are up against Foucault because he questions the key conclusions which feminists have come to about the nature of gender relations, and men's possession of power. This book is an appraisal of how seriously we need to take this challenge. The book will be of interest to undergraduates in sociology, cultural studies, philosophy and women's studies.

Caroline Ramazanoğlu is Senior Lecturer in Sociology, Goldsmiths' College, University of London.

Up Against Foucault

Explorations of some tensions
between Foucault and feminism

Edited by
Caroline Ramazanoğlu

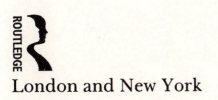

London and New York

First published 1993
by Routledge
11 New Fetter Lane, London EC4P 4EE

Simultaneously published in the USA and Canada
by Routledge
29 West 35th Street, New York, NY 10001

Typeset in Baskerville by
NWL Editorial Services, Langport, Somerset

Printed and bound in Great Britain by
T.J. Press (Padstow) Ltd, Padstow, Cornwall

British Library Cataloguing in Publication Data
A catalogue record for this book is available from the
British Library.

Library of Congress Cataloging in Publication Data
Up against Foucault: explorations of some tensions
   between Foucault and feminism / [edited by] Caroline
   Ramazanoğlu.
   p. cm.
Includes bibliographical references and index.
1. Feminist theory. 2. Feminism. 3. Power (Social
sciences). 4. Sex role. 5. Foucault, Michel.
I. Ramazanoğlu, Caroline, 1939–   .
HQ1190.U6 1993   93–9861
305.42′01 – dc20   CIP

ISBN 0–415–05010–3 (hbk)
ISBN 0–415–05011–1 (pbk)

Contents

Part III Bodies and pleasures: power and resistance

      Susan Bordo   179

9   Violence, power and pleasure: a revisionist reading
      of Foucault from the victim perspective
      Dean MacCannell and Juliet Flower MacCannell   203

10 Women's sexuality and men's appropriation of desire
      Caroline Ramazanoğlu and Janet Holland   239

      Name index   265
      Subject index   267

Contributors

M.E. Bailey is a graduate student at the Johns Hopkins University, studying political theory. In what passes for her spare time she reads science fiction, romance and mystery novels, draws lots of vagina dentatas and plays bass for a feminist rock band, uberWENSCH.

Susan Bordo is Joseph C. Georg Professor of Philosophy at Le Moyne College. She is the author of *The Flight to Objectivity: Essays on Cartesianism and Culture*, SUNY Press (1987), and *Unbearable Weight: Feminism, Western Culture and the Body*, University of California Press (1993). She is also the co-editor (with Alison Jaggar) of *Gender/Body/Knowledge: Feminist Reconstructions of Being and Knowing*, Rutgers University Press (1989).

Maureen Cain is currently Professor of Sociology at the University of the West Indies, St Augustine, Trinidad. She has published widely in the fields of sociology of law and criminology, but in the last few years has concentrated her efforts in the fields of feminist criminology and feminist methodology. Her most recent works are an edited collection on the social control of adolescent girls, *Growing up Good*, Sage (1989), and *Translation and Transgression*, Open University Press (1993).

Jean Grimshaw teaches philosophy and women's studies in the Faculty of Humanities of the University of the West of England, Bristol. She is the author of *Feminist Philosophers: Women's Perspectives on Philosophical Traditions*, Wheatsheaf (1986), and the author of numerous articles and reviews, mainly concerning the relationship between women/feminism and philosophy.

Janet Holland is a Senior Research Officer at the Institute of

Education, London. She has undertaken numerous research commissions for a wide range of organisations and institutions in the United Kingdom and abroad. Publications include *Gender and Class: Adolescent Conceptions of the Division of Labour* (1986), *Equal Opportunities in the new ERA* (1990), *Hard to Reach or Out of Reach* (1991) and *Sexuality and Ethnicity: Variations in Young Women's Sexual Knowledge and Practice* (1992).

Dean MacCannell is Professor of Applied Behavioral Sciences and Sociology at the University of California, Davis. His work on the re-arrangement between the sexes includes essays on sexuality in advertising, Marilyn Monroe, pornographic film and women's face work, and (with Juliet Flower MacCannell) on the 'beauty system'. He served on the California Governor's Commission on the Status of Women in Agriculture. His 1976 book, *The Tourist: A New Theory of the Leisure Class*, helped found tourism studies globally, and one of his recent books, *Empty Meeting Grounds: The Tourist Papers* (1992), continues his concern for failed encounters in nomadic postmodernity. He co-edits *The American Journal of Semiotics* with Juliet MacCannell. He is currently working on film noir and the homeless and Baudrillard's *America*.

Juliet Flower MacCannell is Professor of English and Director of Comparative Literature at the University of California, Irvine. She was the first Director of The Program Emphasis in Women's Studies and currently directs the Organised Research Initiative in Women and the Image. She is author of *Figuring Lacan* (1986), *The Regime of the Brother: After the Patriarchy* (1991), editor of *The Other Perspective in Gender and Culture* (1990), and co-author (with Dean MacCannell) of the *The Time of the Sign* (1982). She has translated the theatrical work of Helen Cixous. She is currently working on women and war.

Maureen McNeil is a Senior Lecturer in Cultural Studies at the University of Birmingham. Her teaching, research and publication have focused on (but not been restricted to) the social relations of science and technology and she is currently writing a book about science, technology and popular culture.

Caroline Ramazanoğlu is a Senior Lecturer in Sociology at Goldsmiths' College, University of London, and has a general interest in explaining power relations. Publications include work on labour migration, *Feminism and the Contradictions of Oppression*,

Routledge (1989), and articles on sexuality and feminist methodology. She has been working with colleagues on young people and heterosexuality.

Janet Ransom has taught at Goldsmiths' College, University of London, and is currently a Lecturer at the London Guildhall University. She is completing a study of the relationship between feminist conceptions of women's autonomy, and women's own accounts which substantively question poststructuralism as a basis for feminist research.

Kate Soper is a Senior Lecturer in Philosophy at the University of North London. Her latest book is *Troubled Pleasures*, Verso (1990). She has written extensively on gender issues, and is currently preparing a work on the theme 'What is nature?'.

Chapter 1

Introduction
Caroline Ramazanoğlu

COMING TO TERMS WITH FOUCAULT

I arrived late at a women's meeting towards the end of the annual conference of the British Sociological Association a few years ago, to find some women expressing indignation at finding session after session of the conference dominated by men talking in terms of 'postmodernism'. These women said they felt silenced, intimidated, excluded, put down and angry. They did not know whether 'postmodernism' was something they should take seriously, because they could not engage with a debate which made the issues inaccessible to them. In her chapter, Susan Bordo describes her own negative encounters as a graduate student with the 'elitism' of poststructuralist thought.

The general areas of thought which have been defined (in various ways) as postmodernist and poststructuralist are, however, the intellectual context of Foucault's work. Much of the work in this area has been characterised by intellectual elitism, and a level of abstraction from experience which makes it far removed from most English-speaking feminist work. This has turned discussion of the wider relevance of Foucault's thought into a demanding academic specialism which has had little impact on feminism outside academic circles. In discussions of Foucault, those most sympathetic to his work tend to disappear into his terminology.

French feminism has been closer to engagement with the work of Foucault, within a shared intellectual context which incorporates debates over poststructuralism and postmodernism (Duchen 1986). Recent French feminist social theory has taken a distinctive approach to sexual politics and differs in its relation to women's experience from most of English-speaking feminism, although their respective concerns have some common threads (Braidotti 1991). In this book, the focus is on the implications of particular tensions around power, knowledge, identity and the body between English-speaking feminism and the work of Foucault.

It is quite feasible for feminists to come to terms with Foucault, and increasing numbers of academic feminists, particularly in North America, Australia and the United Kingdom, are doing this, even though some may initially have felt hostile to his approach to social theory. Some key concepts which are necessary for making sense of Foucault's ideas are commented on in the last section of this chapter. These are marked in the course of the chapter by the symbol '*'. Further definitions are given by individual contributors in the course of their arguments.

Coming to terms with Foucault can be a confusing process since, at some levels, Foucault appears to have much to offer in enhancing feminist understandings. He has enabled feminists to look in new ways at the control of women and especially at sexuality and women's bodies. At other levels, though, Foucault can be said to challenge or even undermine feminism. Directly or indirectly, he questions many of the conclusions which feminists have come to about the nature of social life, and so disintegrates collective political strategies for transforming gendered power relations. This book is intended as an appraisal of how seriously we need to take this challenge.

The contributors comment on Foucault's lack of interest in gender, which raises the question of why feminists should want to make the effort of paying attention to his work. In different ways, however, and with different degrees of warmth towards him, they explore three grounds for claiming that what Foucault is saying should be attended to.

First, his approach to understanding power* relations can offer feminists new and productive insights into women's relations with men and with one another. While feminists have been developing theories of the social construction of gender, sexuality and the body, Foucault has opened up a parallel but rather different theory of social construction through new ways of deconstructing history* and of analysing present power relations.

A second reason for taking Foucault seriously is his challenge to a number of the key assumptions about the nature and causes of women's subordination on which various versions of feminism are based. Foucault's ideas on power, knowledge*, the self* and sexuality, for example, are not compatible with feminist ideas in any simple way, and suggest considerable problems in feminist uses of these terms. Foucault is not simply offering interesting ideas which we can add on to feminism if we wish. The implications of his argument suggest that feminist political practices are based on a misunderstanding of the power relations that feminism aims to transform.

Feminists cannot afford to ignore Foucault, because the problems he addresses and the criticisms he makes of existing theories and their political consequences identify problems in and for feminism. In her chapter, Jean Grimshaw comments that Foucault's work is useful in pointing out that theories of emancipation tend to be blind to their own dominating tendencies, and feminism is not innocent of power. There is a strong case for women to respond to the ways in which Foucault challenges feminism, by thinking again across our social divisions about what we mean by, for example, autonomy, empowerment, justice, sexual politics, oppression and liberation.

A third reason for attending to Foucault is that feminist knowledge poses a considerable challenge to the validity of his work. Because feminism, until recently, has developed largely outside poststructuralist and postmodernist thought, and because Foucault largely ignored feminism, there has been very little engagement between Foucault's ideas and those of English-speaking feminism. The force of this feminist challenge has, as in other areas of social theory and philosophy, been inadequately recognised. Recently there has been growing interest in Foucault's work among academic feminists, with both enthusiastic applications of his ideas, and more critical evaluations of his work (for example, Diamond and Quinby 1988; Fraser 1989; Bartky 1990; Butler 1990; Nicholson 1990; Hekman 1990; Braidotti 1991; Sawicki 1991; Barrett and Phillips 1992). There is no equivalent literature from male scholars sympathetic to Foucault, which provides a comparable critical assessment of feminism.

In this book, the focus is specifically on appraisal of the work of Foucault, rather than more generally on poststructuralism or postmodernism, because of the distinctive contribution Foucault has made to thinking on issues of importance to feminism. The contributors invite us to consider what it means to analyse power relations, sexuality or the body, without also thinking about gender and other social divisions in the light of women's experience. There is no attempt here to cover all the diverse areas of history, literature or cultural studies in which Foucault's ideas have been influential, nor all the diverse political standpoints from which his work could be appraised. The contributors focus, from their different locations in social theory and philosophy, on the same core issues; the ways in which Foucault provokes feminists into questioning their grasp of power relations, and the implications of the absence of gender in his work.

FOUCAULT'S CHALLENGE TO FEMINISM

Although Foucault offered no particularly direct challenge to feminists himself, and seemed personally sympathetic to women's desire to change power relations, his work has particular implications for feminist thought and feminist politics. Feminists are up against Foucault in the sense that his work, like that of some of his contemporaries, invites us to think differently about the nature of knowledge and power, and questions in particular the ways in which feminists have thought about men having power over women.

Looking at power relations with Foucault's insights upsets key assumptions in feminist thinking. Feminism developed in reaction to established ways of western thought, which subordinated, separated or devalued everything female. At the same time, feminists were constrained in how they could think about power and knowledge by the categories of thought that already existed (Acker 1989: 73; Hekman 1990: 188). There are, in particular, assumptions about reality and truth, cause and effect, freedom and the nature of human agency, which have become so taken for granted since the period of the Enlightenment* in western thought, that many feminists have adopted them more or less uncritically. Foucault intentionally disturbs and upsets what we have taken to be true.

The ways in which Foucault's work challenges feminism, however, is by no means straightforward. While Foucault might criticise feminism for the limitations and rigidities of its conception of the 'truth' of patriarchy, feminists could criticise Foucault because he did not recognise that his supposedly neutral analysis of truth, power and sexuality as produced in discourses*, comes from a male perspective. It is not a simple question of feminism being able to counter Foucault's masculinist analysis with an alternative woman-centred analysis. Rather, the inter-action between Foucault's penetration into the nature of power, and the grounding of feminist explanations in women's diverse experiences, confront us with peculiarly difficult problems of explanation.

Foucault's deconstruction of abstract schemes of power, such as patriarchy or capitalism, led him to emphasise the unstable ways in which power is constantly created. Although he certainly recognised domination – for example, in the prison system – he thought it was a mistake to study it as a system benefiting a particular group, and analyse it from the top down. He conceptualised people's experiences of domination and subordination as 'effects' of power rather than as proceeding from a specific source of power. This view has enabled feminists to look at power relations with new eyes, but, where feminists ground their conceptions of power in women's accounts of their experiences, it also opens up a potential gulf between followers of Foucault and his feminist critics. Taking women's diverse experiences of subordination as a source of knowledge, however, is a complex business. The contradictions and inconsistencies of feminist thought should alert us to see that feminism is deeply contradictory because women's lives are contradictory (Ramazanoğlu 1989). This is not because of any intellectual fragility of feminist thinkers, but because close examination of the diversity of women's experiences poses immensely difficult problems of explanation which have not been adequately tackled by existing social theories, including Foucault's. The tensions between Foucault and feminism bring out fundamental problems of explaining power relations which social theory has failed to resolve. It is this complex interaction that is pursued with different emphases by the contributors to this volume.

Foucault's work provides a sharp critique of some of the ways in which feminists have set about explaining gendered power, but Foucault's impact on feminism has also been positive, as all the contributors acknowledge. What he has usefully done is to provide new means for thinking through some of the areas of understanding social life which have proved contradictory and problematic. These contradictions and problems are not necessarily specific weaknesses of feminism, but the consequences of feminism's somewhat pragmatic and *ad hoc* approach to some of the most profound problems of explanation confronting social theory.

The work of Foucault has been influential in supporting the view that not only gender, but also sex and bodies, are social constructions. Foucault takes aspects of our selves which in western culture have come to be taken as fixed, and analyses them as historical effects of power which are constituted by shifting social forces, rather than by our fixed, physical being. Sex and bodies can then be seen as social productions rather than as material; as giving us the possibility of multiple social identities, rather than confining us to an essential self which is 'truly' us. Although he may not have intended to abstract his analysis from material existence (Rabinow 1991: 10), feminists have found his emphasis on social construction both useful and problematic.

Whereas feminists have, in recent years in particular, been paying attention to what Foucault has said about the social construction of sexuality, power and pleasure, Foucault himself, and poststructuralists and postmodernists more generally, have tended to ignore, simplify or distort what feminists have said about sexuality and power. This risks leaving feminist theories as rooted in rather simplistic forms of biological essentialism which can easily be dismissed. Such interpretations make Foucault's challenge to feminism an overwhelming one, and reinforce feminist fears of being caught out as guilty of implicit essentialism or reductionism.

Various conceptions of social construction are characteristic of all versions of feminism, but the bugbear of biological essentialism – the idea that there is an essential femaleness or essential maleness in our physical being that might help explain social differences between women and men, has proved a persistent problem for the potential coherence of feminist thought. Different feminists have taken radically different attitudes towards such claims. Relatively few have ever taken on these views explicitly, wholeheartedly and persistently in the face of criticism. As Maureen Cain's chapter shows, there is now a much more careful consideration of issues of epistemology, methodology and philosophy of social science in attempts to explain gender relations than was the case in the 1960s. But as feminism has diversified over the last twenty years or so, there is little sign of more agreement on whether, or how, to regard material bodies as more than social. Feminist criticisms of Foucault raise again the problem of how we can take our feelings and material existence into account without reducing explanation of social life *to* biological determinants.

Rather than feminists having to choose between being either biologically essentialist or not, the possibility of biological nature, or material bodies, playing some part in explanation of gender difference runs under the fields of feminism like a camouflaged sewer into which the unwary may trip and so be contaminated without fully realising their danger. It is not that feminist assumptions, in contrast to those of Foucault, are built on biological essentialism, or particular versions of materialism, but that many feminists, by paying close attention to women's daily lives, and to common elements in diverse women's experiences, have found the odour of biological essentialism clinging to them. This stumbling over how best to understand the material levels of our existence has been taken as a critical weakness of feminism.

Foucault offers us a theory that bodies and sex are social constructions and are produced as effects of power. This has seemed attractive to many who want to escape any charge of biological essentialism. It enables them to view bodies as only explicable in terms of truths that are socially produced. However, treating material bodies as wholly irrelevant to explanations of sexual and other social relations remains an area which has perhaps been the subject of too much assumption and too little analysis. Foucault's version of social construction does not resolve problems about how we understand the body from the vantage point of subordinated women's bodily experiences.

Feminists are divided over what 'truth' status should be accorded to feminist knowledge, as continuing debates over feminist methodology indicate. The simplest position is that a women's subjective knowledge is 'true' because it directly articulates women's experience. This position is problematic because it poses no challenge to the dualisms of thought that western culture has inherited from the Enlightenment. Claiming that women's subjectivity produces 'true' knowledge of, for example, domestic violence, is simply the other side of the argument that men's knowledge is 'true' because it is rational, objective and neutral. A more logical position for feminists is that, since subjectivity and objectivity cannot ever be separated in the way that the dominant scientific models of western social theory proposed, we always have to interpret and conceptualise accounts of women's disparate experiences. Knowledge of domestic violence cannot then be produced without taking account of women's experience, but such knowledge is not confined to that experience, it is simultaneously always also embodied and conceptualised.

DIFFERENCE IN DANGER – THE POLITICS OF RELATIVISM

Using Foucault for feminist purposes is complicated by the fact that his position shifted in some respects between his major works, and again in the many interviews and discussions with him which have been recorded. His later reflections on his earlier work can be particularly confusing for those seeking consistency in his thought. If consistency is looked for, feminists are at risk of being lured into some version of political pluralism in which feminist politics are undermined by political relativism. There can be a further slippage here between the complexity, inconsistencies and contradictions of Foucault's work and the tendency of some of those attracted to his ideas to simplify and unify his thought.

Just as feminism is becoming a significant intellectual force in the production of knowledge, it is in danger of being thwarted by an elitist, but academically respectable, relativism and pluralism which ignores gender, disempowers women and diminishes difference. Since academic social theorists are increasingly under some pressure to acknowledge feminist social theory, those unsympathetic to feminist politics are offered a level of engagement between feminism, poststructuralism and postmodernism which is intellectually challenging, but extremely abstracted and also insensitive to the political point of feminism. Feminists need to take seriously the political uses Foucault's thought can be put to, and the possible uses of his work in supporting male dominance by ignoring 'gender' in social relations, and appearing to rise above the political implications of social divisions between women.

Feminism is in danger of being shifted from an emancipatory global movement, to a philosophical specialism which provides legitimation for political pluralism. Women can then fragment politically according to their local and specific interests in class, ethnicity, degree of physical challenge, sexual orientation, age or any other social difference. In Chapters 6 and 7, Janet Ransom and Maureen McNeil explore the problem of feminism losing its political force when both similarities and differences between women become abstracted deconstructions and do not have to be continually addressed at the level of experience.

Feminist theories that men have power over women are undermined by claims from many categories of women that they are marginalised, constituted as silent, absent or 'other' in relation to women who exercise power over them through such agencies as class, domestic service, racism and sexual orientation (Collins 1990; Spelman 1990). Foucault's analysis of power has seemed to offer a way in which these differences can be taken into account, but the nature and extent of women's power over one another is still disputed and contested.

Foucault, having stated that the way in which 'power is exercised and functions in a society like ours is little understood' (1988a: 103), goes on to say: 'the questions "Who exercises power? How? On whom?" are certainly the questions that people feel most strongly about.' He considers the example of wanting to explain poverty, but adds that, 'I don't believe that this question of "who exercises power?" can be resolved unless that other question "How does it happen?" is resolved at the same time' (ibid.). From this position he advises focusing on specific techniques of power to show how those in power arrive at particular decisions. In this way he can show that the exercise of power cannot be reduced to a single causal factor. Following his claim to be an empiricist (1988a: 106), he has to deal with the problem that 'The relations of power are perhaps among the best hidden things in the social body' (1988b: 118).

The political problem with this approach is that it does not 'discover' the hidden and institutionalised power relations which differentiate the lives of black lesbian women in Britain from those of white heterosexual women, or the lives of middle-class housewives with ethnic roots in the Indian sub-continent from those of, say, service workers from the African diaspora; or the lives of such service workers from 'black British' professionals. Without some systematic understanding of such inter-relationships we cannot grasp the complexity, the contradictions and the unpredictability of the interplay of social differences.

Foucault's deconstruction of power releases feminism from rigid conceptions of, for example, universal patriarchy, racism or heterosexism. By seeing power as everywhere and, at some level, as available to all, it can encourage us to overlook women's systematic subordination of other women, as well as systematic domination by men. Using Foucault means acknowledging the multiplicity of difference, and claiming the end of 'woman' as a universal category. But it can also lead to a tendency to revert to speaking in abstracted terms of deconstructed 'women', because of the absence of, for example, class, racism or gender as categories of power relations in his thought. The conceptual deconstruction of 'difference' is too easily abstracted from practical politics rooted both in women's differences and in women's common interests. Foucault's challenge to feminist theories of power catches feminism in the same weak spot as challenges which have come from women who assert their experiences of subordination by other women. It can privilege intellectual women and disintegrate the politics of difference.

If analysis is abstracted from a feminist grounding in women's different experiences, there is always the danger of slipping back into an undifferentiated sense of 'women'. This problem needs to be continually addressed and contested from women's different standpoints, and it is here that problems about emancipation lie.

NEUTRAL THEORY AND POLITICAL STRATEGY

In May 1968, the year and month of student revolts that served to shake the intellectuals of much of Europe into new modes of political thought, Foucault published an article in which he responded to a direct question about the political implications of his work (Foucault 1991a: 53). The questioner asked whether Foucault agreed that his theory removed the basis for progressive political intervention. This meant either accepting the existing political situation or waiting for some sort of threat to the system which could come from outside. Foucault says he chose to answer this question because it surprised him at first, then because it went to the heart of his work and because it posed a challenge which no social theory could avoid. His reaction to the challenge that his work is conservative and precludes the possibility of improving the social world is positively emotional.

> With diabolical pertinence you have succeeded in giving a definition of my work to which I cannot avoid subscribing, but

for which no one would ever reasonably wish to assume responsibility. I suddenly sense how bizarre my position is, how strange and illegitimate . . . how jarring it was bound to seem.

(Foucault 1991a: 53)

With relief he pounces on some objections to the way the questioner has phrased the question, and devotes most of his response to specifying the value of his own achievements. He returns later to the troubling question of the political implications of his work:

after all how can grubbing about in the origins of philology, economics or pathological anatomy be of concern for politics, or be counted among the problems which matter to it today?

(Ibid.: 65)

His reply becomes a detailed defence of his work as analysis of scientific discourses. He argues that when he studies specific discourses he can clarify their relationships with political practices. He can show how political practices interact with the emergence of discourses and what political practices make of the discourses that emerge. His own method, he says, is not just an intellectual game but a serious attempt to explain how the 'knowledge which is ours today' and especially knowledge of man [sic] could come to exist (ibid.: 70).

What feminists mean by politics could then be distressing to Foucault, just as he recognised (ibid.: 71) that his method could be distressing to others. He gives a vivid image of himself, with his back to the wall, forced by this questioning of the politics of his work to recognise the gap between his own liberal impulses and the implications of his 'neutral' theory of power.

In criticising Marxist analysis, Foucault notes that Marxists speak of class struggle as the mainspring of history but, with the exception of some of Marx's own historical texts, they do not focus on 'the nature of the struggle' (Foucault 1988b: 123). In turning on Foucault, feminists might throw the same question at him. Where is his focus on political struggle? But Foucault slips away through his argument that the intellectual is only asking in passing whether the revolution is worth the trouble (1988b: 124). While Foucault's position on the role of intellectuals shifted over time and was somewhat ambiguous, he favoured a stance from which intellectuals should 'disturb people's mental habits' (Foucault 1988c: 265) but not tell them what to do. He says his question can only be answered 'by those who are willing to risk their lives to bring it about' (1988b: 124).

Some women do risk their lives in struggling for autonomy, against rape and male violence, racism, victorious armies, corrupt policing, lawless landlords and the many other manifestations of domination and violence. More commonly they risk their relationships, their livelihood, their homes, the custody of their children, their sanity, their pleasures, their health and the integrity of their bodies. Feminists need to go beyond Foucault's analysis of power, by hanging on to radical feminism's sense of moral outrage, while modifying this with recognition of the diversity of women's conditions of life.

UP AGAINST FOUCAULT

In exploring where the tensions between Foucault and feminism might lead us, it is not surprising, given the current diversification of feminist social theory, that the contributors to this book do not share a common position. Their different appraisals of how feminists can usefully draw on Foucault and where they might draw a line do, however, focus on a number of common issues which arise when feminists confront Foucault. Considering power from the perspective of women's experience gives the contributors a critical approach to Foucault's work, but they also note Foucault's very productive ways of deconstructing power relations which feminists have found useful.

In the first section, Kate Soper, Jean Grimshaw and Maureen Cain reflect on what can be made of specific points of tension in looking at how useful Foucault might be for feminism. Kate Soper argues that Foucault's apparent clinical detachment veils a male-centred outlook which is insensitive to feminist concerns, but his work has been positively received by feminists because of the fertility of the contradictions in his thought. Feminists, she feels, can acknowledge Foucault's work, but should do this without too much deference.

In considering the tensions between Foucault's thought and feminist politics, Soper argues strongly against too easy an acceptance of bodies as entirely cultural forces. Foucault is useful in identifying bodies as objects of power, but in looking from this perspective, we may miss why it is that women are at the mercy of this power in the first place. In considering how we may resist power, Soper considers that Foucault sees liberation too much in terms of how individuals can make themselves, thus encouraging an identity politics as a privilege for a minority.

Soper explores a second area of tension with feminism, in which Foucault's views question the coherence of feminist ideas of emancipation. She analyses the inconsistencies in his own work in this respect. If we take Foucault as saying that oppression is constituted in discourses and so oppression cannot exist prior to discourses, then Foucault's accounts of discourses become arbitrary in their severance from material circumstances. The paradoxes in Foucault's account of knowledge and power are responsible for the specific tensions in his work for feminism. Soper argues that Foucault tells us relatively little about power and its sources. He does not offer an account of women's oppression or women's resistance* to oppression, but he invites us to think more deeply and self-critically about feminist 'realism' and what we mean by oppression and liberation.

Jean Grimshaw draws on Foucault's image of his ideas as a 'tool box' to see whether his work can be useful for feminism. But she also considers whether feminism can clarify problems in Foucault's work. She comments on Foucault's opposition to the Enlightenment conception of 'man' as an autonomous, self-determining human subject* and explains his conception of the 'self' as a historical product created by discourses. Feminists can find this approach useful in analysing the extent to which women are constructed as subjects in discourses and so in power relationships. If 'sex' is a product of discourse and not a 'true' identity in Foucault's view, women's liberation cannot take the form of liberating our selves. Since Foucault sees power as everywhere, it is difficult for him to distinguish between malign and benign forms of power. This gives him a problem in developing an adequate theory of women's resistance to power. Foucault can make us attend to the dangers of our political strategies, but his own position is not a neutral one.

In commenting on Foucault's later writings on ethics, Grimshaw argues that his analyses of Greek morality revolves around the care of the self, producing the self somewhat like a work of art. In his later work, power is seen as installed in the self and it is here that Grimshaw finds Foucault disappointing for feminists. Greek morality was elitist and male-dominated, but Foucault assumed the Greeks to be free and so did not attend to gendered differences in the care of the self, or questions about morality and the effects of different codes of conduct. Trapped in his masculinist view of ethics he seems to forget his own earlier deconstructive practices and sidesteps the crucial questions which his work raises for feminism.

Maureen Cain builds on recent debates within feminism by looking specifically at Foucault's theory of knowledge, feminist theories of knowledge and what the two have in common, in order to consider how knowledge which is helpful to women can best be produced. Cain does this by looking at three aspects of Foucault's work. First, she assesses the problems raised by the idea of social existence which is extra-discursive in the sense of existing prior to or outside discourses. Here she finds the work of Foucault useful in considering that relationships can exist which are not wholly within discourses. Cain argues that we cannot now leave discourse analysis out of feminist research, but we cannot leave relationships out of discourse analysis. She sees Foucault as proposing a radical methodology which enables discursive processes and powers to be made available as never before.

Secondly, Cain considers concern with 'repressed knowledges'; the voices of those silenced by, or excluded from dominant discourses. This raises one problem of whether it is possible for women to have experiences of which there is no existing knowledge and another of how it is possible to 'know' realities which have not been thought of. She comes to the conclusion that we do need to recognise the existence of unformulated experience and that some experiences may have no voice at all.

Finally, Cain argues that standpoint feminism and a realist feminist position, is compatible with Foucault's genealogical method* in recognising the place of power in the production of knowledge. Feminists can use Foucault's method to 'know' sub-jugated knowledges, but the concept of 'knowing' as coming from particular standpoints exposes a tension between feminists and Foucault. Cain argues that feminists must go beyond Foucault in theorising feelings that have no discourses and in exploring the unspeakable.

In the second section, M.E. Bailey, Janet Ransom and Maureen McNeil look at both the delights and the dangers of getting too close to Foucault. In an argument which is perhaps the most sympathetic to Foucault in this collection, M.E. Bailey claims that different feminist interpretations of the social significance of bodies have different political implications and that any conception of the body or the self as fixed or biologically stable, as opposed to socially variable, circumscribes feminist political strategies. In her view, seeing the body as natural constitutes a trap for feminism. She argues that Foucault used his genealogical method to show that the supposed truths of sexuality exist in a material world where power is brought to bear on all the forms they take. This implicitly deconstructs the idea of a monolithic patriarchy as a source of power. Rather, women make their bodies conform to historically specific ideas of femininity. Bodies are then usefully seen as variable sites of power/knowledge* relations.

Bailey follows Foucault in taking the forms of modern sexuality to be social and historical in the sense that they are variably determined by techniques of power. There is no universal category of woman, but women can discover common interests in their locations in networks of power relations. Foucault, like feminists, identifies bodies as battlegrounds, but he leads women towards politics based on multiple socially constructed identities. These identities can develop through local and specific resistance in the politics of difference, but no particular identity will be more basic than others.

In responding to Foucault's question of whether it matters 'who is speaking' in creating 'truths', Janet Ransom takes up a position which is more critical of Foucault, by questioning whether feminism can be absorbed into this kind of pluralism. She argues, against Foucault, that we do not disappear from our theories and so it does matter who is speaking when we conceptualise power. Although postmodernism can deconstruct feminism into a variety of different feminist identities, this focus on difference and multiplicity threatens the political disintegration of feminism.

Ransom explores the problem of whether Foucault's method of analysing discourses can help feminism find a theory which can accommodate the plurality of women's experiences. She argues that Foucault severs the moral link between the theorist and the theorised which feminism has insisted on. He does not see it as his task to address the complexity of the world as it is experienced by women and so undercuts feminism's insistence on theory being grounded in experience. Whereas feminism starts from how it feels to be subordinated, Foucault's theory is unable to distinguish between the different kinds of power relations that cut across women's lives.

Maureen McNeil takes the image of dancing with Foucault to represent the complexity of the possible interactions between Foucault and feminism. She focuses on Foucault's criticisms of the ideas derived from the Enlightenment which feminism has accepted somewhat uncritically. In particular, Foucault was critical of the idea that increasing knowledge means increasing freedom. McNeil investigates possible connections between knowledge and power by looking at two main streams of feminist thought which have emerged over the last twenty years. In versions of feminism which depend on therapeutic models, self-knowledge is seen as an end in itself. But Foucault was critical of the idea that self-knowledge meant greater freedom, since he thought subjects were created in and through discourses and discursive practices. Another trend in feminism has served to split an academic specialism from more popular versions of feminism. This puts some feminists in danger of standing as apparently detached and neutral intellectuals apart from political activism. This power–knowledge relation remains at the centre of current feminist uncertainties. Like Ransom, she argues that feminist 'knowers' are not abstracted from their experience. The power relations in which women themselves are caught up still need to be questioned.

In the final section, Susan Bordo, Dean MacCannell and Juliet Flower MacCannell, and Janet Holland and I appraise Foucault's concepts of power and resistance from the perspective of women's experience. Susan Bordo reflects on the extent to which feminists had constructed a politics of the body independently of Foucault. Foucault's work challenged the notion that women are oppressed through men's possession of power. This extended the need to consider women's collusion in their own subordination, and the ways in which men get caught up in being powerful. Bordo particularly questions Foucault's concept of resistance. She argues that Foucault has two sides to his views of resistance. Like Marxism and feminism he emphasises the grip of power on the body, but in his later work he puts more emphasis on the power of bodies to resist this grip. Bordo argues that both arguments are essential to a theory of power and the body, but she illustrates the confusions that have arisen between women's resistance to the grip of power, and the pressures on them to try to conform to dominant body images. The coercion of slenderness is confused with cultural resistance. Such pressures as sexism and racism do not deprive us of agency, but they exert strong pressures over our bodies and our selves and must remain central to the politics of the body.

Dean MacCannell and Juliet Flower MacCannell take accounts of experiences given by women who have been 'victims' of male violence and assault, and evaluate Foucault's theory of power from the perspective of these 'victims'. This leads them to question the neutrality of Foucault's analysis of power, and the utility of his distinction between power and force. They interpret the examples of violence which they document as attacks on women's experience of their own pleasures. It is the extent to which knowledge of this violence is suppressed that privileges some to think of their power as neutral and themselves as free. Foucault conceived power as spreading through networks of relationships with a capillary action; wherever there was power, resistance was possible. MacCannell and MacCannell, in contrast, argue that though resistance may go with power, capillary power is accompanied by capillary violence. This violence can be backed by force and various forms of force are backed by much wider systems of authority. Foucault opened up the possibilities of multiplicity, but he had no real model of feminine pleasure and did not explore the dark possibilities of the new subjective forms being daily created by violence. His critique has not really disturbed the power to define the subjugated.

In the final chapter, Janet Holland and I look at the tensions between Foucault and feminism raised by trying to interpret young women's accounts of their sexuality. Foucault did acknowledge men's exercise of power over women, but denied that men can hold power. We argue that there has been insufficient analysis of the 'middle ground' of power relations, between the micropolitics of struggles around bodies and the consolidation of deeply entrenched male privilege throughout social life. There is a tension in Foucault's work between his later emphasis on shifting, fracturing, unstable power relations to which all have access, and his acknowledgement, especially in his earlier work, of more stable concentrations of power. Feminism demands some tracing of the connections between women's experiences of sexual subordination and the persistence of male power. These connections are critical for grounding feminism's political strategies and preserving some understanding of women's agency and the possibilities of empowerment.

Foucault's work is useful for seeing the active parts young

women play in disciplining* their bodies into subordinated
femininity, but he does not look at the connections between men's
ability to dominate sexual encounters and male power over
women more generally. The variable distinctions between power
inside and outside discourse which he makes at various points in
his work do not discriminate sufficiently between resistance to
power and the ability to transform power relations.

Academic feminists have political responsibilities in
undertaking the deconstruction of gender, knowledge and power
(Cain and Finch 1981). One of the continuing problems for
feminism is that the persistence of social divisions which cut across
women's common interests ensure that, since women do not
necessarily share their politics, neither do they agree on these
responsibilities. Contradictions in feminist thought will linger,
because women's lives and the ways in which we know diversity
are persistently contradictory. At the same time, there are
common threads in women's experiences of gender relations and
in the ability of men to exercise power over women, which have
still not been adequately explained. This book is presented as a
contribution to understanding what gender means and why it still
matters.

COMING TO FOUCAULT'S TERMS

Throughout this book, the contributors have tried to make
Foucault's terms reasonably accessible to those not already
conversant with his work. There are no simple definitions in this
area and shifts in meaning in the course of Foucault's work make
the pursuit of exact meanings difficult. In the rest of this
introduction, I comment briefly on some key terms which are
helpful in considering the relevance of Foucault for feminism. It
is not possible in a few words to cover the range of uses and
qualifications of these terms in Foucault's work.

Genealogy, genealogical method

Genealogy was Foucault's method of studying history through
analysis of discourses (see p. 19). As Maureen McNeil explains in
her chapter, his genealogical method was designed to explore not
who had power, but rather the patterns of the exercise of power
through the interplay of discourses. Maureen Cain shows how

through this genealogical method Foucault arrived at the position that it was the exercise of power that created knowledge, while knowledge itself produces the effects of power. This genealogical method enables Foucault to map the discontinuities of history and the play of power relations in the production of knowledges.

Discourse

The point of Foucault's genealogical method was to analyse discourses. His concept of 'discourse' is a key term both in understanding Foucault's work, and in differentiating his theory from feminist thinking on power. He identified discourses as historically variable ways of specifying knowledge and truth – what it is possible to speak of at a given moment. They function (especially scientific discourses) as sets of rules, and the operation of these rules and concepts in programmes which specify what is or is not the case – what constitutes insanity, for example. Discourses are, therefore, powerful. Those who are labelled insane, or hysterical women or frigid wives, are in the grip of power. This power may be exercised by officials through institutions, or through many other practices, but power is constituted *in* discourses and it is in discourses, such as those of clinical medicine, that power lies. Discourses produce truths and 'we cannot exercise power except through the production of truth' (Foucault 1980: 93).

The term 'discourse' gives rise to a number of related terms since they exist in 'discursive fields', giving rise to 'discursive formations' or groups of regulated practices (Foucault 1991a). He specified:

> we must not imagine a world of discourse divided between accepted discourse and excluded discourse, or between the dominant discourse and the dominated one; but as a multiplicity of discursive elements that can come into play in various strategies. . . . Discourse transmits and produces power; it reinforces it, but also undermines and exposes it, renders it fragile and makes it possible to thwart it.
>
> (1984: 100)

He continues (1984: 102) that the point is not where discourses come from, nor what interests they represent, but what 'effects of power and knowledge they ensure' and what makes their use necessary. There is no all-powerful subject which manipulates discourse; rather 'discoursing subjects' (that is, people who produce and deploy discourses) form part of the 'discursive field' (Foucault 1991a: 58). He is not interested in what discourses mean, but in what makes them possible.

This view makes it problematic as to whether power can exist prior to discourse, whether we cannot think in terms of a 'pre-discursive reality' such as the existence of the human body before it is socially constructed – in medical discourses, for example. This point is taken up by Kate Soper in Chapter 2 and Maureen Cain in Chapter 4 in rather different ways. In Foucault's view, power cannot be possessed by men. The exercise of power is not a matter of equality, but power has no particular source and, since it is constituted in discourses, power is everywhere.

Resistance to power (see p. 23) comes through new discourses producing new truths. These may be 'counter discourses' which oppose dominant truths, or 'reverse discourses'. Foucault gives an example of a reverse discourse as that of homosexuality. The idea or 'truth' of homosexuality appeared as discourse which did not counter the prevailing medical discourse. It claimed homosexuality as natural, in the terms of the dominant discourse (Foucault 1984: 101).

History

Because Foucault thinks of genealogical method in terms of analysing and recovering discourses, he rejects the view of history as being about the unfolding of a continuous narrative. His interest is rather in the multiple histories of particular discourses and their complex interrelations which define particular truths at particular times. History is about recovering the discontinuities of the transformations of discourses and their variable relationships to one another.

Episteme

Rather than writing a history of discourses, Foucault thought in terms of discourses being located in epistemes. An episteme was not a period, nor a slice of history, but a complex relationship between ensembles of discourses; 'an *open and doubtless infinitely describable field of relationships*' (Foucault 1991a: 55). Foucault uses episteme to emphasise discontinuity, change and the 'intensity of difference' in and between discourses (ibid.: 56), rather than historical unity or continuity.

Power/knowledge

Because Foucault defines power as constituted through discourses, his concept of power is very different from that of feminism, and it is this theme in particular which runs through the chapters which follow. Foucault's early work is concerned with domination and physical power, but he moved increasingly to a position which denied that power was a repressive force, or came *from* a dominating class. While feminists define men's power as repressive and illegitimate, Foucault moved towards a position which defined all power as productive – that is, as producing knowledge rather than repression.

> In general terms, I would say that the interdiction, the refusal, the prohibition, far from being essential forms of power, are only its limits, power in its frustrated or extreme forms. The relations of power are, above all, productive.
> (Foucault 1988b: 118)

This view raises considerable problems for feminist theories of women's subordination to patriarchal power. As Janet Ransom explains, Foucault treats power as co-extensive with knowledge. There is no single truth – for example, about our 'true' sexual selves – but many different truths situated in different discourses, some of which are more powerful than others. Foucault did ask, though, for some care in how we interpret this:

> I know that as far as the general public is concerned, I am the guy who said that knowledge merged with power. . . . If I had said, or meant, that knowledge was power I would have said so, and having said so, I would have had nothing more to say, since, having made them identical, I don't see why I would have taken the trouble to show the different relations between them.
> (Foucault 1988c: 264)

The relation between knowledge and power is then something that has to be established through investigation. Power struggles are about the deployment of power; how power is exercised. A number of feminists have found this a creative way of approaching power differences between women, and in accounting for the ways in which men get caught up in the exercise of power. This theme is critically evaluated in different ways by all the contributors.

Analyses of women's experience of men's power underlie feminist criticisms of Foucault. They lead feminists to suggest two aspects of power which can conflict with Foucault's understanding. First, women's experiences suggest that men can *have* power and their power is in some sense a form of domination, backed by force. Secondly, this domination cannot be seen simply as a product of discourse, because it must also be understood as 'extra-discursive' or relating to wider realities than those of discourse.

Discipline, docility, bio-power, normalisation, the disciplinary gaze

In Foucault's earlier work there is considerable emphasis on the ways in which power is deployed to get people to conform. He notes the historical changes in administration and thought in seventeenth- and eighteenth-century Europe which led to the disciplining of bodies in terms, for example, of making the best use of workers, and also to the docility of bodies as people were integrated into new systems of controls such as education and the prison system. In these apparatuses, power was exercised as discipline through a number of techniques, including surveillance (for example, of prisoners, inmates, schoolchildren) and the 'eye of power' in the disciplinary gaze.

He also notes the general regulation of populations, which he terms 'bio-power'. He sees discipline and docility exercised on bodies, on the one hand, and bio-power exercised on populations on the other, as two poles around which the management of life became organised.

The related concept of normalisation indicates the extension of control and self-regulation. Discourses define what is normal, and what is not normal is then seen as in need of normalisation, or conformity to the norm. Feminists have found these concepts useful in indicating social pressures on women not only to submit to discipline, but also to conform to norms by producing their own docile bodies. Susan Bordo, in her chapter, discusses some of the complexity of trying to distinguish between normalisation and resistance.

Resistance

The concept of 'resistance' is part of Foucault's definition of power since he defines all power as producing resistance. Resistance takes the form of counter discourses which produce new knowledge, speak new truths, and so constitute new powers. The implications of this concept of resistance are problematic for feminism, and these problems are explored throughout this book.

Enlightenment

The term 'the Enlightenment' characterises a shift in European thought largely from the eighteenth century. During this period the notion of reason as superior to other modes of thought became dominant (although never unified or unchallenged), together with a belief in the progress of humanity and the superiority of scientific method as a means of discovering the truth. The social sciences carried these ideas into the study of social life. Although these ideas have been contested on many counts, they have remained powerful in affecting common-sense assumptions about what is true, how we discover truth; the superiority of reason over emotion, objectivity over subjectivity, mind over body. Feminism has attacked Enlightenment thought as concealing masculinist bias beneath the appearance of neutrality and objectivity.

Foucault's theory upsets the Enlightenment assumptions which have been absorbed into feminist theories of power, knowledge, truth and causation, but Foucault's sexism, and his own ambivalence in freeing himself from some Enlightenment assumptions, is a recurrent theme in the chapters which follow. Foucault was critical of Enlightenment assumptions, but especially towards the end of his life he also acknowledged the Enlightenment as the source of a critical tradition on which we still depend (Hoy 1986; Foucault 1991b).

The human subject, the self

The dominant ideas of the Enlightenment incorporated various concepts of a human nature which lies within us as the core of an essential self. People could empower themselves by liberating their selves, and so achieve autonomy, justice, independence, freedom from repression. In moving beyond the assumptions of the Enlightenment, Foucault had no need to think in terms of the agency of the human subject who uses reason progressively to discover the truth about the world and so can emancipate himself from oppression.

Foucault rejected this way of thinking as approached through the wrong questions. In his view, power is generally productive rather than repressive. People are, therefore, social selves, and these social selves are not essential, but historically variable. They are also produced in power relations. People are constituted as subjects in discourses, and disciplinary practices, and also (whether knowingly or not) contribute themselves to the process of turning themselves into particular kinds of subjects. From Foucault's perspective, it does not make sense to think of political change, as feminists conventionally have done, in terms of emancipation from oppression. It does make sense to think of transforming political relations through the production of new discourses and so new forms of power and new forms of the self.

BIBLIOGRAPHY

Acker, J. (1989) 'Making gender visible', in R. Wallace (ed.) *Feminism and Sociology*, London: Sage.

Barrett, M. and Phillips, A. (eds) (1992) *Destabilizing Theory: Contemporary Feminist Debates*, Cambridge: Polity Press.

Bartky, S.L. (1990) *Femininity and Domination: Studies in the Phenomenology of Oppression*, London: Routledge.

Braidotti, R. (1991) *Patterns of Dissonance: A Study of Women in Contemporary Philosophy*, Cambridge: Polity Press.

Butler, J. (1990) *Gender Trouble: Feminism and the Subversion of Identity*, London: Routledge.

Cain, M. and Finch, J. (1981) 'Towards a rehabilitation of data', in P. Abrams, R. Deem, J. Finch and P. Rock (eds) *Practice and Progress: British Sociology 1950–1980*, London: Allen & Unwin.

Collins, P. Hill (1990) *Black Feminist Thought*, London: Harper Collins Academic.

Diamond, I. and Quinby, L. (eds) (1988) *Feminism and Foucault: Reflections on Resistance*, Boston: Northeastern University Press.

Duchen, C. (1986) *Feminism in France: From May 1968 to Mitterrand*, London: Routledge.

Foucault, M. (1980) 'Two lectures', in C. Gordon (ed.) *Power/Knowledge: Selected Interviews and Other Writings 1972–1977 by Michel Foucault*, London: Harvester Wheatsheaf.

——(1984) *The History of Sexuality*, vol.I: *An Introduction*, London: Penguin.

——(1988a) 'On power', in L. Kritzman (ed.) *Michel Foucault: Politics, Philosophy, Culture: Interviews and other writings 1977–1984*, London: Routledge.

——(1988b) 'Power and sex', in L. Kritzman (ed.) *Michel Foucault: Politics, Philosophy, Culture: Interviews and other writings 1977–1984*, London: Routledge.

——(1988c) 'The concern for truth', in L. Kritzman (ed.) *Michel Foucault: Politics, Philosophy, Culture: Interviews and other writings 1977–1984*, London: Routledge.

——(1991a) 'Politics and the study of discourse', in G. Burchell, C. Gordon and P. Miller (eds) *The Foucault Effect*, London: Harvester, Wheatsheaf.

——(1991b) 'What is enlightenment?', in P. Rabinow (ed.) *The Foucault Reader: An Introduction to Foucault's Thought*, London: Penguin.

Fraser, N. (1989) *Unruly Practices: Power, Discourse and Gender in Contemporary Social Theory*, Cambridge: Polity Press.

Hekman, S.J. (1990) *Gender and Knowledge: Elements of a Postmodern Feminism*, Cambridge: Polity Press.

Hoy, D.C. (1986) 'Introduction', in D.C. Hoy (ed.) *Foucault: A Critical Reader*, Oxford: Blackwell.

Kritzman, L. (ed.) (1988) *Michel Foucault: Politics, Philosophy, Culture: Interviews and Other Writings 1977–1984*, London: Routledge.

Nicholson, L. (ed.) (1990) *Feminism/Postmodernism*, London: Routledge.

Rabinow, P. (ed.) (1991) *The Foucault Reader: An Introduction to Foucault's Thought*, London: Penguin.

Ramazanoğlu, C. (1989) *Feminism and the Contradictions of Oppression*, London: Routledge.

Sawicki, J. (1991) *Disciplining Foucault: Feminism, Power and the Body*, London: Routledge.

Spelman, E. (1990) *Inessential Women: Problems of Exclusion in Feminist Thought*, London: The Women's Press.

Part I

Reflections on the value of Foucault's argument for feminism

Chapter 2

Productive contradictions

Kate Soper

In one sense, Foucault is rather fortunate to have attracted the attention he has from feminists, since it is not clear that he has done that much to deserve it. His own engagement with feminist writing is minimal. He has not focused on 'the woman question', in the forms in which it has been posed in poststructuralist theory, to anything like the degree that is true of Lacan and Derrida – the two other comparable influences on feminism at the present time. His overall argument, however, encourages as much scepticism as theirs about the theoretical coherence and practical viability of feminist emancipation. At the same time, the hallmark of Foucault's style of approach is a clinical detachment which has both recommended his work to his followers, but also veils a somewhat less than objective male-centredness of outlook. In this covert androcentricity, then, Foucault arguably reveals himself as peculiarly indifferent, even insensitive to feminist concerns.

In another sense, however, the feminist interest in Foucault is both perfectly appropriate and readily explained. For not only is his stature as a theorist such that he cannot be ignored, but he has also centred his work on themes which are extremely germane to those of feminism, and pursued them in a way which must command a certain feminist sympathy. One may cite in this connection the tribute of his critic Jürgen Habermas (1986: 107): 'Within the circle of philosophers of my generation who diagnose our times, Foucault has most lastingly influenced the *Zeitgeist* [spirit of the times] not least of all because of the seriousness with which he perseveres under productive contradictions.' Though Habermas himself has shown little more interest than many other male commentators on Foucault in pursuing his possible value for feminism, he does, I think indicate here two of the main

justifications for the feminist engagement with Foucault's work:
the extent of his influence and the fertility of the contradictions
within his thinking. Let us, then, acknowledge Foucault's
importance in this respect, and the fact that it gives him as much
claim to feminist attention as that of the other contenders for the
palm of most enduring influence on the *Zeitgeist*: Lacan, Derrida
and Habermas himself.

If we are thinking, however, not so much in terms of individual
theorists and their magnetism, but more in terms of collective
bodies of work, it is difficult not to feel that the deepest and most
persistent impact on the *Zeitgeist* will have been that of feminism
itself. Let us therefore also acknowledge the degree to which
feminist theory has informed the context in which any male
philosopher has been working in recent years, and adjust our
perspective on the Foucault-feminism connection accordingly. For
this must be seen as reflecting not only what Foucault has to offer
feminism, but also the interest Foucault has himself acquired in
virtue of the feminist climate of his times. I suggest, then, that as
feminists engage with Foucault they pay themselves the tribute of
having prepared some of the discursive space for his emergence.

I make this point in part in answer to those who may be inclined
to view collections such as the present volume as a somewhat
dubious preoccupation with a single male super-star. For what is
really at issue here is not the propriety of feminist engagements of
this kind, but questions of a rather deeper and more general
aspect: Foucauldian questions about the making and dissemin-
ation of 'influence', and feminist questions about how it is that
even in these profoundly anti-subjectivist, postmodernist times,
the creation of the philosophical *Zeitgeist* is likely to be attributed
to a handful of individual male talents. If all this seems a little
shocking and heretical to Foucault's more ardent disciples, so be
it. They should content themselves with the compliment that it is
Foucault himself who has helped us to become more questioning
about the production of these kind of knowledge 'effects' within
our culture.

One cannot dispute that Foucault has been responsible for a
remarkable and justly admired body of work, much of which can
be clearly seen to confirm and consolidate feminist critique. It is a
body of work, however, which for the reasons cited in these
opening remarks, I believe – along with other contributors to this
book – feminists would be wrong to approach with too much

deference. I shall therefore focus here on what I think are the main problems with any feminist appropriation of Foucault's argument. This means I shall be addressing two types of tensions: those which arise in virtue of feminism's emancipatory aims, and those which arise in virtue of Foucault's male-orientated, or androcentric, perspective. The first set of tensions relate to contradictions internal to Foucault's account of power and the role accorded discourse in constituting social 'reality' and the formation of subjectivity. Though they take specifically feminist forms, such tensions would arise for any movement seeking to combine Foucauldian insights with an overall commitment to the removal of inequalities and oppressive constraints on self-realisation. Foucault's androcentricity, on the other hand, is obviously the source of more particular tensions between his argument and that of feminism.

TENSIONS BETWEEN FOUCAULT'S THOUGHT AND FEMINIST POLITICS

Essence, nature and authenticity

Where Foucault and feminist thinking most obviously come together is in their emphasis on the culturally constructed, rather than naturally dictated, quality of 'sexuality' and its norms and codes of behaviour. Here Foucault can be seen to have deepened and extended the challenge to the idea of gender as natural which provided the initial springboard for feminism. Thus, if feminism may be said to have prefigured Foucauldian theory in its deconstruction of the supposedly natural and inevitable order of male supremacy and its sexual arrangements, it is Foucault who has laid the groundwork for current feminist denunciations of the 'naturality' not only of existing gender attributes and relations, but of sexuality and the body themselves.[1] One may cite, in this connection, his influence on the argument of Judith Butler (1987, 1990a, 1990b), and on several of the contributors to the American collection *Feminism and Foucault* (Diamond and Quinby 1988). A relevant example here is Susan Bordo's preamble to her Foucauldian treatment of anorexia nervosa:

> Throughout my discussion, it will be assumed that the body, far from being some fundamentally stable, acultural constant to

which we must *contrast* all culturally relative and institutional forms, is constantly 'in the grip', as Foucault puts it, of cultural practices. Not that this is a matter of cultural *repression* of the instinctual or natural body. Rather, there is no 'natural' body. Cultural practices, far from exerting their power *against* spontaneous needs, 'basic' pleasures or instincts, or 'fundamental' structures of body experience, are already and always inscribed, as Foucault has emphasised, 'on our bodies and their materiality, their forces, energies, sensations and pleasures'. Our bodies, no less than anything else that is human are constituted by culture.

(Bordo 1988: 90)

But while arguments of this kind do remind us of the need to respect the extent to which the body, and bodily experience, are culturally formed, there is surely something too glib about their formulation. Indeed, it is not clear what sense we are to make of their political critique, if we do not presuppose the body as a pre-discursive entity subject to those constant and continuous natural processes which allow us through dieting, or body-building, or surgery or cosmetics, to alter bodily shape and appearance in accordance with socially prescribed norms of beauty or gender identity. Both in Foucault's own argument, and in that of some of the feminism he has influenced, the notion of a 'discursive construction' is, in fact, employed in ways that are too facilely anti-naturalist. For it is one thing to argue that we do not have experience of the body other than as symbolically and culturally mediated; it is quite another to suggest that bodies are 'constructed' out of cultural forces in the same manner that, say, telephones are put together. One crucial difference here is that the body exists as a physical entity prior to any cultural work of production in a way that a telephone does not. Another is that, whereas telephones are once and for all made, bodies are not, but remain in continual transformation, either as a result of what we deliberately contrive ourselves, or as a result of involuntary processes.

To make these points is not to deny the importance of Foucault's emphasis on the discursive formation of our corporeal existence. It is to suggest that this emphasis ceases to be productive if it is pressed at the expense of proper recognition of the impossibility of dispensing with any reference to a pre-discursive reality. Difficult as it may be to sustain the tension between these contrary insights on the quality of our experience, it must be acknowledged that the invitation to view ourselves as cultural 'constructs' always contains within it a claim upon a self conceived as an autonomous centre of pain and pleasure, need and desire.

Feminists appealing to Foucault's arguments should therefore be wary of their anti-naturalist rhetoric. For to dismiss the idea of 'spontaneous' feeling is to undermine the feminist demand for a 'reclamation' of the body and the expression of an 'authentic' desire. Foucault's radical anti-essentialism can even be seen to lend itself to the forces of reaction in so far as it offers itself as a pre-emptive warning against any politics which aims at the removal of the constraining and distorting effects of cultural stereotyping.

What Foucault does, however, reveal is the dialectic at work in our discourses of the 'normal' and the 'natural'. His discussion of homosexuality is particularly instructive in the light it sheds on the ways in which societies legitimate their conventions of sexual behaviour by casting all those who do not conform as 'perverts' transgressing against the 'natural' order. He has also drawn attention, through his concept of the 'reverse discourse', to the way in which any suppressed and marginalised group will seek to contest its demonisation by insisting on its 'naturality', and hence be invoking, even as it challenges, the legitimating discourse of the oppressor. In this sense, he has invited us to view what is constituted as 'normal' as dependent upon, and even incorporating, what it seeks to exclude as 'perverse'; and to view what is castigated as 'perverse' as problematically reliant on the discourse of 'naturality' which it hopes to subvert. As Jonathan Dollimore has commented apropos of Foucault's discussion of homosexuality:

> We know that the centre remains vulnerable to marginality because its identity is partly created and partly defined in opposition (and therefore also *at*) the margins. But the concept of reverse discourse suggests another dialectic sense that the outsider may be said to be always already inside: a return from demonized other to challenging presence via containment, and one involving a simultaneous, contradictory, yet equally necessary appropriation and negation of those dominant

notions of sexual identity and human nature by which it was initially excluded and defined.

(Dollimore 1991: 225)

The pertinence of this 'dialectic' to an understanding of the social positioning of minority groups, and of the political moves available to them is, I think, incontestable. But it also has its bearing for feminism in so far as the gender hierarchy has been sustained through a discursive construction of 'woman' as 'other' and by an insistence on the 'naturality' of her subordinate and excluded status. It has generally been by means of a 'reverse discourse', in which women proclaim the 'perversity' of the constructed norms of feminine identity, that this situation has been challenged.

Suggestive as it is, however, of the discursive dependencies which govern our appeals to what is 'normal', 'natural' and 'authentic', this 'dialectic' is by no means adequate to a full understanding either of the forms taken by feminist resistance, or of the complex processes whereby the position of marginal and subordinate groups comes to be changed. First, it is by no means clear that either gay culture or feminism has always stated its resistance in the discourse of the 'oppressor' (indeed, a great deal of current feminist discourse deliberately attempts to sidestep or transcend its 'masculinist' logic). Secondly, the force of the idea that 'resistance' is always re-contained within dominant culture relies on an undialectical conception of society itself. For it invites us to overlook the transformative and progressive potential for 'dominant culture' of the margins it comes to 'contain'. For example, in so far as feminism has succeeded in breaking down earlier prejudices against women, it has also altered the 'excluding' and 'normalising' social parameters themselves.

Finally, however, it is important not to be seduced by the dialectic of the 'reverse discourse' into forgetting that the fate of oppressed groups is not decided simply at the level of competing discourses. What is critical to their advancement is the specific economic and political climate in which they are expressing their resistance, and this can be more or less favourable to their reception. Both gay and feminist opposition is quite experienced enough to know that it can be differently received in time of war than in time of peace, that the nature and quality of its success is tied very closely to prevailing economic conditions, and so on.

Granted these qualifications, the fact remains that Foucault has invited us to think about the nature and efficacy of the discourses of resistance in ways that are illuminating for any politics of emancipation. They are illuminating in part, and paradoxically, because they have helped to reveal what is unsatisfactory about glib left rejections of 'essentialism'. If Foucault's contradictions are 'productive', this is not because they show us the wisdom of rejecting 'essence', 'nature' and 'authenticity', but because of the light they shed on the self-defeating quality of the attempt to do so.

In this connection, it is relevant to note that Foucault has, in fact, provided some considerable ammunition to feminists seeking to 'reclaim' the body from 'medicalisation' and subjection to an intrusive 'male' science. He has also prompted a rediscovery of the 'authentic' body which comes of seeing it as the object of forms of power which work primarily through the agency of the subject. For if Foucault himself has focused on the body as a site of an 'objectivising' disciplinary power exercised through the various medical, educational, military and penal institutions and their associated forms of scientific know-how, he has also alerted us to the co-opted and collusive role of the subject, as a dutiful and desiring individual, in the operation of this bio-politics and its routinising and confessional techniques. Feminists have not been slow to see the relevance of this dimension of his argument to the understanding of the more 'unofficial' processes of genderisation. Hence the studies they have offered of the ways in which 'femininity' is subjectively 'inscribed' on the body through various forms of voluntary self-policing and surveillance (slimming, electrolysis, distorting and painful clothing, and so forth).[2]

This Foucauldian attention to the cultural 'construction' of women in their bodily and sexual being is, however, not without its snares and limitations. For it risks retaining that obsession with female corporeality which has been so prevalent in patriarchal culture itself, and is thus arguably lending itself to the same procedures of masculine power which it is seeking to overthrow. The emphasis, moreover, on the body and sexuality as *effects* of power encourages a theoretical absorption in the *phenomenology* of those effects at the cost of any serious analysis of why women are at the mercy of this 'power' in the first place. It therefore fails to offer any clear picture of the interrelationship between the bio-political and socio-economic dimensions of female subordination. In this respect, Foucault may be said to advocate an individualistic and even narcissistic conception of liberation. The focus is on the politics of 'self-making' and the 'aesthetic of the self' (of the kind, in fact, to which Foucault devotes a good part of his *History of Sexuality*) rather than on those structural determinants of women's lives which still tend today to make this kind of 'identity' politics the privilege of a minority of feminists.

Such cautions, of course, are rooted in materialist premises from which Foucault himself stated his distance. They may not deter those who value Foucault's work not only for the insights it sheds on female experience, but also for his iconoclastic rupture with the two 'grand narratives' of Marxism and psychoanalysis to which so much feminism has linked its own story and provided the women's supplement. For these feminists, it is a key attraction of Foucault's approach that it in principle frees the subject from the fixity and determination of both economic circumstances and infantile experience. Yet the under-theorised nature of Foucault's concept of 'power' is nowhere more clearly revealed than in the clash between this existentialist impulse of his argument and his otherwise relentless deconstruction of the autonomous Enlightenment subject.[3] This brings us to a further, paradoxical, area of overlap between feminist and Foucauldian interests: that of what one might term 'gender Utopianism'.

GENDER UTOPIANISM

I speak of this convergence as paradoxical because, although a concern with emancipation is clearly central to the feminist project, the very coherence of any such concern is in many ways called into question by the Foucauldian logic. Foucault has on the whole desisted from 'progressivist' talk, and this is consistent with his genealogical disengagement from an evolutionary-revolutionary historical perspective. He has not, however, entirely forgone all speculation on the quality of liberation and on what is desirable in the way of future agendas, at least in regard to sexuality. Even as he advises us to think only in terms of a history of differing regimes of power, and a succession of knowledges whose only purpose is to continue, at the same time he beckons us towards a society which has transcended all normalising sexual codes and gender regulations, and whose members encounter one another only in the depoliticised experience of 'bodies and pleasures' (Foucault 1978: 159).

Such a gesture towards transcendence of the power/knowledge axis is, of course, both clearly implied and, in a sense demanded, by the explicitly pejorative vocabulary in which Foucault describes the operation of modern power. For to speak of power as 'disciplinary' and 'regimental', to depict it as rooted in 'dividing practices', 'individualising techniques' and modes of 'surveillance', is surreptitiously to invoke a desire which aspires to be free of this subjectifying machinery and its panoptical gaze. In this sense, the 'Utopian' element in Foucault's thinking is consistent with the critical edge of his own discourse. But there is no doubt that there is some considerable tension between the normative-political Foucault who aspires to an anarchic freedom from governance, and the theoretical-analytical Foucault who speaks to us only of the inevitability of domination.

It should therefore be acknowledged that it is only in this anarcho-existentialist dimension of his argument that Foucault coincides with the emancipatory and Utopian logic of feminism, or indeed can offer the latter any protection against a Foucauldian account of its own 'normalising' and 'disciplining' role as a discourse which invites us always to scrutinise and police our behaviours in the light of the 'truth' and 'knowledge' it has offered us about gender relations. Feminists drawing on Foucault's work will therefore need to emphasise the deregulating potential, rather than the politicising aspects of feminist discourse – its capacity to destabilise sexual identity rather than to re-shape it. But in doing so, they will also come up against the same 'productive' contradiction, between the promise of liberation and its prohibition, which lies at the heart of the Foucauldian conception of power. This contradiction is here met in an acute form, since the 'promise' of women's liberation would seem to return Foucault and his feminist followers to precisely that 'repressive hypothesis' about the blocking of a 'natural' desire, which the prohibition has deconstructed. The alternative, of course, is to maintain that ambivalent position between scepticism and libertarianism which has prompted Terry Eagleton to remark that it allows Foucault

> to combine, in a manner typical of much post-structuralism, a kind of secret apocalyptic ultra-leftism with a dry-eyed, pragmatic political reformism. It protects Foucault at once from the reactionary and the romantic – the latter being a vice to which

French intellectuals, one might claim, are peculiarly allergic, preferring on the whole to be thought wicked rather than gullible.
(Eagleton 1991: 386)[4]

This is not to deny that it is always open to feminists to shift the
balance of the ambivalence towards the romantic pole, and open
themselves rather more fully than perhaps Foucault does himself
to the prospect of a degendered, 'polysexual' future. If we do,
however, retain any element of pragmatism at all, then I think it
does require us to consider how far this is a realisable, or even
desirable, future. So far, it seems to me, these issues have been
rather little explored in feminist writing. But two points suggest
themselves. First, it would seem clear that many men and women
will react to the idea of degenderisation as quite threatening to
their own identity and, to that extent, view it as an illegitimate
policing of their own desire and pleasure. The advocates of
'bodies and pleasures' may in this sense need – if they are being
consistently Foucauldian – to consider their own discourse as a
potential 'discipline' upon the subject.

There is also a problem about the individualistic, even
solipsistic, conception of the self which seems to underlie the idea
of 'gender invention' and 'polysexual' pleasure. This not only
seems to credit us with an implausible degree of control over our
affections, but also to suppose it desirable that we are freed of all
ties and duties in the pursuit of our 'pleasures'. It would appear
to rely, that is, on a valorisation of ourselves as sexual monads
accountable only to the dictates of our personal tastes and
dispositions, and hence to abstract entirely from questions of
inter-personal dependency and need. In fact, it is difficult not to
suspect that behind this fantasy of future gratification stands the
familiar isolated individual of liberal theory. Of course, if this is
the case, it is profoundly contradictory, since it is this supposedly
autonomous individual whom Foucault has invited us to view as
the construct of the individualising techniques of modern power.

This Foucauldian equivocation around the subject can in itself,
however, be seen to reproduce some of the ambivalences and
anxieties of the classic liberal conception, at least in the sense that
this, too, focuses on the policing function of the social, and seeks
to protect the individual from its incursions. As we shall see, this
covert appeal to an 'autonomous' subject is not without its bearing
on Foucault's androcentricity.

FOUCAULT AS ANDROCENTRIC

Greek and Greco-Roman sexual ethics

Several critics have remarked on Foucault's androcentric bias,[5] though its various dimensions have not been as fully noted as they might be. Foucault has been justly charged with offering an account of power which not only ignores those highly specific forms in which it is exercised in any sexually hierarchical society, but also overlooks the differential impact on the lives of men and women of the general 'disciplining' procedures to which he does attend. In this sense, it can be said that he retains at the very heart of his critique of the liberal-humanist and Marxist accounts of power something of that same universalising and gender-blind approach to humanity which, for feminism, is a central failing of these theories. Foucault, in other words, might be said to be somewhat implicitly reliant on a masculinist conception of the subject as the support for his polemic with humanism.

There is also something markedly androcentric in the quality of the attention Foucault brings to his study of the Greek and Greco-Roman sexual ethics in his history of sexuality (Foucault 1986, 1988). It is important, however, to be clear about the nature of this charge. Clearly Foucault does immerse us in the mores of highly patriarchal and patrician societies from which women were a priori excluded as significant ethical subjects; his genealogy of ethics is thus very much concerned with the desire and comportment of an elite of male citizens. But in a very real sense, the historian (or genealogist) of ideas has no option but to reflect the social pre-eminence of this group since it was largely responsible for the dominant culture. This is particularly true of anyone charting the mores of the ancient world, given the almost total absence of any documentation of the subjective forms of experience of other sectors of this community. The extensive attention paid to the ethics of antiquity and the early Christian period is quite justifiable in view of the influence of this legacy and the large-scale and comprehensive nature of the study to which Foucault was committed – and which was very much still an evolving project at the time of his death.

The complaint, then, is not that his work is too much weighted towards the study of these early historical formations. Nor would it be appropriate to accuse Foucault of being unaware of the sexism and elitism, and hence limited social reference, of the ideas about sexuality and the 'aesthetics' of the self, with which he is engaged in *The Use of Pleasure* and *The Care of the Self* since these are qualities to which he draws attention himself, and has remarked on forcibly. Thus in the course of one of his interviews with Paul Rabinow and Hubert Dreyfus, he notes that

> The Greek ethics were linked to a purely virile society with slaves, in which women were underdogs whose pleasure had no importance, whose sexual life had to be oriented toward and determined by, their status as wives, and so on.
>
> (Foucault in Rabinow 1984: 344)

Or again that

> The Greek ethics of pleasure is linked to a virile society, to dissymmetry, exclusion of the other, an obsession with penetration, and a kind of threat of being dispossessed of your own energy, and so on. All that is quite disgusting!
>
> (Ibid.: 346)

The charge of 'androcentricity' relates rather to the effects of Foucault's treatment of the history of ethics as a registering of the differential modes in which the (male) subject experiences his desires, sets rules of conduct for the self, and conceives his purposes in life. For this is to distract attention from another kind of history which Foucault in fact relies on for his argument, and continuously refers to, though always in a rather glancing fashion. This is the history of the causes of the changes – particularly the changes, as Foucault puts it, in 'marriage, society and so on' (Foucault in Rabinow 1984: 357) – whose impact on the male ethics of the self Foucault takes to be the central matter of concern. He focuses on the way in which this ethics of the self can be seen to reflect changed attitudes to boys or women, but not on what might have stimulated such changes of attitude in the first place. He draws attention to the shifts within this ethics – notably between the Greek, and Greco-Roman and early Christian responses to sexuality and the conduct of the 'good life' – and he suggests that there are socio-economic factors behind these which have their impact on the function and importance of marriage and the status of women in society.[6] But since he attends only to the effects of these at the level of the man's personal duties and comportment, we are offered a history whose primary object of study is the male perception of this more subterranean and relatively unexamined ethical development. Why after all, *does* marriage change, what, as it were, has been going on behind the scenes which issues in the more 'austere' requirements regarding the husband's marital fidelity, or the marginally more reciprocal nature of the relations between men and women on which Foucault remarks? Why by the time of Pliny has the relationship of at least some men to their wives (Pliny's own, for example) become much more a matter of love, passion and dependency, than appears to have been possible in Plato's day?[7] These questions surely point to changes in ethical relations which cannot be grasped simply through a behaviourist scrutiny of differences of a *reactive* kind in respect of masculine self-regulation?

Foucault certainly offers a wealth of scholarly knowledge on this 'ethics' of the self, and orders the material in ways that illuminate the differential forms in which this was pursued. But it is difficult, all the same, not to feel that some part of the story is missing: that part which might at least consider the role of inter-personal relations in prompting these mutations of a masculine ethics, and how far the doubtless expressed, though unrecorded, feelings of the women themselves may have been a contributory factor. It is, after all, an implication of Foucault's account that the ethical status of women has undergone some alteration, albeit rather minimal, over the historical span with which he is dealing. But if this is the case, does it not say something more about the changing forms of interaction between men and women than is registered in Foucault's emphasis on male rules and prohibitions? Would we not have to relate these changes more closely than Foucault wants to allow, to changes of an economic, political and social character? Foucault, in short, by abstracting as much as he can both from the social context of the ethical codes he is charting, and from the dialectic of personal relations, defines the ethical so as to make it appear a very private – and masculine – affair: a matter primarily of self-mastery and authorial creation.

To this one might add that, despite Foucault's noted disgust with the phallic quality of Greek sexuality, there is also the occasional slippage in that direction in his own discourse. His remark that 'in our society the main field of morality, the part of ourselves which is most relevant to morality, is our feeling (you can have a girl in the street or anywhere, if you have very good feelings towards your wife)' (Foucault 1984: 352) is hardly unprejudiced. The same goes for a number of other rather casual assumptions that when we are talking about 'our' morality we are talking about *his*.

The significance of the Lapcourt incident

There is, however, a further, and for me more worrying, dimension of Foucault's androcentricity which resides in his choice of what is 'significant' in the history of sexuality. In illustration, let me cite the anecdote which Foucault relates in the course of his discussion of the 'repressive hypothesis' in Volume I of *The History of Sexuality*. It tells of a simple-minded farmhand from the village of Lapcourt who in 1867 was reported to the mayor for obtaining, as Foucault (1978: 31) puts it, 'a few caresses from a little girl, just as he had done before and seen done by the village urchins round about him; for, at the edge of the wood, or in the ditch by the road leading to Saint-Nicholas, they would play the familiar game called "curdled milk" '. The mayor reported the incident to the gendarmes, who led him before the judge, who indicted him (though he was eventually acquitted), and turned him over to a doctor, who contacted two other experts, who eventually wrote and published a report on the case. What is significant about this story, asks Foucault – a question to which he responds (1978: 31–2) as follows:

> The pettiness of it all; the fact that this everyday occurrence in the life of village sexuality, these inconsequential bucolic pleasures, could become from a certain time, the object not only of a collective intolerance but of a judicial action, a medical intervention, a careful clinical examination and an entire theoretical elaboration. [. . .] So it was that our society – and it was doubtless the first in history to take such measures – assembled around these timeless gestures, these barely furtive pleasures between simple-minded adults and alert children, a whole machinery for speechifying, analyzing, and investigating.

But has Foucault offered us the true moral of this tale? Could it not be that what is significant about *his* discourse upon it is the extent to which it may be exonerating, displacing and repressing the 'event' that it is really about: this 'alert' (terrified?) little girl, who runs to her parents to report her 'inconsequential bucolic pleasures' (her distress at being slavered over in a ditch by a full-grown, mentally disturbed male?), thus summoning forth a 'collective intolerance' (alarm and sympathy?) over an episode remarkable only for its 'pettiness' (for the fact that something of this kind was for once accorded the attention it deserved?)? Foucault is surely right here: discourse is of the essence, and his own as nicely chosen as that of the exculpatory judge on a case of sexual harassment. How successful is it, too, in shifting our attention from the reality to the rhetoric, from the fright of the child victim to the phallic discipline of the academic luminary, whose vision is so dazzling on the issue of 'significance' that it all but blinds us to what may really be of most moment. At any rate, it would seem rather clear that child abuse neither preceded not gets constructed in this discourse.

This, it may be said, is an intemperate, even mildly hysterical, response to what is, after all, a mere trifle of a narrative when viewed in the context of Foucault's work as a whole. In any case, perhaps Foucault is right. Perhaps nothing very serious was going on at the edge of that field, and Foucault precisely targets, therefore, the degree to which 'sexuality' is summoned into being out of a lot of discursive fuss about nothing.

But the problem is to know how Foucault knows that 'nothing' was going on. Why should we accept the word for it of one who was not there, who never interviewed the child, who is arguably himself caught up in the discourse of 'inconsequential bucolic pleasures', and who in the end is inviting us to accept the 'truth' of his own account only on the basis of his personal sense of the significance of these events? What does 'nothing' mean in this context? Nothing that was being talked about? That we may accept. But Foucault would seem to imply here something further than this: that there was nothing to *justify* the talk, and this surely is a rather different point, and one that suggests that Foucault contra Foucault does, after all, think that the discourses of sexuality are about some extra-discursive reality which they may be said to represent more or less adequately (in this case, according to him, very distortingly).

But let us pursue a rather different tack. Why not take the same line on feminism? There were all those women getting on with their rather inconsequential female roles at the margins of society and not finding too much to complain about, indeed rather enjoying their furtive existence, when suddenly some Mary

Wollstonecraft or Simone de Beauvoir starts wondering whether it is all quite as pleasurably in order as she had been led to believe up till then, and goes off to pen a few notes. The notes extend into a book, which is handed over to a publisher, who discloses it to the world at large, and lo and behold, a whole machinery of discourse comes into being, spawning literally thousands of other studies and that collective female intolerance which comes to be known as 'feminism'.

Would Foucault here too want us to remark the 'pettiness' of it all? Would he want to address us with that same rhetorical gesture he brings to the discussion of the Lapcourt incident, as if to say: 'how extraordinary it is how societies acquire these *idées fixes* at times, and suddenly begin to scrutinise all those innocuous and timeless arrangements to which they had previously turned a blind eye – and no one can say quite why, because there is not anything really which the fixations are about, nothing other than the talk, the fuss and their effects?'

I suspect, in fact, that Foucault would not want to dismiss the emergence of feminism in these terms, since he clearly deems it to be a significant and enlightening development. But there is surely something of a dilemma here. For if we do want to claim that feminism is an important event in the history of sexuality, there would seem to be only two ways of accounting for it. Either the whole machinery of speechifying, analysing and investigating which constitutes feminism is remarkable because there is something here that is worthy of attention, it is not simply trivial. The discourse is *about* something in that it is justified by a condition (of oppression) which precedes it and to which we are alerted in its feminist representation. In this case feminism as a discursive formation would seem analysed in terms which transgress the Foucauldian claims about the discursive construction of 'sexuality' (as offered, for example, apropos of the Lapcourt incident).

Alternatively, we stay with the Foucauldian line of argument, which means denying that there is any 'reality' extrinsic to our systems of belief (or any 'oppression' which precedes its discourse), and therefore insist that the importance of feminism resides in the reality it constitutes: in the new set of beliefs, norms and values it brings into being. Feminism's significance then lies in the fact that it exposes (and thereby comes to replace) the purely normative and political character of a pre-feminist 'reality' – that is, a reality which had viewed the subordination of women and the differential treatment of the sexes as pre-ordained by nature and therefore incontestable.

But if we take this line, why should we not approach the discursive formation generated around the Lapcourt episode in some similar fashion in order to remark, not on its 'pettiness', but on its normative impact? Why, for example, should we not view all that 'intolerance' and 'surveillance', those numerous studies and disquisitions, all that *knowledge* which exposed the normalising role of the discourse of 'inconsequential bucolic pleasures' and 'timeless gestures' in keeping us quiet about child abuse, as a deconstruction of a sexuality previously claimed as of no import?

Conversely, however, if we are prepared to allow Foucault to decide for us that little, if anything, was really to be remarked upon in what we may at least suspect was a case of child molestation, why should we not equally respect the decision of all those who have wanted to react to feminism as an unreasonable and over-blown form of 'intolerance'? Would it not have been perfectly in accord with Foucault's own procedure in the case of the Lapcourt events for feminism to have been found 'significant' – as indeed it has tended to be by its opponents – only in the fluster and histrionics it precipitated around previously timeless, natural arrangements?

Now it may be said in response to all this that in failing to detect the irony in Foucault's 'nostalgic' description of the Lapcourt incident, I have overlooked its critical force in exposing the disjuncture between earlier and contemporary attitudes to sexual deviation.[8] Where Foucault's approach has the advantage, it might be said, over more conventional treatments, is that it precisely does not appeal to modern sensibilities, but rather exposes us to the 'shock' of their difference from prior perceptions. It thus also serves to highlight what does appear to be an arbitrary and purely discursive element in our moral changes of heart.

It is certainly true that by emphasising the 'productive' dimension of knowledge, Foucault alerts us to the element of reflexivity involved in our 'moral panics' and shifts of ethical focus, thereby exposing the deficiency of attempts to explain these wholly in terms of a pre-discursive reality. What I have tried to expose, however, is the deficient – and all too arbitrary – character of any Foucauldian account of discursive formations which severs them from the material circumstances of their emergence and from the impact of these on human experience.

We should understand, moreover, that even if knowledge is productive of new norms and 'disciplines' upon the subject, it is also the force which releases the subject from the coercion of ignorance and superstition. Indeed, Foucault can only convince us of the specific forms in which knowledge is employed in the co-option of the modern self, by implicitly invoking its power to liberate us from earlier, more bigoted, attitudes.

One might cite as an example here the parallels which Foucault has invited us to draw between the inquisitional procedures of modern medicine and psychotherapy, and the religious confession. These have certainly been illuminating of our contemporary faith in science, and of our trust in the power of knowledge to bring salvation. They have suggested, that is, that getting at the 'truth' of our experience, and naming its name, may neither be as voluntary nor as liberating as we have been led to believe. But these parallels between priest and lay practitioner are reliant for their force on the light shed by the secular and scientific discourses of modernity on theological mystification, and the guilts and superstitions encouraged by the Church. The rhetorical power of the comparisons, between the clinical and white-coated gaze of the contemporary therapist and the unctuous probings of the religious confessor,[9] rests on a liberation from our awe for the latter which the former has helped to dispel. For it is only as the discourses of science have discredited the discourse of 'sin' and 'grace', 'divine wrath' and 'eternal felicity' that we have been placed in a position to appreciate the idea that religious confession has functioned as a technique for the worldly co-option of souls – as a disciplining strategy which worked through the promise of salvation. But without this appreciation, Foucault's analogies would have no purchase on our understanding.

If this is right, it suggests that we may need to readjust the bias of Foucault's account in order to recognise not only the power of knowledge in constructing the self, but also its disintegrative effects on the constituting powers of ignorance and silence. Moreover, if power re-invests us, by means of a continuous disinvestment of the powers of discourse to which we have previously been held in thrall, then this suggests that it relies for its operation on a certain continuity of experience – of a kind to allow us to see that what we had not seen before is relevant to our former experience. In so far as Foucault appeals to our capacity to understand cross-cultural references – to understand, for example, the similarity in the operation of secular and religious discourses on sexuality – he tacitly acknowledges more of a trans-historic core to human sensibilities and powers of understanding than his emphasis on the dislocation and radical discontinuity between epistemes might seem to imply.

It is certainly good to be reminded of these cultural disjunctures of experience, and of how far we are the creatures of our own particular time and place. But our very awareness of these shifts of rationality presupposes a capacity to detect the lines of communication between our own experience and that of our predecessors. Strange as we are to the past, and it to us, we are not so strange as not to perceive the nature of our separation. One is tempted here to appeal to the rather distant figure of Chaucer, who, in Foucauldian vein, remarks on how oddly the expressions of sentiment used in an earlier age now strike the ears of his contemporaries. But, as he also points out, those who employed this archaic language of love fared no less well in their amours: 'Ek for to wynnen love in sondry ages/ In sondry londes, sondry ben usages.'[10]

CONCLUSION

If I have dwelt in these last remarks on some of the more general paradoxes of Foucault's account of knowledge and power, it is because it is these which are ultimately responsible for the specific tensions his work presents for feminism. Feminism, after all, is about dismantling a gender hierarchy which is patently trans-cultural and trans-historic. But if we were to attend only to Foucault's explicit polemic against conventional historical understanding, it would seem impossible that we could detect any sameness in the forms of oppression to which women have perennially and in almost all cultures been subjected. Feminism is about freeing men and women from distorting and disabling conceptions of themselves and of their relations to one another. But if we pay heed only to Foucault's reminders of the co-opting and disciplining role of discourse, it is not clear how we can even state, let alone aspire to emancipatory aims of this kind. Feminism is about contesting the multiple forms of power responsible for female subordination. But though Foucault everywhere refers us to power, he has very little to tell us about its nature and sources other than to inform us that it is an effect of discursive formations which are themselves theorised as the effect of power.

I state these points baldly here and in deliberately prejudicial fashion. They are not intended as dismissals of the relevance of Foucault's argument to feminism, whose value lies precisely in the extent to which he has invited feminists to think more deeply and self-critically about the formulation of their classic 'realist' case. But if discourse theory has served to expose some of the naïveties in standard forms of feminist reasoning, it is equally the case that it itself can offer no adequate comprehension of the oppression of women or of the resistance to it. Feminism then, can best benefit from a Foucauldian mediation by remaining very aware of the limitations of its particular bias and self-subverting dimensions. A gender politics which ignores or rejects this mediation will be the weaker for it. But a feminism which posits an unanchored 'power' as the precipitating force behind all changes in gender relations will be no more explanatorily satisfactory than a realism which is insensitive to the constitutive role of discourse.

NOTES

1 This is not to suggest that feminist denunciations of the importance of biology, or culturalist accounts of sex (of the kind, for example, to be found in the writing of Christine Delphy or Monique Wittig), have necessarily drawn on Foucault's argument or evolved under its influence.
2 See, for example, Bordo (1988) and Bartky (1988) and cf. Frigga Haug's more critical discussion (1987: 190–208). For a Foucauldian-influenced discussion of sexual advice, see Brunt (1982); cf. Heath (1982).
3 For a relevant discussion which stages a confrontation between Foucault and the psychoanalytic feminism of Dorothy Dinnerstein, Nancy Chodorow and Jane Flax, and argues the superiority of the latter position, see Isaac Balbus (1987). Cf. also Morris (1988); Dollimore (1991); Dews (1987, 1989).
4 Cf. Eagleton 1991: 387; 390–2.
5 See Diamond and Quinby 1988: xiv–xvii; Bartkowski 1988: 43–6; Morris 1988: 26; cf. Balbus 1987.
6 Foucault remarks of the Roman Imperial period that
    It does seem, however, that the art of leading the married life was considered and defined in several important texts in a relatively new way. The first change appears to consist in the fact that the art of matrimonial existence, while continuing to be concerned with the household, its management, the birth and procreation of children, places an increasing value on a particular relationship

between husband and wife, the tie that joins them, their behaviours toward each other.

(Foucault 1988: 148)

Marriage thus comes to be defined by a 'stylistics of the individual bond' (ibid.). (Foucault's behaviourist circumlocution for what the rest of us might refer to as 'love'?) (See Foucault 1988: 148; 1986: 166–84 and more generally, Part III, Chapter 1 and Part V.)

7 Cf. Pliny's yearning letter to his wife (cited in Foucault 1986: 78–9). Foucault's failure to address these questions directly speaks to a refusal to acknowledge the ethical relevance of the subject as a centre of affections, impulses and resistances. Cf. Terry Eagleton's remark that Foucault

still cannot quite bring himself to address the subject as such. What we have here, rather than the subject and its desires, is the body and its pleasures - a half-way, crab-wise, aestheticising move towards the subject which leaves love as technique and conduct rather than as tenderness and affection, as praxis rather than interiority.

(1991: 395)

8 I am grateful to Peter Dews for raising this point with me.
9 Cf. Foucault 1986: 158–9. For a discussion and critique of Foucault's tendency to neglect differences between religious and secular confessional techniques, see Cousins and Hussain (1984: Part III, Ch. 8) (though, as Cousins and Hussain note, Foucault does himself suggest that we ought in fact to respect these differences). Relevant here is Peter Dews's point that

Foucault does not explain how the 'effort in discipline and normalization' is *enhanced* by the application of scientific knowledge. The reason for this failure is not difficult to discover. For, were Foucault to admit that the application of scientific knowledge increases the effectivity of action, he would be obliged to abandon his underlying relativist stance, and to admit the reality of 'progress' in at least one dimension of rationality: the cognitive-instrumental dimension. Hence the crossing of the 'technological' threshold by disciplines, the spiralling reinforcement of power and knowledge which Foucault evokes, remains theoretically unexplained.

(Dews 1989: 37)

10 The passage in question is from Chaucer's *Troilus and Criseyde*, Book II, 22–8:

Ye knowe ek that in forme of speche is chaunge
Withinne a thousand yeer, and wordes tho
That haden pris, now wonder nyce and straunge
Us thinketh hem, and yet thei spake hem so,
And spedde as wel in love as men now do;
Ek for to wynnen love in sondry ages,
In sondry londes, sondry ben usages.

BIBLIOGRAPHY

Balbus, I. (1987) 'Disciplining women: Michel Foucault and the power of feminist discourse', in S. Benhabib and D.Cornell (eds) *Feminism as Critique*, Oxford: Polity Press.

Bartkowski, F. (1988) 'Epistemic drift in Foucault', in I. Diamond and L. Quinby (eds) *Feminism and Foucault: Reflections on Resistance*, Boston: Northeastern University Press.

Bartky, S.L. (1988) 'Foucault, femininity and the modernization of patriarchal power', in I. Diamond and L. Quinby (eds) *Feminism and Foucault: Reflections on Resistance*, Boston: Northeastern University Press.

Benhabib, S. and Cornell, D. (eds) (1987) *Feminism as Critique*, Oxford: Polity Press.

Bordo, S. (1988) 'Anorexia nervosa: psychopathology and the crystallization of culture', in I. Diamond and L. Quinby (eds) *Feminism and Foucault: Reflections on Resistance*, Boston: Northeastern University Press.

Brunt, R. (1982) 'An immense verbosity: persuasive sexual advice in the 1970s', in R. Brunt and C. Rowan (eds) *Feminism, Culture and Politics*, London: Lawrence & Wishart.

Butler, J. (1987) 'Variations of sex and gender', in S. Benhabib and D.Cornell (eds) *Feminism as Critique*, Oxford: Polity Press.

—— (1990a) 'Gender trouble', in L. Nicholson (ed.) *Feminism and Postmodernism*, London: Routledge.

—— (1990b) *Gender Trouble: Feminism and the Subversion of Identity*, London: Routledge.

Cousins, M. and Hussain, A. (1984) *Michel Foucault*, London: Macmillan.

Dews, P. (1987) *Logics of Disintegration*, London: Verso.

—— (1989) 'The return of the subject in late Foucault', *Radical Philosophy*, 51: 37–41.

Diamond, I. and Quinby, L. (eds) (1988) *Feminism and Foucault: Reflections on Resistance*, Boston: Northeastern University Press.

Dollimore, J. (1991) *Sexual Dissidence, Augustine to Wilde, Freud to Foucault*, Oxford: Clarendon Press.

Eagleton, T. (1991) *The Ideology of the Aesthetic*, Oxford: Blackwell.

Foucault, M. (1978) *The History of Sexuality*, vol. I: *An Introduction*, Harmondsworth: Penguin.

—— (1984) 'On the genealogy of ethics: an overview of work in progress', in P. Rabinow (ed.) *The Foucault Reader*, London: Penguin.

—— (1986) *The History of Sexuality*, vol. II: *The Use of Pleasure*, London: Viking Penguin.

—— (1988) *The History of Sexuality*, vol. III: *The Care of the Self*, London: Penguin.

Habermas, J. (1986) 'Taking aim at the heart of the present', in D.C. Hoy (ed.) *Foucault: A Critical Reader*, Oxford: Blackwell.

Haug, F. (1987) *Female Sexualisation*, London: Verso.

Heath, S. (1982) *The Sexual Fix*, London: Macmillan.

Morris, M. (1988) 'The pirate's fiancée', in I. Diamond and L. Quinby (eds) *Feminism and Foucault: Reflections on Resistance*, Boston: Northeastern University Press.

Rabinow, P. (ed.) (1984) *The Foucault Reader*, London: Penguin.

Chapter 3

Practices of freedom

Jean Grimshaw

The ambivalence that many feminists have felt towards Foucault's work is brought out strikingly in the following passage, written by Toril Moi in 1985.

> What could be more seductive for feminists than a discourse which, like that of Michel Foucault in *La Volonté de Savoir* (*The History of Sexuality*), focuses on the complex interaction of power and sexuality? . . . Alluring as they may seem, however, the apparent parallels between Foucault's work and feminism ought not to deceive us. Feminists ought to resist his seductive ploys since, as I shall argue in this essay, the price for giving in to his powerful discourse is nothing less than the depoliticisation of feminism. If we capitulate to Foucault's analysis, we will find ourselves caught up in a sado-masochistic spiral of power and resistance which, circling endlessly in heterogeneous movement, creates a space in which it will be quite impossible to argue that women under patriarchy constitute an oppressed group, let alone develop a theory of their liberation.
>
> (Moi 1985: 95)

Moi moves from this passage to a blistering critique of the ways in which Foucault constructs a picture of nineteenth-century French sexuality that seems to ignore the power structures within which feminists have claimed that women were oppressed by men. Foucault argued that the human subject is constituted within a complex network of discourses and power relationships which allow for no resistance that is not situated within these. There is no 'single locus of great Refusal, no soul of revolt, source of all rebellions, or pure law of the revolutionary. Instead there is a plurality of resistances, each of them a special case' (Foucault 1981: 95–6). To accept Foucault's analysis, Moi argues, commits feminism to the view that we can neither answer the question of what resists power, nor give any fundamental critique of the notion of 'power' itself.

It is interesting to contrast Moi's (strikingly sexualised) view of Foucault as a potential 'seducer' of feminism with his own conception of his work. Foucault sometimes saw his own writing as a 'tool box', from which the tools might be bent and distorted in ways not envisaged by their creator. Despite Foucault's own distance from feminism, a number of feminist writers have seen aspects of Foucauldian methods or theory as capable of being usefully appropriated for feminist purposes. 'Foucault' and 'feminism' should not, however, be seen as two wholly discrete blocks of theory which might or might not be brought into a relationship. Conflicting readings of Foucault abound, and there are times when Foucault himself seemed to encourage this. In addition, there is no easy set of indicators of usefulness to feminist theory; whether 'tools' are useful or not depends on the job which one wishes them to do. Those who attempt to theorise the situation of women sometimes have very different theoretical and political allegiances, and amongst them there is no clearly agreed set of 'tasks' which theory should perform. Whether or not one finds Foucault useful will depend on whether the tasks that one sees as important for feminist theory *already* bear similarities to the enterprises that Foucault undertook. And perhaps whether or not one sees Foucault as a potentially dangerous 'seducer' depends on whether one starts from a set of problems or a theoretical framework to which Foucault's writings are antithetical.

With one further qualification, however, the toolbox metaphor can be useful. The qualification is this: it is just as important to ask whether there are respects in which Foucauldian analysis raises difficulties which can be addressed by an understanding of the problems faced by feminist theory. It is not so much a question of whether 'Foucault' can be useful to 'feminism' (or vice versa) – or whether some 'synthesis' of the two can be found. It is rather a question of what affinities there are between some of the questions that feminist theory has addressed and those that Foucault addresses, and what sort of dialectic can be created between these.

FOUCAULT, FEMINISM AND THE 'DECONSTRUCTION' OF SUBJECTIVITY

Foucault took issue with all notions of 'man' as an autonomous and self-determining agent. The self, as it appears in many of Foucault's writings – notably in the introduction to *The History of Sexuality* (1981) – is seen as created by discourses.[1] Foucault explores, for example, the idea of the 'deep self' as an effect of historical practices and discourses such as the Christian confessional, psychoanalysis and much contemporary discussion of sexuality. The task of 'genealogy', the name which Foucault gave to his method of researching history, is to enquire into these practices and discourses. But one of the major enterprises of feminist theory has been the 'deconstruction' of female subjectivity, and the analysis of the extent to which women's experiences of themselves as subjects may be constructed within discourses, practices and power relationships.[2] It is not surprising that some feminist writers have drawn on Foucault's writings. Susan Bordo (1989), for example, has shown how Foucault's analysis of disciplines of the body might help to illuminate the phenomenon of anorexia. Sandra Bartky (1990a), in a discussion of the relationship of women to the fashion and beauty industry, draws on Foucault's analysis of power as not located in any single source. She notes the apparent 'facelessness' of many of the imperatives of fashion and beauty, which appear to emanate from nowhere in particular, and to the ways in which these lead women to practise endless forms of self-surveillance in order to be 'feminine'. But if some writers have found Foucault useful in what might be called the 'deconstructive' tasks of feminist theory, others have suggested that there are dangers and gaps in Foucault's analyses of power and subjectivity.

It has been argued that there are acute problems with Foucault's conception of power – see, for example, Fraser (1989), Dews (1986), Taylor (1986), Best and Kellner (1991). In *Discipline and Punish* (1979), Foucault was concerned with the ways in which the modern subject was constituted by disciplinary technologies of power, which operated primarily through the body, producing 'docile bodies' which were traversed through and through by power.[3] The book presents us with a striking image of 'the carceral society'; of modern societies as characterised by an erosion of older freedoms by processes of 'normalisation' or the increasing marginalisation of deviance, and by the increasing colonisation of human subjectivity. But it has been suggested that this image is unbalanced and distorted; it cannot sensibly be taken for an image of modern societies, period. Society is *not* adequately to be compared to a gigantic prison, and Foucault's broad use of the concept of 'discipline' may serve to conceal extremely important differences between so-called 'disciplinary' practices – or differences between liberal democratic and fascistic societies.

It has been asked, in addition, whether Foucault can adequately theorise resistance. In *The History of Sexuality* Foucault criticised the repressive conception of power. Power, he argued, has to be understood as 'productive'. Sex, for example, is not essentially a true identity in some fixed sense; rather, techniques of power/knowledge have *produced* the idea of sex as 'the secret' of human identity. Practices such as the confessional and psychoanalysis have produced a 'hermeneutics of the deep self'; the desire to ferret out its innermost and hidden secrets. Rather than seeing these things as potentially liberating, Foucault sees them as involving forms of normalisation and subjection. In his view, power is 'everywhere'; it cannot be understood as having any particular source, or as imposed from above, hence it cannot be the possession of any particular social group. It is 'capillary'; it operates from below.

But if the subject is constituted by relations of power in this way, what space can there be for resistance? If norms of 'femininity', for example, cannot be understood as simply imposed, how can women resist them? Foucault has responded often in his more recent writings to these kinds of objections, and has frequently claimed that power and resistance go together; there is never power without resistance. Precisely because he does not see power as located in a single source, precisely because he thinks that the concept of power as the *possession* of a particular group is not adequate to characterise the operations of power in modern societies, he argues that power can never be uniform, total or smooth in its operations. It is always shifting and unstable, and it always generates resistance.

But even if power necessarily generates resistance, then on what grounds do we (or can we) resist? Can norms of femininity, for example, be resisted in the name of a 'true' female nature which has been suppressed? Questions such as these lead to the second main type of problem that critics have seen with Foucault's concept of power. There is (especially perhaps in *Discipline and Punish*), an implicit sense of moral outrage at the oppressiveness of modern disciplinary techniques. But if resistance is ever to be seen as something more than a spontaneous and anarchic refusal of the power relations implicit in any particular network, how is it to be justified? And how might we distinguish between effective and ineffective forms of resistance?

Critics – for example, Dews (1986), Fraser (1989) and Taylor (1986) – have made two particular points. First, if the concept of 'power' is extended so widely that power becomes, in effect, a constitutive principle of *all* human relationships, then power cannot be seen *in itself* as a bad thing. It would be as pointless to complain, in principle, about the operations of 'power' as it would be to complain about the 'restrictiveness' of the conventions of human language. In that case there are two problems about Foucault's implicitly condemnatory attitude towards power. Do we not need to make crucial distinctions between malign and benign forms of power? And does not the critique of power require some independent critical stance or perspective? Nancy Fraser (1989), for instance, argues that a crucial defect of Foucault's work lies in the absence of a clear normative framework. The force of his implicit condemnation of disciplinary practices derives from an unacknowledged acceptance and use of 'Enlightenment' values of freedom, justice and so forth, which Foucault has also apparently set out to demolish. Although it may for certain purposes be methodologically legitimate to suspend a normative framework, in the end, Fraser argues, if he is to be consistent, Foucault has a choice. He can either admit that his theoretical framework can only lead to nihilism and pessimism, or he has to come up-front, and admit that he is appealing to certain values of freedom and justice, and to an idea of 'liberation' which, if accepted openly, would force him profoundly to modify his conception of power, and acknowledge that power is held by some over others. The fundamental charge here is that Foucault's work, although maybe useful to some extent in contributing to the feminist 'deconstructive' project, in the end offers nothing to the projects of articulating a vision of the future, a critical feminist ethics, or a coherent feminist politics.

This perception of Foucault's work distinguishes, then, between the 'deconstructive' and the 'reconstructive' project. Foucault can offer some useful 'tools' from time to time in the task of providing a 'genealogy' of female subjectivity. But beyond this he has little to offer.

PRACTICES OF FREEDOM

The perception of Foucault that I have outlined in the previous section of this chapter depends at least partly, however, on the view that it is possible clearly to distinguish the 'deconstructive' from the 'reconstructive' project. But some feminist writing on Foucault suggests, implicitly at least, that there is no sharp boundary between the two. Jana Sawicki's work on Foucault is a case in point. Sawicki (1991) argues that a Foucauldian approach can offer a useful alternative to feminist analyses which adopt over-monolithic notions of male power and male control of women, or which retain Utopian visions of the total reconstruction or autonomy of female desire.

In an interview given in 1983, Foucault wrote: 'My point is not that everything is bad, but that everything is dangerous, which is not exactly the same as bad. If everything is dangerous, then we always have something to do. So my position leads not to apathy, but to a hyper- and pessimistic activism' (1986: 343). Foucault constantly points out in his writings how traditional emancipatory theories have been blind to their own dominating and oppressive tendencies. Sawicki argues that this recognition is crucial for feminism, for two reasons. First, women themselves are implicated in many forms of domination and oppression. The white woman, for example, on the Southern slave plantation, was caught in a complex web of gender and racial oppression, in which images of 'woman' were closely linked with images of 'race'. Or the highly paid woman executive who struggles against discrimination may earn herself a place in a system which is itself premised on the continuing exploitation of low-paid workers.

In addition, feminist thinking and practice itself has not been innocent of divisive, exclusionary and oppressive tendencies. Some examples will illustrate this. First, one of the most important themes of feminist writing in recent years has been the way in which certain forms of feminist theory and practice have marginalised many women; not merely by the unthinking use of the concept of 'woman' itself in a manner that elides difference, but by the very use of the sign of 'difference', which may construct some women as 'Other' – and thus, in a different way, still marginalised. Secondly, the concept of 'autonomy' has, for good reasons, been a central one in feminist thinking. But attempts to theorise the ways in which women might gain greater autonomy and resist aspects of the common construction of female subjectivity have sometimes led to views of an 'authentic' feminist self which have been implicitly contemptuous of any woman who does not conform to some ideal of 'feminist' behaviour or lifestyle (see, for example, Daly 1979 and 1984). Thirdly, the common feminist dislike of hierarchy, which has often resulted in strenuous efforts to be wholly democratic and abolish formal modes of leadership, has sometimes resulted in what can be called 'the tyranny of structurelessness'; a pragmatic domination by the more experienced and articulate which may sometimes be less easy to oppose than more formal modes of procedure.

Feminist debates about sexuality have brought to light a series of problems in feminist conceptions of power and freedom. Sawicki argues that a Foucauldian approach can offer an alternative to both radical and libertarian approaches. Libertarian approaches either suppose a 'natural' sexuality which merely has to be released, or they see the issues around sexuality simply as those of 'freedom of choice'. Neither of these recognise the ways in which sexuality is not simply a 'given' in human life, and the ways in which all human choices are constrained. On the other hand, radical feminist analyses which operate with a social constructionist model of sexuality may also operate with an over-centralised notion of power, and suggest that female sexuality, as currently constituted, is solely an effect of male power and ideology; see, for example, Dworkin (1987) and MacKinnon (1987). Writers such as Dworkin and MacKinnon seem to suggest that women should have total self-determination before they can be said to be 'free' in their desires, and total autonomy over the question of defining or constructing their own sexuality. A totalistic view of power is allied with an almost wholly negative attitude towards any current forms of sexual desire. Sawicki argues that this Utopian conception of freedom has nihilistic consequences for the present. The ambiguity and multiplicity of current sexual practices is totally denied; male desire itself is usually left unanalysed, and there is an over-emphasis on the victimisation of women, who tend to be seen as passive containers of male ideology. Sexuality, she suggests, should neither be seen as a site wholly of resistance nor of domination, and it is crucial for feminist analysis to recognise the irreducible plurality, ambiguity and multiplicity of sexual practice and sexual desires.

The 'politics of desire' is an extremely difficult issue for feminism. On the one hand, many feminists have objected vociferously to what they see as the 'policing' of desire, the potentially dangerous consequences of censorship, and the implausibility of supposing that desire and fantasy could ever fall completely into line with some stringent set of political ideals – see Cornell (1991) and Segal and McIntosh (1992). On the other hand, why should desire and fantasy be seen as *wholly* given, or totally unamenable to change; and may there not be forms of these things which *are* damaging to women – see Bartky (1990c)? But whilst a Foucauldian approach may not, indeed, resolve these questions, it can be used to suggest that certain radical feminist approaches to them can be of little help in resolving the political or ethical problems involved. Take, for instance, the work of Sheila Jeffreys (1985, 1990) on sexuality. Jeffreys' view of sexuality depends on a number of presuppositions about sexuality, subjectivity and male power which are not compatible with a Foucauldian approach. She supposes that sexuality/ heterosexuality are *the* central site of male oppression of women; in other words, she tends to see power as located in a single source. She supposes that all heterosexual relationships are irredeemably marred with general structures of domination and subordination, and her analysis of heterosexuality allows for none of the ambiguity and ambivalence which a Foucauldian approach might want to recognise in sexual desire. She supposes it possible for there to be an autonomous and wholly self-recognising form of female desire. She also supposes that it might be possible to reconstruct sexual desire on terms of 'perfect equality'. A Foucauldian approach to questions of sexual nature, power and politics is not compatible with any of these suppositions. Although Foucault frequently stressed that his views did not, in themselves, recommend specific ethical or political practices concerning sexuality, they nevertheless rule some other views out as ethically and politically undesirable as well as impossible. And they implicitly suggest a politics which includes, at the least, a recognition of ambiguity, contradiction and complexity at its heart. In this sense, a Foucauldian approach to questions of sexuality is not merely 'deconstructive'.

The recognition that feminist practices have not been

'innocent' of power relationships might be seen as a counsel of pessimism or despair; and indeed, Foucault described himself as a pessimist. But this 'pessimism' is better seen not as a belief that no change is possible, but as a caution against the potential dangers and deceptions involved in certain kinds of Utopian optimism. Sawicki argues that those critics who have seen Foucault's work as lacking any normative framework have seen it wrongly. For one thing, Foucault did not always say the same thing. He *was* engaged; he wanted to defamiliarise forms of life and experience which have sometimes become 'second nature' to us, and suggest that there could be new ways of thinking and acting. The idea of inventing a completely new ethical scheme would in any case be foreign to Foucault's thought; we *can* only start from where we are, and where we are includes the continuing relevance and importance of the 'Enlightenment' ideals of which Foucault was critical. Sawicki argues that Foucault's 'negative freedom' does not deny us the option of using a discourse of rights, liberties and justice; he just points out its potential dangers. But there is nothing in Foucault which stops us having positive strategies as well – provided that we recognise their dangers.

> Freedom lies in our capacity to discover the historical links between certain modes of self-understanding and modes of domination, and to resist the ways in which we have already been classified and identified by dominant discourses. This means discovering new ways of understanding ourselves and one another, refusing to accept the dominant culture's characterisations of our practices and desires, and redefining them from within resistant cultures.
>
> (Sawicki 1991: 44)

The theme of 'liberation' remains a central one for feminism. But it is important not to suppose that there is any *one* central site of liberation, and to remain constantly aware of the ways in which new modes of resistance and self-understanding run the danger of re-instating, in some way, aspects of that against which they have been struggling. In an interview given in 1984, Foucault said:

> I've always been a little distrustful of the general theme of liberation. . . . I do not mean to say that liberation or such and

such a form of liberation does not exist. When a colonial people tries to free itself of its colonizer, that is truly an act of liberation, in the strict sense of the word. But we also know that, in this extremely precise example, this act of liberation is not sufficient to establish the practices of liberty that later on will be necessary for this people, this society and these individuals to decide upon receivable and acceptable forms of their existence or political society.

(Foucault 1988: 2–3)

The theme of 'practices of freedom' seems to me to be an extremely important one for feminism. Another way of putting it is to say that questions about 'how one should live' are not answerable wholly by reference to highly general ethical ideals. In addition, it can never be assumed that any particular kinds of 'liberation' will establish freedom, equality or mutuality permanently or without ambiguity, either in women's relationships to men or to other women. Consider, for example, a situation in which a woman experiences a strong need to re-evaluate her relationships to men, including her sexual ones. Such a need may well have arisen from an emerging feminist consciousness. Sandra Bartky (1990d) has argued that the experience of acquiring a feminist consciousness is commonly one which may be very disorientating. Old guidelines for behaviour and practice become open to question; old interpretations become subject to a radical kind of doubt. And a new 'repertoire' of behaviour may not lie ready to hand; furthermore, new forms of behaviour and emotion may themselves be difficult to interpret. How is one to distinguish, for example, between justifiable anger and unreasonable self-justification? How is one to distinguish between behaviour on the part of a male partner which should merely be seen as supportive, and behaviour which should be read as implying female dependence or incapacity? When does need for another itself become a sign of undue dependence and lack of a necessary autonomy? When, in a sexual relationship, does the need for another's desire shade into a problematic kind of sexual objectification? If sexual desire is closely related to the desire of another person for oneself, to what extent and in what contexts does one's own desire for another's desire shade into a subordination of that desire to another's?

These sorts of questions plainly arise in other areas of human life as well. The question of feminist pedagogy provides an example. Suppose that one wishes to avoid oppressive hierarchies of expertise, of those who 'know', who are always advantaged relative to those who do not. What practical forms of pedagogy should one adopt? This is not an easy question. One response to this has been to argue that all feminist education should be student-centred, in the sense that pedagogy should always be seen as arising out of and as providing a response to the immediate experiences and needs of students. Yet if knowledge can be seen not merely in terms of 'power over' but also of 'empowering', then sometimes a failure to provide and make accessible more structured forms of knowledge might itself be seen as failing to provide resources for empowerment which some have and others do not.

The point about these sorts of dilemmas is that they are never resolvable in any final kind of way, and that they cannot be resolved by a simple appeal to very general principles. Thus, although it is plain that principles of equality and mutuality might be central ones in such re-evaluations of practice, they need constant interpretation and re-interpretation.

In this sense, Foucault's view of 'practices of freedom' does not constitute a wholly 'negative' view of freedom. Rather, it suggests that feminism might often need to combine an adherence to regulative principles with an attitude of somewhat experimental and cautious pragmatism in the ways in which these are interpreted in particular contexts.

I have argued so far that the 'deconstructive' and 'reconstructive' aspects of feminism cannot be sharply distinguished, and that Foucault's approach does not merely suggest ways in which we can 'deconstruct' female subjectivity, but carries with it a set of (somewhat cautious) political and ethical attitudes which can be of value. In his last writings, however, (which Sawicki does not discuss), Foucault turned more explicitly to questions of ethics. And I want now to ask whether these writings suggest a more explicit normative framework with which the project of developing a feminist ethics can usefully engage.

ETHICS AND THE CARE OF THE SELF

Foucault's last published writings, including the second and third volumes of *The History of Sexuality* (1987, 1990a) and some of his later interviews and essays, have been seen by many critics as marking a 'break' in his work. In books such as *Discipline and Punish* or *Introduction to the History of Sexuality* the 'self' is deconstructed and seen as an effect of discourses and disciplinary techniques to the point where notions of freedom and autonomy seem to have little purchase, and where questions of ethics or normative justification seem to be almost wholly suspended. Suddenly, in the last writings, notions of freedom and of ethics are central.

Foucault's own view of this supposed 'break' seems to have been roughly as follows. He agreed that at times, for heuristic purposes, some of his books concentrated almost wholly on the self and the body under the aspect of their construction and immersion in disciplinary technologies and discourses. But he denied that he had ever presented resistance as impossible, and argued that his theory of power had always implied both the possibility and existence of forms of resistance, and of 'subjugated knowledges' which might struggle for expression. Nevertheless, there is a profound shift in his later work. In the introduction to *The Use of Pleasure*, Foucault describes this shift as a process of development. In the earlier projects he had undertaken, he had looked at the formation of sciences that referred to sexuality, and at the systems of power that regulate its practice.

But, Foucault suggests, this work needed supplementing by what he calls a 'genealogy of the desiring subject'. By this Foucault meant an exploration and analysis of the practices by which individuals were led to focus attention on themselves and acknowledge themselves as subjects of desire, and a search for the forms and modalities of the relation to self by which individuals constitute themselves as subjects. Much of Foucault's analysis was focused on the theme of the 'deep self', which he saw a dominant feature in western civilisation since the era of Christianity. His project of a 'genealogy of the desiring subject' led him to want to trace the historical emergence of this idea from a time when he believed it did not exist. He was thus led back to a study of antiquity, and the ways in which sexuality and the body became the object of moral deliberation and regulation.

But what, Foucault asked, is the object one has in view when one studies 'morality'? One may study the set of values and actions that form a more or less coherent code. One may study the real behaviour of individuals in relation to these rules. But there are also many different ways in which to obey a code, and different ways of thinking about one's relationship to it. A 'moral' act is not reducible to simple conformity to a rule or law. The place a moral action occupies in the scheme of things can be very variable; thus conjugal fidelity might be aimed at self-mastery, or at detachment from the world, or at insensitivity to the passions. Moral action also involves a relationship to the self, a process of self-formation as an ethical subject. It involves

> a process by which the individual delimits that part of himself that will form the object of his ethical practice, defines his position relative to the precept he will follow, and decides on a certain mode of being that will serve as his moral goal. And this requires him to act upon himself, to monitor, test, improve and transform himself.
>
> (Foucault 1987: 28)

In some moralities, Foucault suggested, the main emphasis is on the code, and the process of subjectivation will occur under a strongly authoritarian and quasi-juridical system. But other moralities may have their dynamic elements in the form of subjectivation and practices of the self. The system of codes and rules may be rather rudimentary, and exact observance not so important. Foucault argued that in Greek morality there were few formal or universal prohibitions. Morality revolved around what he calls 'the care of the self', the development of arts of living and of the detailed regulation of sexual pleasure. The aim of Greek practices of austerity and self-mastery was not so much obedience to a universal law as 'a principle of stylization of conduct for those who wished to give their existence the most graceful and accomplished form possible' (Foucault 1987: 250–1). The life of the individual might become something like a work of art.

Foucault was very clear that in no sense can the morality of antiquity be taken as a model or exemplar for ourselves, and that neither was it his intention in any way to tell people what they ought to be, do or believe. Philosophical and ethical thinking, he believed, cannot be thought of as having a 'basis' that can be discovered, a 'ground' from which it has strayed or to which it must be recalled. It is not that the idea of care for self is a missing key, which if rediscovered can set ethics on the right foundation; Foucault was far too much of an anti-foundationalist to suggest such a thing. But he believed nevertheless that the study of morality and the relationship to self in antiquity (to which he was plainly attracted) could be useful to contemporary ethical thinking, for two reasons. First, Foucault argues that a study of ethical praxis and thinking that is different in many ways from dominant western traditions is an important exercise in defamiliarisation:

> As for what motivated me, it is quite simple. . . . It was curiosity
> – the only kind of curiosity, in any case, that is worth acting
> upon with a degree of obstinacy; not the curiosity that seeks to
> assimilate what it is proper for one to know, but that which
> enables one to get free of oneself. . . . There are times in life
> when the question of knowing if one can think differently than
> one thinks, and perceive differently than one sees, is absolutely
> necessary if one is to go on looking and reflecting at all. . . .
> What is philosophy today – philosophical activity, I mean – if it
> is not the critical work that thought brings to bear upon itself?
> In what does it consist, if not in the endeavour to know how and
> to what extent it might be possible to think differently, instead
> of legitimating what is already known?
>
> (Foucault 1987: 8–9)

This aligns Foucault with what I have called the 'deconstructive' task. But secondly, Foucault argues that, despite the historical distance between ourselves and antiquity, there is an important parallel. Antiquity did not, he suggests, operate with a conception of morality as consisting primarily in obedience to a moral code. Today, after a domination of many centuries, this idea of obedience to a moral code is disappearing. The search for an 'aesthetics' of existence must, Foucault argues, correspond to the disappearance of moral codes.

The ethical ideal of antiquity, as Foucault depicts it, is that of a morality which is orientated towards practices of the self and the care of the self. To live well is to transform oneself by a process of intensive self-discipline. Power undergoes a transmutation in Foucault's later work. Terry Eagleton suggests that despite Foucault's apparent dislike of the techniques of modern power, there is also in his work a kind of aesthetic gratification at its 'productivity'. In his late writings:

> The ethical ideal is one of an ascetic, dispassionate mastery over
> one's powers. . . . This position combines the best of coercion –

to produce oneself involves a taxing, punitive discipline – with the best of hegemony; the subject has the autonomy of the hegemonic subject, but now in a more radically authentic manner . . . since this power is directed upon oneself, it cannot be oppressive.

(Eagleton 1990: 391)

Power, in the late work of Foucault, is thus installed within the self. And, given the ways in which women have often experienced severe difficulties in achieving any form of personal autonomy, these notions of self-mastery, self-transformation, the active creation of the self, the concentration on practices of the self and the care of the self, might seem to be ones which could be congenial to feminist thinking. I want to argue, however, that the particular ways in which Foucault maps out his conception of ethics and the self in his later work are profoundly disappointing, and fail even to retain the 'deconstructive' usefulness of some of the earlier work.

AUTONOMY, GENDER AND THE SELF

There are some obvious – and some less obvious – reasons why the ethic of care for the self in antiquity, as described by Foucault, seems light-years from anything that any feminist might want to endorse. The most obvious thing is that, as Foucault himself noted, the Greek morality that he analysed was totally elitist and male-dominated. The 'ethical subject' whom Foucault discusses is always a masculine one. The 'aesthetics' of existence that he describes was the privilege of a very few free males, and was not addressed to women at all. But it is not simply its exclusiveness in this sense that is at issue.

The first thing to note is the 'thinness' of the conception of the subject or the self in the second and third volumes of *The History of Sexuality*. Terry Eagleton (1990) notes that Foucault's stress on sexuality focuses almost entirely on the body – and that, significantly, eating is seen as the nearest thing to sex. The body, Eagleton suggests, stands in for the subject, and the aesthetic for the ethical: 'this individual is a matter, very scrupulously, of surface, art, technique, sensation. We are still not permitted to enter into the tabooed realms of affection, emotional intimacy and compassion' (1990: 391). What Eagleton does not note is the way

in which Foucault's attempt at a defamiliarisation of contemporary modes of relationship to self reads sometimes less like a
defamiliarisation than a repetition of some dominant contemporary themes. A great deal of popular discourse on sexuality
since the late 1960s, for example (including such things as popular
'sex manuals'), has conceived of sexuality precisely as a matter of
surface and sensation; touching the right spot, triggering the right
response, a matter, as it were, of sexual button-pushing, an almost
solipsistic view of sexuality. And critics have often noted the
'performance anxiety' which this may generate, and the view that
without an 'adequate sex-life', as defined by such norms, no one
can possibly lead a happy or fulfilled life. Eagleton notes, in
addition, that the Greek view that self-indulgence might lead to a
depletion of one's vital powers is a familiar male fantasy (which
was endemic in Victorian discussion of sexuality).

However, perhaps even more importantly, Foucault seems
wholly to evade questions, which are crucial to feminism, about
the forms of self-monitoring and self-surveillance which he
characterises as autonomy, or as the power of the self over the self.
In much of his earlier writing, he noted the ways in which
disciplinary practices and techniques operated by means of
internalised self-surveillance, such that external sanctions or
forms of control were no longer necessary to bring the subject into
line. Suddenly, in his last writings, these practices of self-discipline
and self-monitoring are no longer seen as disciplinary practices
which undermine all notions of the autonomy of the self; they are
seen, rather, as constituting autonomy. Why is there this shift? It
remains unexplained in Foucault's writings, and it leads him to
evade the crucial question of *when* forms of self-discipline or
self-surveillance can with any justification be seen as exercises of
autonomy or self-creation, or when they should be seen, rather, as
forms of discipline to which the self is subjected, and by which
autonomy is constrained. Foucault, in fact, evades his own
question about 'practices of freedom'.

It is interesting to consider some of the dominant modes of
'self-surveillance' in contemporary culture – and the ways in
which these are highly gendered. Nowhere does Foucault
consider this issue. The theme of the 'male gaze', and the ways in
which women are constructed as 'objects' not merely of the male
gaze but of a whole apparatus of self-surveillance, has become a
dominant one in cultural studies, for example. Discourses of

fashion, beauty and 'fitness' constantly require women to follow programmes of self-monitoring, and routines and regimens which can verge on the ascetic. We are indeed in the realm of surface, art and technique with a vengeance. Sandra Bartky (1990b) discusses how, in the fashion and beauty industry, there appears to be no 'source' for these imperatives as to how one should 'make the best of oneself', and they may appear as wholly self-imposed. Susan Bordo (1989) shows how the self-perception of the anorexic may be premised on notions of autonomy and control, even though in fact her whole life may in fact be damagingly or even fatally *out* of control.

When should we see a concern for one's body, a programme of monitoring of one's fitness or concern for one's appearance, as an exercise of creative self-mastery rather than as the result of the internalisation of norms of bodily appearance which serve to undermine other forms of autonomy? How should we think about the female body-builder, who in some way transgresses some of the norms of 'femininity', compared with the woman who is told by her doctor to lose 5 stone for her health, or the woman who is unhappy going out without her make-up? Feminist consideration of these things raises questions of 'practices of freedom' which seem almost intractable at times. And they raise questions about gendered differences in such practices. What kind of differences are there, for example, in the politics of male and female body-building, or male and female concern for appearance; are women and men doing 'the same thing' when they go to the gym?

There is a sense here in which Foucault needs turning against himself. The Foucauldian warning that 'nothing is innocent' has been completely lost in his consideration of the ascetic practices and regimens of the ancient Greeks. He writes of an elite class of males who are simply *assumed* to be free; whether their self-mastery and self-surveillance is really that, rather than an internalised disciplinary technique, the classic Foucauldian question in *Discipline and Punish* is wholly evaded. And perhaps the reason that it is so easily evaded brings us to the second central problem with Foucault's conception of self in his later writings.

THE RELATIONSHIP OF SELF TO SELF

What is the relationship of one self to another in Foucault's last work? There are tensions here. In some of his last interviews, he asserted that he believed the self to be social (see, for example, Foucault 1988). But this sociality or mutuality is hard to detect in the second and third volumes of *The History of Sexuality*. Foucault is here considering the relation to self of a few elite males; and it is noteworthy that those with whom they have relationships seem to be thought of as instruments through which they fashion their own freedom. This is particularly true in the case of women. Women were subjected to rules of chastity and fidelity simply because of their inferior political status. For men, chastity and fidelity were not related to concern or love for the woman so much as to the 'stylisation' of their own lives. But it is also true of the relationships of men to one another. The main concern in Greek homosexual relationships seems to have been how to avoid being seen as the 'passive' partner; homosexual relationships had to be precisely orchestrated so that neither the older nor the younger male would lose actual or potential status as a 'dominant' free individual. This was a process in which concern for the feeling of another seems to have been largely irrelevant, except in so far as it concerned questions of individual status.

Although Foucault pays lip-service, as I have said, to the idea of 'the social', there is no sense whatever of the importance of collective goals or aspirations, or the ways in which individual lives might be lived in the light of something that transcended these. Foucault argues that an 'aesthetic' approach to morality, based on the exquisite and somewhat solipsistic fashioning of a regimen for an individual life, is the only alternative to a morality which is based on prescribed adherence to a rigid or universal code. What is missing from this is the idea that there might be a morality, painfully fashioned no doubt, which rejects the idea of unproblematic 'universalism' and recognises the dangers and 'absences' in many so-called 'universal' ideals, but which aims nevertheless for mutuality and collectivity as crucial organising principles for the conduct of individual lives. It is precisely this possibility of mutuality and collectivity which has been at issue in much feminist discussion of ethics.

Feminists have been only too well aware of the 'absences', such as those of race, class or sexual orientation, which have been at the heart of many forms of universalism, and the exclusions that are their sub-text. They have become increasingly aware of the fact that 'nothing is innocent', that apparently 'liberatory' ideals can only too easily be recuperated or undermined by that against which they seem to be struggling. They have been suspicious of 'codes' that have all too often been masculine, and have consigned women to a place of inferiority, or depicted them as mere lack or absence. They have seen the need for regulative ideals of freedom or equality or justice, yet also become aware of the immense difficulties in translating these into 'practices of freedom'. Above all, perhaps, they have struggled to conceptualise a view of morality which is not rooted in individualism, but which is still able to respect individuality and autonomy. It is a problem of how to realise ideals of community and mutuality while preserving the forms of autonomy, individuality and care for self without which ideals of community and mutuality can sometimes be as coercive and constraining as those forms of individualism they have wished to replace.

Foucault fails even to recognise these problems and possibilities. I think it is because his conception of a class of free beings who make works of art of their own lives is 'always already' premised on a distinction between those who do and those who do not have such freedoms. The minute *any* regulative ideal of equality or mutuality is introduced, then a Foucauldian conception of the individual life as a 'work of art' can no longer be sustained.

The third central problem is this. As Eagleton (1990) points out, the ethic depicted by Foucault in his last writings is highly and troublingly formalistic. What matters, he claims, is not so much the code of conduct one follows, as the control over and prudent exercise of one's powers and capacities. It is a wholly subject-centred morality. But is something morally bad only if it signifies immoderacy or imprudency on the part of the agent? Are there not questions about the effects on the other to consider? 'What', Eagleton asks, 'would a stylish rape look like, precisely?' (Eagleton 1990: 394). Are there not some things which are inherently bad in all circumstances, because of the devastating effect they may have on others?

The question of whether there are 'moral absolutes' is, again, one that has been much debated in feminist ethical theory – see, for example, Gilligan (1982), Grimshaw (1986), Ruddick (1990), Young (1990). It has been argued, for example, that an approach to morality which sees this as primarily a question of rights and principles which have to be ordered in a hierarchy is one which is paradigmatically male rather than female. Women, it has been suggested, are less likely to think in terms of 'absolute' rules and principles, and more likely to think contextually, in the light of an awareness of the nuances of situations and relationships, and of the effects a course of action might have upon others. Debates about whether women, through time and across cultural and other differences, have a different approach to morality from men are fraught with difficulties, and I do not want here to defend any particular perspective on them. It should also be noted that many women have indeed insisted that certain acts, including rape and sexual assault, cannot be justified in any circumstances; there have been strands in feminist ethical thinking which have been highly 'absolutist'. The important thing to note here is that Foucault allows us no space in which to raise these questions; they are blocked from the outset.

CONCLUSION

In general, then, Foucault's late work on ethics is disappointing, and somewhat depressingly unaware of anything that feminists have written about ethics or morality. It seems trapped in a highly masculinist view of ethics as the concern of a male elite to stylise their own lives. It sees this stylised aestheticisation of life as the only alternative to a morality based on adherence to a rigid or universal code. Its perception of sexuality as *the* central question for ethics is, again, a recapitulation rather than a reversal of an almost banally familiar theme in traditional discussions of morality. In addition, it might be argued that there is indeed a 'break' in Foucault's last work. The enterprise of considering the 'genealogy of the desiring subject' may, it is true, bear an important relation to Foucault's earlier work. But in undertaking it, Foucault's own previous 'deconstructive' practices seem to have been forgotten. I have suggested that Foucauldian questions about 'practices of freedom' are of great importance to feminism. So, indeed, are questions about the 'care of the self', about personal self-creation or transformation, and about the relationship of self to ethical codes. But I have argued also that Foucault's later work offers a masculinist conception of the self which sidesteps many of the most crucial questions in ethical thinking which feminism needs to confront.

NOTES

1 Exactly what Foucault meant by 'discourse' is not an easy question to
answer, and the meaning of 'discourse' is not necessarily the same in
all of his writings. In *The History of Sexuality* (1981) Foucault
investigates what he sees as the concepts and assumptions that are
crucial to much contemporary thinking about sexuality (for example,
the assumption that homosexual behaviour flows from a homosexual
'nature'); but these concepts and assumptions have to be understood
in the context of the social practices which involve relationships of
power (such as the relationship between analyst and analysand in
psychoanalysis).
2 Feminists have drawn, for example, on various forms of
psychoanalytic theory to try to understand the ways in which
'femininity' and female subjectivity are shaped and constructed; see,
for instance, Mitchell (1974), Chodorow (1978), Mitchell and Rose
(1982).
3 Foucault discusses, for example, the crucial importance of bodily
discipline and demeanour to institutions such as the modern army,
factory or school.

BIBLIOGRAPHY

Bartky, S.L. (1990a) *Femininity and Domination: Studies in the Phenomenology of Oppression*, London: Routledge.
—— (1990b) 'Foucault, femininity and the modernization of patriarchal power', in S.L. Bartky, *Femininity and Domination: Studies in the Phenomenology of Oppression*, London: Routledge.
—— (1990c) 'The politics of personal transformation', in S.L. Bartky, *Femininity and Domination: Studies in the Phenomenology of Oppression*, London: Routledge.
—— (1990d) 'Towards a phenomenology of feminist consciousness', in S.L. Bartky, *Femininity and Domination*, London: Routledge.
Best, S. and Kellner, D. (1991) *Postmodern Theory: Critical Interrogations*, London: Macmillan.
Bordo, S. (1989) 'The body and the reproduction of femininity', in A. Jaggar and S. Bordo (eds) *Gender/Body/Knowledge*, New Brunswick, NJ and London: Rutgers University Press.
Chodorow, N. (1978) *The Reproduction of Mothering*, Berkeley: University of California Press.
Cornell, D. (1991) *Beyond Accommodation: Ethical Feminism, Deconstruction and the Law*, London: Routledge.
Daly, M. (1979) *Gyn/Ecology: The Metaethics of Radical Feminism*, London: The Women's Press.
—— (1984) *Pure Lust: Elemental Feminist Philosophy*, London: The Women's Press.
Dews, P. (1986) 'The nouvelle philosophie and Foucault', in M. Gane (ed.) *Towards a Critique of Foucault*, London: Routledge.

Dworkin, A. (1987) *Intercourse*, London: Martin Secker & Warburg.

Eagleton, T. (1990) *The Ideology of the Aesthetic*, Oxford: Blackwell.

Foucault, M. (1979) *Discipline and Punish*, Harmondsworth: Penguin.

—— (1981) *The History of Sexuality*, vol. I: *An Introduction*, Harmondsworth: Penguin.

—— (1986) 'On the genealogy of ethics: an overview of work in progress', in P. Rabinow (ed.) *The Foucault Reader*, Harmondsworth: Penguin.

—— (1987) *The History of Sexuality*, vol. II: *The Use of Pleasure*, Harmondsworth: Penguin.

—— (1988) 'The ethic of care for the self as a practice of freedom', in J. Bernauer and D. Rasmussen (eds) *The Final Foucault*, Cambridge, MA: MIT Press.

—— (1990a) *The History of Sexuality*, vol. III: *The Care of the Self*, Harmondsworth: Penguin.

—— (1990b) 'An aesthetics of existence', in L. Kritzman (ed.) *Michel Foucault: Politics, Philosophy, Culture: Interviews and other writings 1977–1984*, London: Routledge.

Fraser, N. (1989), 'Foucault on modern power: empirical insights and normative confusions', in N. Fraser *Unruly Practices: Power, Discourse and Gender in Contemporary Social Theory*, Cambridge: Polity Press.

Gilligan, C. (1982) *In a Different Voice: Psychological Theory and Women's Development*, Cambridge, MA: Harvard University Press.

Grimshaw, J. (1986) *Feminist Philosophers: Women's Perspectives on Philosophical Traditions*, Brighton: Wheatsheaf.

Jeffreys, S. (1985) *The Spinster and her Enemies*, London: Pandora.

—— (1990) *Anticlimax: A Feminist Perspective on the Sexual Revolution*, London: The Women's Press.

MacKinnon, C. (1987) *Feminism Unmodified: Discourses on Life and Law*, Cambridge, MA: Harvard University Press.

Mitchell, J. (1974) *Psychoanalysis and Feminism*, London: Allen Lane.

Mitchell, J. and Rose, J. (1982) *Feminine Sexuality*, London: Macmillan.

Moi, T. (1985) 'Power, sex and subjectivity: feminist reflections on Foucault', *Paragraph*, 5: 95–102.

Rabinow, P. (ed.) *The Foucault Reader*, Harmondsworth: Penguin.

Ruddick, S. (1990) *Maternal Thinking*, London: The Women's Press.

Sawicki, J. (1991) *Disciplining Foucault: Feminism, Power and the Body*, London: Routledge.

Segal, L. and McIntosh, M. (eds) (1992) *Sex Exposed: Sexuality and the Pornography Debate*, London: Virago.

Taylor, C. (1986) 'Foucault on freedom and truth', in D. Hoy (ed.) *Foucault: A Critical Reader*, Oxford: Blackwell.

Young, I.M. (1990) *Throwing Like a Girl and Other Essays in Feminist Philosophy and Social Theory*, Bloomington and Indianapolis: Indiana University Press.

Chapter 4

Foucault, feminism and feeling
What Foucault can and cannot contribute to feminist epistemology
Maureen Cain

I believe too much in truth not to suppose that there are different truths and different ways of speaking the truth . . . we can demand of those who govern us a certain truth as to their ultimate aims, the general choices of their tactics, and a number of particular points in their programs: this is the *parrhesia* (free speech) of the governed, who can and must question those who govern them in the name of the knowledge, the experience they have, of what those who govern do.

(Foucault 1988b: 51)

INTRODUCTION

This chapter considers Michel Foucault's theory of knowledge, feminist theories of knowledge and what the two have in common. I examine whether a reconsideration of Foucault, twenty years on from the publication in English of *The Archaeology of Knowledge* and four years since the appearance of his last posthumous work (Volume III of his *History of Sexuality*) can help sort out some of the issues about how we know what we know, which contemporary feminists are debating. Implicit in my argument is the assumption that we are not and can never be beyond epistemology. All social theories, including feminist accounts of social life, entail some theory of knowledge, and some theory of how we come to know social life. All feminists are concerned with how knowledge which is helpful to women can best be produced and with what such knowledge should be like. These are epistemological questions.[1]

More specifically, this chapter addresses three themes in the works of Foucault which are relevant to feminist concerns. First, I look at his uneasy and constantly changing relationships with the 'extra-discursive'. This concept of 'extra-discursive' refers to some conception of social existence which cannot be grasped in the analysis of discourses; it is literally what is outside discourse. Secondly, I consider Foucault's concern with repressed knowledges; that is, with the existence and voices of those who are silenced or subordinated by, or excluded from, dominant discourses. This is an area in which feminism has been particularly active in recovering women's voices. Thirdly, I consider the extent of the compatibility of Foucault's discovery of the genealogical method with the progressive politics of a realist feminism.

I have chosen these issues for particular consideration because they connect with epistemological questions which are central and problematic both in feminism and in interpretations of Foucault's work.

First of all, the realist position which I and others have developed denies the strong postmodern position that social life derives in its entirety from a play of communications resulting sometimes in temporary sedimentations of meaning. Such a view gives ontological primacy to discourse, it being impossible to 'have' a relationship which is not expressible in, and ultimately constituted by, some discourse or other. I argue instead (see especially Cain 1990) that whereas such transitive relations obviously exist (the taxpayer–state relation is a good example), other relations exist which have not, or have not as yet, been formulated in discourse. Following Bhaskar (1979) I call these 'intransitive relations'. The problem for the exponent of such a position is that she cannot give an example of an intransitive relation, for once a relation is formulated by a sociologist, a participant or anyone else, it by definition becomes transitive, a part of a world of cultural meanings.

The argument that not all relationships in which people live are expressible in discourse is a difficult one philosophically and, I believe, a necessary one politically for feminists and subjugated people generally. It is necessary to establish the possibility of an unthought relationship in order to make sense of feminist work which appears to expose, for the first time, the relationships in which women are placed, while yet claiming to know that the relationship preceded the exposure which 'brought it to light'. Sandra Harding (1983) uses the example of the 'discovery' of sexual harassment to illustrate a similar point. I discuss the twin questions of unthought relationships and their discovery, at the end of the section in which I consider what Foucault has to say about the extra-discursive.

This possibility of unthought relationships is fundamental to my discussion of repressed knowledges: was there a female knowledge which was silenced, or is the problem a deeper one, that a knowledge of the relationships in which women are placed was never allowed to be formulated consciously at all?

In the final section, I argue that formulating the unthought is an extremely dangerous and political business. Here we are fully into Foucault's world of knowledge/power. *How* we formulate relations will shape our lived experiences as well as our political strategies. So it matters very much who makes the formulation. I argue that this is why feminist researchers have emphasised the importance of sharing a standpoint with those they investigate. It is because knowledges are so dangerous and powerful that the relational and political credentials of their producers must be understood and open to scrutiny.

DISCOURSE AND THE EXTRA-DISCURSIVE

When Marxism was the only radicalism on the menu, the radical positions which centralised communication were always questioned as to their relationship to Marx's theories. Foucault's work did not escape this largely Anglo-Saxon preoccupation. It is central to the exegetical accounts of both Smart (1983) and Poster (1984), and perhaps also of Balbus (1988, discussed in Sawicki 1991: 50–6).

My concern with the extra-discursive in Foucault is a little different, certainly less grand, and possibly less legitimate. I need to work out where Foucault stood on the question of the ontological primacy of discourse; that is, on the question of whether or not only those relationships exist which are somehow or other known in discourse. His only extended discussion of the extra-discursive seems a sensible place to start.

The Archaeology of Knowledge (1972) was the first book by Foucault that I ever read. It provided a key enabling me to move forwards and backwards in his works; it was an explosion of recognition of the limits and potential of understanding, and also a touchstone in terms of which his own discursive development can be judged. Foucault must have influenced my thinking: so many hours of my life have been spent reading, noting, teaching, talking and thinking about him. So a stock-taking is over due. And although *The Archaeology* is no longer my favourite text, it was my first love: for this reason too it is a place to begin.

Foucault's only serious problematisation of the relations between discourse and the extra-discursive appears in *The Archaeology of Knowledge* (1972). In this, his only purely methodological work, Foucault explores primarily the internal relations of discourse, the structure which enables discourse to have meaning. Discourse is to be examined in itself, not in terms of why it is as it is. It must be read from the inside, in terms of the rules governing the relations between its elements.

He no longer seeks to explain discourses in terms of their causes or origins, or even the sense they make; rather, he seeks to explore the internal relationships between the 'elements' such as subjects, objects, concepts and so on, relationships which make any specific discourse into what it is. Foucault's aim is to make these relations visible, by a process that has come to be known as 'deconstruction'. Deconstruction implies a preoccupation with the elements. Foucault's fascination is with the way the elements have their existence in and through their relationships within the discourse which they constitute.

In *The Archaeology* Foucault argues that a discourse is identified by the *rules* which govern the *relationships* between the various items which the discourse constitutes and deploys. These rules constitute the discourse, and are recognised by their use within it. They are not regulations imposed from outside. The 'items' constituted in terms of the rules are objects of the discourse (for example, crimes, convicted people, defences, mitigating circumstances and so on), subjects of the discourse (for instance, the law), enunciators of the discourse (such as judges, attorneys), sites of enunciation (like the courts and so forth). Discourses make *statements* possible, and discursive formations are made up of groups of statements. The statement (which of course can be repeated)

> appears as an asset that has its own rules of appearance but also its own rules of appropriation and operation; an asset that consequently . . . poses the question of power; an asset that is, by nature, the object of a struggle, a political struggle.
>
> (Foucault 1972: 119)

Discourse itself has no external subject who speaks or makes it.

Possible spokespersons, who have the authority to speak it, are created within it.

Some of these rather difficult ideas may become clearer if Foucault's discussion of how discourses may be analysed using the method of archaeology is considered. Foucault uses the form of a negative definition, distinguishing his archaeological approach from the more conventional history of ideas (1972: 138–9):

1 Archaeology 'tries to define not the thoughts, representations, images, themes, pre-occupations that are concealed or revealed in discourses, but those discourses themselves, those discourses *as practices obeying certain rules*' (my emphasis). Thus a discourse is not a document, or a sign of something else: it is a monument. It 'does not seek another, better hidden discourse'. A discourse is its surface.

2 Archaeology seeks 'to show in what way the set of rules that they [discourses] put into operation is irreducible to any other'. A discourse can only be revealed in terms of itself, not explained in terms of antecedents.

3 Archaeology does not acknowledge 'the authority of the creative subject as the *raison d'être* of an *oeuvre* and the principle of its unity'. A discourse cannot be explained in terms of its author: only revealed in terms of the relationships between its internal items.

4 Archaeology 'does not try to restore what has been thought, wished, aimed at, experienced, desired by men in the very moment in which they expressed it in discourse'. People's purposes, interests, intentions cannot be identified as the origin of the discourse. A discourse must be examined in itself to see *how* it means.

Because Foucault insists throughout *The Archaeology* that a discourse cannot be explained in terms of anything except its own internal relationships it is easy to see how this can be interpreted as proposing a radical autonomy for discourse. By the time he wrote *The Archaeology* he had already shown that causality, as part of the 'search for origins' is just one culturally and historically specific way of explaining things (Foucault 1970: 197). His alternative method of 'mapping' as displayed in *The Archaeology* leaves his work open to the interpretation that discourses are not only self-generating but also generative of all the relationships of which they speak.

And certainly, as far as knowledge goes, they do constitute the relationships of which they speak. Logically, however, even this does not preclude the possibility of relationships of which no discourse speaks. Nor does the fact that Foucault chooses a method which radically refuses to consider in detail the extra-discursive. Nor does an argument that discourses are best studied and understood in radical independence from the extra-discursive mean that they entirely subsist in such a state of radical autonomy.

I prefer to interpret Foucault as proposing a radical *methodology*, one which enables discursive processes and powers to be made apparent as they have never been before. On this reading, *The Archaeology* is a methodological work which says that discourses must be studied and examined in their autonomy, that is, in their uncausedness. It is not an ontological work, arguing that because discourse itself is uncaused, all other relationships are constituted/caused by it. Foucault is not offering us discourses as the new subjects of history. He is saying that discourses are important, they are potent, they must be exposed and explored rather than explained. Explaining them, in terms of contemporary notions of origins and causes, mislocated the powers of discourse in authors, in speakers, in other structures. But to mislocate the powers of other structures in discourses would be just as problematic.

Depending on how they are interpreted, Foucault's remarks in *The Archaeology* about the extra-discursive make different kinds of sense. His discussion occurs early in the book, as part of the presentation concerning 'objects' (1972: 44–6). Foucault argues that discursive relations must be distinguished from

> 'primary' relations which, independently of all discourse or all object of discourse, may be described between institutions, techniques, social forms, etc. After all, we know very well that relations existed between the bourgeois family and the functioning of judicial authorities and categories in the nineteenth century. They cannot always be superposed upon the relations that go to form objects: the relations of dependence that may be assigned to this primary level are not necessarily expressed in the formation of relations that makes discursive objects possible. But we must also distinguish the secondary relations that are formulated in discourse itself: what, for example, the psychiatrists of the nineteenth century

could say about the relations between the family and criminality does not reproduce, as we know, the interplay of real dependencies; but neither does it reproduce the interplay of relations that make possible and sustain the objects of psychiatric discourse. Thus a space unfolds articulated with possible discourses: a system of *real* or *primary relations*, a system of *reflexive* or *secondary relations*, and a system of relations that might properly be called *discursive* [Foucault's emphasis]. *The problem is to reveal the specificity of these discursive relations, and their interplay with the other two kinds* [my emphasis].

(Foucault 1972: 46)

According to the above passage, primary relations are not necessarily expressed in discursive relations at all. Relationships, Foucault tells us, such as those between the bourgeois family and the judicial authorities in the nineteenth century, are not 'necessarily expressed in the formation of relations that make discursive objects possible'. There is something of the extra-discursive about them. Foucault describes these relationships as 'real or primary'.

In his later works, he discusses how the bourgeoisie re-appropriated the law and re-instituted the legal form in post-revolutionary France, which helps make clear what a relationship might be between the bourgeoisie and legal categories, techniques and so on, which is not expressed or expressible in legal discourse.[2]

Dreyfus and Rabinow (1982: 64) express it this way: 'Although what gets said depends on something other than itself, discourse dictates the terms of this dependence.' If that means that discourses cannot break their own constitutive rules, by definition, then I am happy with it. Discourse (formed by its internal relations) also organises and binds together unspoken or differently spoken relations external to it.[3] But it is clear that Foucault is trying to make an important distinction here and, in the passage cited above, he takes space to argue very clearly that discursive relations do not constitute the entirety of possible social, political relations.

Secondary relations are more difficult. Foucault uses the example of the nineteenth-century psychiatrist; there is psychiatric discourse proper, with its own objects, subjects and concepts, and internally constituted, authorised spokespersons;

there are 'real dependencies' or relationships; there are also things that the psychiatrists 'could say about the relations between family and criminality'. Foucault seems to be talking about occupational relations. He calls them reflexive, implying the way groups of people think about themselves and their projects, and relate to one another. Discourse organises and gives a voice to these as well.

To recognise an organising role for discourse does not imply that other relations, between people or institutions, are impotent (Foucault indicates that the occurrence of some of the objects which appear in discourse is made possible by extra-discursive relations). Nor does such a recognition give the discourse ontological primacy; it does not imply that discourse calls the other relations into being or that they exist only through discourse. Such a recognition does, however, have epistemological implications. It means that primary and secondary relations may not exist wholly as they appear in the discourses available to the researcher. It probably means that these primary and secondary relations have a being that cannot be captured in its ontological fullness (that is, in the whole of its existence) in any discourse. I will return to the implications of this argument. But first I must complete the discussion of Foucault and the extra-discursive.

Foucault argues that his enterprise, or the problem he faces, is 'to reveal the specificity of these discursive relations and their interplay with the other two kinds' (1972: 46). The autonomy, or uncaused character, of discursive relations does not mean that their articulations with primary and secondary relations cannot be mapped, in the same way that the intra-discursive relations discussed in *The Archaeology* are mapped, rather than explained (or explained away). Such mappings are sketched in at many points in Foucault's analyses of discursive relations; connections and disconnections, comings into contact or abutments between discursive and primary relations, all these occur quite frequently, as we shall see. They are not illegitimate, as Balbus (1988) appears to have argued.[4] Nor are they the focus of careful conceptual analysis on Foucault's part. However, as indicated by the quotation on page 76, these points of articulation (and statements in particular) do seem to be sites of political action, of struggle and power and resistance. So it may be that feminists need to explore and map the moments of articulation more than Foucault did. Feminists too may need to examine the relations between the bourgeoisie and the courts, as well as the discourses in terms of which say juvenile justice or family law are dispensed.

These abutments appear in all Foucault's post-*Archaeology* writings. Of course, the extra-discursive appeared in the earlier works too, but in *Madness and Civilisation* (Foucault 1967) it had a causal role. His discussion of the 'great confinement' of the seventeenth century is explained in terms of a combined expression of absolute and bourgeois power, leading to a marriage of labour and morality. The meanings of madness change over time, but the political economic mode of explanation persists. Foucault's lifelong fascination with the constitutive powers of professional discourse starts here, albeit not yet freed from modernist causal frameworks. Unreason, however, even in this early work, cannot be captured by such superstructural explanations. It emerges in a wild refusal, a challenge to contemporary civilisation. It seems probable that Foucault's position on this issue was not clearly worked out until he took time out to reflect on his emerging research practice in *The Archaeology*.

Foucault's colleague Robert Castel finds analysis of the articulation between secondary relations and discursive relations extremely revealing in *I, Pierre Rivière . . .* (which is discussed further below).[5] Intra-professional discord over the treatment of the murderer Rivière, between local and elite Parisian practitioners, and inter-professional rivalry with the judges, intersecting with and expressed in emerging discourses, combine to shape the destiny of Rivière and those who come after him.

The king and the people, capitalism and social classes connect at a range of points with the emergence of the new scientific disciplines which were 'formed at the same time as a new class power' (Foucault 1977a: 232). In chapter 2 of *Discipline and Punish*, the French Revolution is explicitly connected with the shift from 'mass criminality to marginal criminality', and the 'shift from a criminality of blood to a criminality of fraud'. The development of production, increasing wealth, the higher juridical and economic value placed on property relations, stricter surveillance, better information techniques and 'a tighter partitioning of the population' form a complex of relationships in mutual play. The first two are primary relations, the third is a secondary relation, and the last two are practices arising from discursive relations.

The abutments continue to appear all through *The History of Sexuality*. In Volume I (1978b), Foucault argues that the most rigorous techniques of control developed within the bourgeoisie and were later promulgated to the working classes as part of an expanding hegemony. First birth control was advocated, then in the 1830s in France, the family was recognised as an 'indispensable instrument of political control and economic regulation'. By the 1870s, the control of perversions for the good of the race was deemed important. 'Bio-power', argues Foucault, was 'an indispensable element in the development of capitalism. The latter would not have been possible without the controlled insertion of bodies into the machinery of production and the adjustment of the phenomena of population to economic processes' (1978b: 141).

Volume III (1988a) discusses the articulations between the Roman Empire, identity, sexuality, the economic place of the household, conjugal relations and medicine. (I have jumbled the order.) Foucault is interested in identity/subjectivity, discourse and experience (1985: 4). But his invocation of these relationships (here they are largely common-sense concepts of relationships) provides a useful example of how a map can be constructed which focuses on discursive relations. It is not an illegitimate invocation. He is not saying that the Empire caused a discursive shift from one which problematised relations with boys to one which problem-atised relations with spouses. Nor is he saying that this discourse or any discourse 'caused' the Empire. *That* indeed, would be an impossible statement for Foucault, who explicitly historicised explanations in terms of relations of causality in *The Order of Things* and insists that they have no place in his modes of explanation. To ask which set of relations causes the others is impossible for a Foucauldian. The extra-discursive is not invoked as an *explanation* of discourse. Its appearance is necessary from time to time as part of the process of historical *mappings*. Nor did Foucault ever claim that discourse creates the entirety of its context. The mountains do not make the towns, and towns do not make the mountains. But there may be connections/articulations between them which are illuminating. This is what non-causal theory is about.

FEMINISM AND THE EXTRA-DISCURSIVE

The ontology (theory of being or of how things 'are') which I briefly presented in the introduction to this chapter can now be explored a little further, in relation both to Foucault's position and to feminism. Furthermore, the ontology must be connected to an epistemology (theory of how things can be known) in order for its relevance for feminists to become clear. The epistemological issue is dealt with in the next section.

Foucault has bracketed the more usual concern with primary relations, the more readily to reveal the independent potency of discursive relations. But the abutments with primary relations too are neither innocent nor without effect. This is why Foucault has needed to map them and, as I have argued, why we do too.

In a recent paper (Cain 1993), I have argued that extra-discursive relationships are also potent, so that in the politics of knowledge (the politics of which view of a matter is to count as the best) there may be a clash of qualitatively different kinds of forces; competing discourses and competing relations; forces capable of methodological separation, but forever intertwined. Since Foucault wrote, we can never again leave discursive relations out of our analyses; nor can non-causal theorists claim to know or predict in advance what the outcomes of such clashes will be. But since feminists began to produce knowledge of the previously unthought relationships in which women live, we cannot leave intransitive (or 'primary') relationships out of the analyses either.

Where does this leave feminists? In a place which feminists themselves have invented, in a place in which they can legitimately claim to have discovered relationships which no one 'knew' about, to have identified relations which pre-existed their identification. Sexual harassment may be one such; the widespread nature of incest may be another; but the best recent example which I know is in the work of Liz Kelly (1988).

Kelly discovered the possibility that virtually all women in the United Kingdom had experienced sexual violence. Her respondents spoke of encounters which Kelly conceived as pressurised sex (everyone in Kelly's volunteer sample), through coerced sex to rape. Because all these encounters were experienced as abusive to a greater or lesser extent, Kelly writes of a 'continuum of violence' from pressurised sex through coerced sex to rape. Her respondents could not speak of pressurised sex, but once it was discursively arrived at in feminist theory, all of them recognised it. And I too recognised it with a great feeling of emancipation: I had always felt an unease, an inexplicit consciousness of something wrong. This is an example of an intransitive relationship, pre-existing its possible utterance.[6]

What has Foucault got to do with this? Very little, in so far as Kelly's work stands alone, needing authentication from no man, however dead, or eminent or European. Quite a lot, in that it demonstrates the critical importance of the unthought relation, of the extra-discursive, to precisely those vulnerable and subjugated people for whose concerns Foucault so passionately wished to create a space of legitimacy.

Fortunately for feminists, who need the Foucauldian theory of discourse to understand some of the most powerful relations holding them in place, there is not, after all, an incompatibility between accepting and using much of Foucault's argument, while at the same time holding on to our certainty that many of the relationships which bind us down are not yet available to politics because they are not yet available to anyone's knowledge.

REPRESSED KNOWLEDGES

Kelly's work leads us directly to the problem of repressed knowledges, to the question of how women can be given a voice. Foucault had a passionate concern for those whose ways of being cannot be spoken. But because he never told us in so many words, we do not know whether he believed that such ways of being cannot be spoken because the people who live them have no language for them, or because the language in which they express their existence is politically subjugated; that is, rendered illegitimate by dominant discourses.

Foucault produced two books which are quite often simply not mentioned in the critical commentaries. They are important here because both re-present 'lost' documents for the reader to interpret. *I,Pierre Rivière, Having Slaughtered My Mother, My Sister, and My Brother* (1978a) is allowed to roar through the centuries its demand that the author's rage and pain be heard in its own terms. *Herculine Barbin* (1980a) tells her tale of being discovered to be a hermaphrodite and forced to change from a female to a male identity, more quietly, more simply, more sadly and more poignantly. Physically, she flouted the boundaries of approved sexual identity. There could be no place for her, nor is there still.

Interpreting these texts is the more difficult because Foucault directed his analytic efforts to serious and elaborated discourses rather than to common-sense knowledges (although plainly the two overlap: Foucault 1970, 1985, 1988a). But he does offer us both implicit and explicit methodological guidance here. This is fortunate, for there are few areas where feminism has made as many inroads as in its identification and re-presentation of the subjugated knowledges of women.

Behind this issue, of which discourse wins in a clash of ways of knowing, lies an even more important question for women, and especially for women who have sometimes felt they are going mad. Is it possible to *have* an experience without a knowledge (let alone a developed discourse) to have it in? *I, Pierre Rivière, Herculine Barbin* and some of the essays and interviews help here.

The editorial team of *Pierre Rivière* make both arguments.[7] Their central concern was the 'battle among discourses and through discourses' (Foucault 1978a: iii), but in the event it was not the debates within the medical profession, nor those between the various tiers of medical and legal practitioners, which captivated them. Although three of the accounts do indeed explore discursive clashes between judges, lawyers and medics, or between medical practitioners in hierarchic relations with one another, the team as a whole, says Foucault, 'fell under the spell of the parricide with the reddish brown eyes'.[8]

On the side of the possibility of there being an experience without a language, we have Peter and Favert arguing that Rivière had 'come to utter that insensate laughter . . . which speaks of the intolerable' (Foucault 1978a: 175).[9] The 'prodigious reversal of all signs' (ibid.: 187) that was the Revolution had promised human status to the peasants, a human nature the experience of which was scarcely tolerable, and the frontiers of which were un-explored. 'Only to those who are excluded from the social nexus comes the idea of raising a question about the limits of human nature' (ibid.: 188). The 'clumsy psychiatry' which tried to cheat Rivière of the triumph of his death was a declaration that 'the native's speech had no weight' (ibid.: 198). But now the authors have moved to the second meaning: political repression of a speech which already is there.

Foucault's own Note (the second) argues that Rivière's text was 'profoundly committed to the rules of popular knowledge' namely that of the broadsheets, full of history of how 'murder frequents power' (ibid.: 205) – and hungry for knowledge of how people have been able to rise against power. But to Rivière's discourse, wherein he occupied the 'lyrical position of the murderous subject . . . there was applied a question derived elsewhere and administered by others' (ibid.: 211). The political silencing of the repressed discourse of the peasantry was achieved by the discursive supremacy of law and medicine.

Moreover, as Barret-Klegel notes in her commentary (ibid.: Note 4) these two supreme discourses were constructed from the depositions of witnesses. Rivière's account is absent, as it was not requested until later.

Note 5 offers a more hopeful interpretation, for those with political stamina. 'Precisely because it was kept out of circulation for so long, this memoir . . . has lost nothing of its strange power of trapping any interpretation which has the pretension to be a total one' (ibid.: 250).

Feminists do not want, and perhaps cannot afford, to wait so long for our voices to be heard. What this text does give us is an enhanced confidence in our unthinkable experiences, and the beginnings of another technique, that of multiple discontinuous interpretation, by means of which our silent voices can be made to sound. The final section of this chapter considers the risks and possibilities in such interpretive relations, of and with other women. The need for such interpreters is made even more apparent by the poignant little tale of Mlle Barbin. 'Herculine Barbin was a French hermaphrodite. Designated female at birth and raised as a girl in religious institutions, she was re-designated male when she was twenty-two'. She committed suicide at the age of thirty.[10]

Foucault himself describes this nineteenth-century French tale as an almost banal account of that insistence that there must exist one deeply true sex for each person which has figured so largely in psychological, medical and ultimately common-sense discourses from the eighteenth century to the present day.

In his introduction to *Herculine Barbin* Foucault suggests neither the excitement at the discovery of a method and an approach to theory, nor the warmth of feeling for the subject of the memoir which exist in *Pierre Rivière*. It is as if, having given us *The History of Sexuality*, Foucault now gives us the memoir and dossier as an exercise in do-it-yourself discourse analysis. His introduction suggests an interest only in the discourses constituting the dossier, not a concern with either the subject of the memoir, or the ultimate fate of the psychiatrist 'who went in his own manner towards his own madness' (Foucault 1980a: xvii). Hermaphroditism lacks its own discourse in the modern world.

Herculine Barbin's breathless and 'girlish' (in a stylised sense) writing lacks the power or the audience to ground such a discourse, even for a sympathetic reader. But as a demonstration of the policing of a discourse before it can be spoken, of the struggle to express an experience in a language which lacks authenticity because it does not quite 'fit', this little book stands rather sadly alone.

Foucault spoke more clearly about suppressed knowledges in his interviews and occasional papers, both before and after *Herculine Barbin*. In 'Intellectuals and power' (in 1977b), he argues that the masses do not need to gain consciousness, 'they know perfectly well, without illusion' (ibid.: 207). The trouble is that their discourse is blocked by a system of power. Thus the task of intellectuals is to resist uttering these blocking and therefore politically neutralising discourses. The discourse of the masses will have less to struggle against. Such blocking discourses have

> always represented political power as arising from conflicts within a social class. . . . Popular movements, on the other hand, are said to arise from famines, taxes, or unemployment; and they never appear as the result of a struggle for power, *as if the masses could dream of a full stomach but never of exercising power* [my emphasis].
>
> (Foucault 1977b: 219)

In the first of 'Two lectures' (in 1980b), Foucault constructs a more elaborate concept of subjugated knowledges, in which he includes 'two things: on the one hand I am referring to the historical contents that have been buried and disguised' in academic discourses: 'blocs of historical knowledge which were present but disguised' (ibid.: 81–2). 'On the other hand in addition there is a whole set of knowledges which have been disqualified as inadequate to their task or insufficiently elaborated', or even 'directly disqualified', such as the knowledge of the psychiatric patient.

Foucault argues that the re-appearance of these localised and popular knowledges makes criticism possible, as one half of the localised, dispersed, power/knowledge struggles makes it possible for suppressed groups to engage with power effectively on their own terrain. The re-emergences of suppressed knowledges are the keys to a multi-faceted, postmodern politics of refusal at the sites of power, which are these engagements. The method whereby the intellectual can assist this process is, as we shall see below, genealogy.

Thus Foucault writes mostly about already constituted discourses which have been suppressed. His account here is surprisingly similar to Gramsci's (1972) discussion of the vulnerability of common-sense knowledges, because of their internal inconsistencies and lack of elaboration. Foucault suggests a humbler, more facilitative role for the intellectual, however: not so much a creative place in the discursive vanguard as the job of clearing the road blocks.

FEMINISM AND FEELING

On this question of repressed knowledges I believe that feminists must read Foucault with considerable caution. First, as I have indicated in my discussion of Kelly, some feminisms imply a pre-discursive experience, lacking all voice. Secondly, feminists have followed Gramsci in arguing for researchers (intellectuals?) to share a standpoint with those they investigate, or to place themselves 'in the same critical plane' (Harding 1987). Standpoint feminisms are not, of course, all the same. Some attach more importance to women's sexual identity, and others are more relational. The gist of the argument is that anyone producing knowledge occupies a relational and historical site in the social world which is likely to shape and set limits to the knowledge formulations produced. This is unavoidable. However,

1　sites may be chosen politically and to some extent changed: I cannot become a black male teenager, but I could work with a group or agency which more authentically speaks with their voice;
2　to produce knowledge for a group of people it is necessary to share their site – to convert your own site into a chosen *standpoint* for the production of knowledge. If this is not done then the researcher may end up as an out-of-touch do-gooder, who may indeed do more harm than good (see Hartsock 1983; Cain 1986, 1990).

Sharing a standpoint is not quite the same as being an 'organic intellectual' in Gramsci's sense, but the attempt to grasp a putting of oneself into another's shoes is the same. And within feminism, researchers like Kelly plainly do more than clearing the junk out of the road, the role Foucault recommended for the intellectual; they do a midwiving job in relation to an emergent discourse. This more active role, of course, is why to occupy the same standpoint is crucial. Those clearing the way can do less harm than those claiming to assist in jointly constituting the new. As Sawicki (1991) says, refusal may be enough, indeed, of fundamental importance for a white male like Foucault. But the subjugated peoples themselves have to build and create discourses and practices which are not yet there.

Which leaves the first point of disagreement as the final point to be explored. Can people have an unthought experience? Is pre-discursive experience possible? Are birthing and infantile experiences possible? Did Kelly's respondents have an experience before they together created a new discourse of the continuum of violence? Did the relations which constitute sexual harassment exist before they were named, and did the women in those relations have an experience? Is not that pre-discursive experience the reason that women wanted to take the personally risky and politically fundamental step of giving the experience a name?

The question of whether pre-discursive reality is possible is not a question of whether the names are 'right'. That is not a possible question, for discourse and primary relations operate on different terrains, are qualitatively different relations. They could not, as it were, mean or be one another. Rather, it is always a question of whether the naming is useful both as a way forward for feminist politics, and as a way of saying something which women feel or recognise as being apt in its expression of the pre-discursive experience. A recognition that a formulation is apt brings immense relief and gratitude that something unsayable can now be said and shared.

At this stage we move from the ontological question of the relationship between discourse and reality, and the possibility of unthought relationships, to the epistemological question, how is it possible to 'know' about this reality?

In relation to epistemology, I lean again on Bhaskar's early (1979) insight, that to argue that things (in our case relationships) exist independently of knowledge of them does not commit anyone to a quite separate argument that these relationships can be known in their 'truth'. First, reality and knowledge of it are forever separated by the capacities of the knowers, which are limited and species-specific. Secondly, these capacities are culturally specific, depending on available modes of thought and discourse. Thirdly, these capacities are 'historically', or relationally, specific, depending on the site occupied by the knower in a relational nexus which provides a social vantage point. Professions do this self-consciously; other locations (class, region, gender, age, for example) also provide social vantage points for knowing. Finally, that which is to be known keeps on changing too, especially for the sociologist whose object of study – namely, social relationships – is more mobile and fluid than most. So although relations may be conceived as real (and existing independently of knowledge of them) and as changing, knowledge of relationships is always produced by someone with a particular set of capacities; these historical and variable capacities shape and constrain the knowledges produced.

This connects with what the early empiricist David Hume argued (1739/1975). Among the simple impressions, as well as those from the senses, he included feelings and emotions. He argued that feelings (like other impressions/sensations) cannot err. Error creeps in when one applies reason to them. I can accept his starting point of the pre-thought experience. Where I cannot join him is in the idea that such an experience can ever, with certainty, be told 'right'. The classical empiricists did not make the distinction between a realist ontology and a relativist epistemology which is so fundamental to modern feminist realism. A realist feminism must maintain this crucial distinction between relativity in epistemology and what might be described as dynamic absolutism in ontology. This moves realist feminism beyond empiricism. Where Hume and his successors aimed for truth, many feminists argue that the most women can do is to reflect upon and make public the way their knowledge was made.

I have now put myself in a position of arguing that we need to recognise the existence of the unformulated experience among subjugated peoples. This means that it is not just that already formed discourses are politically repressed, but also that the play of relations of domination and subjugation means that some experiences do not as yet have a voice at all. When I say this, I may be accused of empiricism. I shall answer that feminism has identified some important things (feelings/emotions/ unformulated experiences) which do exist prior to knowledge of them; that some classical empiricists share the recognition of this problem; that Foucault – sometimes, tentatively, not very often – shared this recognition; and that realist feminists have gone beyond both in elaborating an epistemology and a method which adequately addresses the issue.

In the next section I argue that standpoint feminism is compatible with the Foucauldian genealogical method, showing again that a careful reading of Foucault can help us to expand our methodological and technical armoury without sacrificing our own unique and fundamental approach to the construction of social theory for the use of women.

GENEALOGY, FEMINIST STANDPOINT AND COMMITMENT

Genealogy, as Foucault characterised his later works, has been discussed elsewhere in this volume, as has the interconnected concept of power. Therefore it is necessary simply to sketch in this concept, before exploring its relations to a realist feminism.

The term 'genealogy' means a tracing of descent. Foucault uses it to describe his method of tracing the 'descent' of ideas. Since all such tracings must by definition start in the present, Foucault needed a concept which would distinguish his enterprise from teleological histories of ideas, in which the author's present is pre-constructed as the necessary point of arrival of the descent, as if the always immanently intended purpose of my family tree were to give birth to me.

A genealogical tracing of descent is radically different from this, in three ways. First, 'descent reveals differences, discontinuities, and divisions' (Major-Poetzl 1983). Nothing that has been in discursive or any other relations need have been so. Rather, what Foucault wishes to display is the field of forces which discursive relations in part constitute and in which they change.

To understand this play of forces Foucault elaborates a concept of power as inherent in all discursive relations, so that 'power/knowledge' becomes a possible concept. In other words, power is a necessary part of the concept of genealogy. 'What was missing from my work was the effects of power proper on the enunciative play' – Foucault, cited in Dreyfus and Rabinow (1982: 104). What genealogy does

is to entertain the claims to attention of local, discontinuous, disqualified, illegitimate knowledges against the claims of a unitary body of theory which would filter, hierarchise and order them in the name of some true knowledge . . . it is really against the effects of the power of a discourse that is considered to be scientific that genealogy must wage its struggle.

(Foucault 1980b: 83–4)

In order to develop such a genealogical tactics of insurrection on behalf of those knowledges which were the losers in the play of forces, it is necessary to suspend truth as a possible concept. Some people may call 'true' those knowledges which have been successful until now: that is all.

Armed with a concept which entails and makes possible the mapping of discontinuities and the play of power relations in the relational and temporal/temporary production of knowledges, Foucault's project can be more clearly political. Dreyfus and Rabinow (1982) argue that the extra-discursive plays a more significant role in the genealogical works. I have not noticed this. However, there is no doubt that the genealogies are political. Foucault (1991: 71) argues that a progressive politics is precisely one which historicises (and thus relativises) practices, and which identifies their internal relations, which does not seek to explain them but to expose them, but which considers the way in which discourses 'form a practice which is articulated upon the other practices' (ibid.: 70).

Foucault believes that politics is integral to the process of exposure of the repressed alternatives. He also believes that politics is where one starts from. It is where one starts from because one's own knowledge productions are situated in a field of relations and dependencies, are part of a play of knowledges and powers. As Sawicki says 'He would have been the first to admit that one could do a genealogy of the genealogist. As an engaged critic the genealogist does not transcend power relations' (1991: 50). But more than that, the genealogist works from an intellectually and politically committed place in the present. The genealogist chooses carefully the points at which she will intervene. For Foucault theory is practice, not a translation or interpretation of it (Foucault 1977b: 208).

If we were to characterise it in two terms, then 'archaeology' would be the appropriate methodology of [the] analyses of local discursivities, and 'genealogy' would be the tactics whereby, on the basis of the descriptions of these local discursivities, the subjected knowledges which were thus released would be brought into play.

(Foucault 1980b: 85)

So it seems that the genealogical method is entirely compatible with a realist feminist approach. So far feminists have tended to use the archaeological rather than the genealogical approach to the analysis of discourse, focusing on dominant rather than subjugated discursive relations.

Thus, for example, in my own field of criminology, both Mary Eaton (1986) and Hilary Allen (1987) have analysed in an archaeological fashion the discourses and practices of the criminal courts, clearly revealing how engendered legal equality is. A genealogical approach would consider how these contemporary discourses came into being, and the alternatives that were suppressed along the way. Perhaps it could be said that, while it is possible and useful to do archaeology without genealogy, it is not possible to do genealogy without archaeology, since the internal relations of the discourse must always be explored. But whichever approach is emphasised, the commitment of the researcher and the tactical and strategic use of the genealogies identified is part of feminism's project. Feminism too is an integrally political approach.

Where Foucault and feminisms might have parted company is at the site of the researcher. Foucault would have denied the possibility of a biologically given woman, from whose standpoint genealogies and other relational analyses could be produced. In this sense relational standpointism is a more Foucauldian position. Relational standpointism, deriving as it does from a complex realist ontology and epistemology, argues that the site from which one speaks cannot be given by biology, but can only be given relationally. As discussed in the previous section, the site from which a person generates knowledge is converted into a standpoint by an act of political will, and by changing one's relationships if necessary, so that the site of the research subject can be shared. Such an effort to forge an appropriate relational nexus from which to work is usually necessary for middle-class academics wanting to write on behalf of under-privileged people, for example.

When a standpoint is conceived in this political and relational way, then another corollary is that, for example, men may write as feminists, if they have immersed themselves in the women's movement (Cain 1986). So standpoints can be changed (in part) and chosen. Using this relational conception, a feminist standpoint becomes more problematic, less apparent to those who might wish to use or engage with the knowledge produced.

For this reason it is necessary for a relational standpoint feminist to explore and display her site in a more or less sharable discourse; that is to say, in a theory. In this way it becomes possible for feminists (who need not all be women) to make strategic decisions about differences: both as to which are relevant at a particular conjuncture, as to useful alliances and their limits, and as to how the discourse of difference itself may be developed and deployed. Feminists do not all share a site, a place in a field of relations, but they may, if they choose, all share a standpoint (Cain 1990).

CONCLUSION

Foucault's work has many lessons for feminists, and feminists are using it to good effect. His conception of the mapping of the connections and disconnections between discourses and extra-discursive relations is compatible with much feminist research and with at least the realist strand in feminist epistemology. His understanding of the chosen and committed historical site of the genealogist is compatible with relational versions of standpoint feminism. His concern for the suppressed discourses has been shared in feminist work, yet feminist epistemology must reach beyond Foucault, to theorise how it is possible to have a feeling without a discourse. This is the ultimate subjugation of subjectivity. For this reason we must cling to our unnamed feelings; where else can we start from in exploring the unspeakable? We cannot let even Foucault tell us that our feelings are impossible. Sometimes they are the most important political asset we have.

NOTES

1 How can we be beyond epistemology when we debate the possibility of knowledge(s) all the time? Perhaps it is a bit like being beyond sexual repression, yet compulsively contributing to a culture of

confession. Foucault might have produced a good genealogy of our preoccupation with our knowledge processes.

2   In 'Intellectuals and power' in Foucault (1977b). Also see 'On popular justice: a discussion with Maoists' in Foucault (1980b).

3   This interpretation is found in Dreyfus and Rabinow (1982: 62–7).

4   Discussed in Sawicki (1991), ch. 3.

5   Note 1 by J-P. Peter and J. Favert in Foucault (1978a).

6   Another example of an intransitive relationship becoming conceptualised is that of the social construction of dependency in the creation of the 'third world'. I will not elaborate this, but refer readers to Frank's (1967, 1969) classic studies.

7   The introduction and dossier are followed by seven Notes, only one of which is authored by Foucault himself. The Notes constitute multiple Foucauldian interpretations of the dossier.

8   Namely: Foucault 1978a: Note 5 by Philippe Riot, 'The parallel lives of Pierre Rivière'; Note 6 by Robert Castel, 'The doctors and the judges'; and Note 7 by Alexandre Fontana, 'The intermittences of rationality'.

9   Foucault 1978a: Note 1. See also Note 4 by Blandine Barret-Klegel, 'Regicide and parricide'.

10 Publisher's summary, final (unnumbered) page of Foucault 1980a.

BIBLIOGRAPHY

Allen, H. (1987) *Justice Unbalanced: Gender, Psychiatry and Judicial Decisions*, Milton Keynes: Open University Press.

Balbus, I. (1988)'Disciplining women: Michel Foucault and the power of feminist discourse', in J. Arac (ed.) *After Foucault: Humanistic Knowledge, Postmodern Challenges*, New Brunswick, NJ: Rutgers University Press.

Bhaskar, R. (1979) *The Possibility of Naturalism*, Brighton: Harvester.

Cain, M. (1986)'Realism, feminism, methodology, and law'. *International Journal of the Sociology of Law*, 1: 3 and 4.

—— (1990) 'Realist philosophy and standpoint epistemologies OR feminist criminology as a successor science', in L. Gelsthorpe and A. Morris (eds) *Feminist Perspectives in Criminology*, Milton Keynes: Open University Press.

—— (1993) 'The symbol traders', in M. Cain and C. Harrington (eds) *Lawyers' Work*, Milton Keynes: Open University Press (in press).

Di Stefano, C. (1990) 'Dilemmas of difference: feminism, modernity, and postmodernism', in L. Nicholson (ed.) *Feminism/Postmodernism*, New York: Routledge.

Dreyfus, H. and Rabinow, P. (1982) *Michel Foucault: Beyond Structuralism and Hermeneutics*, Brighton: Harvester.

Eaton, M. (1986) *Justice for Women*, Milton Keynes: Open University Press.

Foucault, M. (1967) *Madness and Civilisation*, London: Tavistock.

—— (1970) *The Order of Things*, London: Tavistock.

—— (1972) *The Archaeology of Knowledge*, London: Tavistock.

—— (1973) *The Birth of the Clinic*, London: Tavistock.

—— (1977a) *Discipline and Punish*, Harmondsworth: Penguin.

—— (1977b) *Language, Counter-Memory, Practice*, C. Gordon (ed.), Oxford: Blackwell.

—— (1978a) *I, Pierre Rivière, Having Slaughtered My Mother, My Sister, and My Brother*, first published 1973, Harmondsworth: Penguin.

—— (1978b) *The History of Sexuality*, vol. I: *An Introduction*, Harmondsworth: Penguin.

—— (1980a) *Herculine Barbin*, Brighton: Harvester.

—— (1980b) *Power/Knowledge*, C. Gordon (ed.), Brighton: Harvester.

—— (1985) *The History of Sexuality*, vol. II: *The Use of Pleasure*, New York: Vintage Books.

—— (1988a) *The History of Sexuality*, vol. III: *The Care of the Self*, New York: Vintage Books.

—— (1988b) *Politics, Philosophy, Culture: Interviews and Other Writings 1977–1984*, L. Kritzman (ed.), New York: Routledge.

—— (1991) 'Politics and the study of discourse', in G. Burchell, C. Gordon and P. Miller (eds) *The Foucault Effect: Studies in Governmentality*, London: Harvester.

Frank, A.G. (1967) *Capitalism and Under Development in Latin America*, New York: Monthly Review Press.

—— (1969) 'The sociology of development and the under development of sociology', in A.G. Frank, *Latin America*, New York: Monthly Review Press.

Gramsci, A. (1972)'The study of philosophy', in A. Gramsci, *Selections from the Prison Note Books*, London: Lawrence & Wishart, pp. 323–79.

Harding, S. (1983) 'Why has the sex-gender structure become visible only now?', in S. Harding and M. Hintikka (eds) *Discovering Reality: Feminist Perspectives in Epistemology, Metaphysics, Methodology and Philosophy of Science*, Boston: D. Reidel.

—— (1987) *Feminism and Methodology*, Milton Keynes: Open University Press.

Hartsock, N. (1983) 'The feminist standpoint: developing the ground for a specifically feminist historical materialism', in S. Harding and M. Hintikka (eds) *Discovering Reality: Feminist Perspectives on Epistemology, Metaphysics, Methodology and Philosophy of Science*, Boston: D. Reidel.

Hume, D. (1975) *A Treatise on Human Nature*, (first published 1739), London: Oxford University Press.

Kelly, L. (1988) *Surviving Sexual Violence*, Cambridge: Polity Press.

Major-Poetzl, P. (1983) *Michel Foucault's Archaeology of Western Culture: Toward a New Science of History*, Brighton: Harvester.

Poster, M. (1984) *Foucault, Marxism, and History*, Cambridge: Polity Press.

Sawicki, J. (1991) *Disciplining Foucault: Feminism, Power, and the Body*, London: Routledge.

Smart, B. (1983) *Foucault, Marxism and Critique*, London: Routledge.

Part II

Identity, difference and power

Chapter 5

Foucauldian feminism
Contesting bodies, sexuality and identity
M.E. Bailey

What is currently in flux in feminist politics is feminist identity – what feminism is and what it means. The 'subject' of feminism is, ostensibly, women, and its aim to improve the lives of women. This notion of improvement has been based on the argument that the ways in which women have been understood in western culture have denied many possibilities to women because men generally exercise power over them.[1] In this analysis, western culture deems women, at best, creatures fundamentally different from, and naturally inferior to, men, whose identity is determined by a relationship of subordinated complementarity with men. At worst, western culture identifies women as inferior or abnormal men and, in order to maintain 'quality control', seeks to 'fix' as many of the defectives as possible and annihilate the rest. Feminists, from the 1960s, have identified and criticised, in different ways, dualistic, patriarchal, heterosexist models of gender identity in western culture, in which men are taken to be the active, strong and moral half of a human whole which has and needs two parts. Women are the other half: evils necessary for reproduction and other male needs (Elshtain 1981: 15–16).

An assumption implicit in some feminist criticisms, however, is of the stability of the dualistic categories 'men' and 'women' as given, natural and eternal categories. This gives some versions of feminism a static notion of patriarchal power as oppression and repression. As soon as this became apparent, the problems and limitations of basing women's resistance to 'patriarchal' power on assumptions about women and men each having an essential sex were raised by many feminists. By assuming that men and women were distinguished from each other by characteristics which correspond to the male and the female, feminist critics of 'patriarchy' were found to be sharing the fundamental 'patriarchal' arguments for differential and hierarchical roles for men and women – that they are essentially and fundamentally different creatures. This left feminist politics confined to a strategy which simply reverses the hierarchical valuation of essential sexes or sexed essences, making women superior to men.

As a way of resolving this problem, distinctions were drawn between 'sex', which was taken to be universal and biological, and the distinctive traits of gender identity, which were taken to be culturally variable – but still, at some level, fundamental. Because these gender differences between male and female roles are then seen as social rather than biological, they are changeable by human agency. The point of an international feminist movement rooted in this gender-based understanding is to liberate women from patriarchy by challenging men's power over women.[2]

The feminist theories which took 'woman' as a universal category quickly came under fire from women of colour, lesbians and non-western women, who emphasised the power of some women relative to others, and identified the experiences and interests shared by some women with some men, such as ending the oppression of racism. The universal 'woman' had to be modified.

More recent feminist analyses have contested the stability of the distinction between the categories of sex and gender, arguing that it has outlived its usefulness. Because it was distinguished from the notion of biological sex, gender served to enable a certain hopefulness. If anatomy was destiny, and gender characteristics could be separated from biological sex characteristics, then one need not be destined for or resigned to gender roles. But this distinction rests on some notion of determinate, fixed and 'natural' biology as clearly distinct and separable from culture and socialisation. The notion of a biological 'nature', prior to culture and eternal, is now for many feminists, poststructuralists, and philosophers and historians of science, thoroughly suspect. It is not just that gender – the social, cultural, historical characteristics which accrue to the biological category 'sex' – is at issue. Rather, the 'sex' of gender, the 'doer behind the deed' of identity, has been subjected to radical critique (Butler 1990; Haraway 1991).

It is at this crossroads – when the stable identity of 'woman' has been called into question by many feminists – that the work of Michel Foucault holds some strategic possibilities for feminism. Foucault has much to offer feminists who put his ideas to work for feminist projects, in part because he gave special attention to analysing sexuality, but also because his genealogical method changes the terms of debate about politics based on identity, sex and bodies.[3] Feminists can go further by studying the gaps in Foucault's works, since these continue to demonstrate the need for all kinds of political action and scholarship which can encompass the diversity of feminist aims.

Different feminist interpretations of the social significance of bodies enable different potential realities. For example if, as I have argued above, bodies are believed to have some sort of pre-social or extra-cultural status, then the arena of feminist political interventions is circumscribed. If biology continues to be understood as prior and to some extent external to what is social, then the differences – and similarities – which biology describes and inscribes will be reified. This means these differences will have a being of their own, a categorical, undeniable, eternal 'natural' status. Sex and gender as systems of division between people will remain, and feminist political projects will continue to revolve around the mutually constitutive axes of sex and gender. The notion of biological sex will remain sacrosanct – and there are some tempting reasons to opt for this model.

Appeals to the distinct biology of the female sex allow for the more immediate realisation of some feminist projects which are defined already, to greater and lesser extent, as 'biological' issues, such as women's health care, rape, abortion, maternity. Obviously, there is some utility in employing the category of 'sex'. Further, as early feminist struggles have clearly demonstrated, there is also strategic use for the distinction between 'sex' and 'gender'. Delineating 'gender' as a category of socialised behaviours has enabled political intervention – because 'gender', unlike 'sex', is taken to be neither 'natural' nor unchangeable, the justification for restricting women from areas of possibility and opportunity reserved to men falls apart. It is questionable whether it is possible to use biological 'sex' and not be trapped by some notion of 'nature'. Is it possible to hold on to some notion of 'gender' without presupposing some essential, biological sex of which it is the learned, acculturated, social expression? Foucault's *History of Sexuality* suggests some avenues feminists could use to explore the advantages of an identity not premised on some pre- or extra-social essence. His historical/theoretical method, 'genealogy', details the ways in which supposedly 'objective' models of 'truth' – for example, western science and metaphysics – are tied, as are the 'discoveries' they deploy, to specific interests.

This chapter is my attempt to explore and perhaps deploy for feminism the theoretical territory of Michel Foucault's reading of bodies in *The History of Sexuality*, volume I, and selected other materials. Although Foucault does not extensively examine the relationship of gender to bodies and identity in this text, his reading of bodies may lend itself quite amicably to a feminist exploration of these issues.

Some justification for my focus on *The History of Sexuality* may be necessary. Certainly, some of his other writings examine interesting aspects of the issues involved (Foucault 1977, 1980a), but what is critical in *The History of Sexuality*, for my purpose, is the specific genealogical positioning of bodies within this text. Foucault used his method of genealogy for recovering or reclaiming alternative historical accounts, 'subjugated knowledges', by scholars and the subjects of history who are directly involved and disqualified – for example, criminals within penal systems. *The History of Sexuality* is expressly a genealogy of sexuality; therefore, bodies will be situated in this text in relation to sexuality and sex.[4] Sexuality and sex are the axes along and through which bodies are theorised. Bodies are understood in relation to the production, transmission, reception and legitimation of knowledge about sexuality and sex. Foucault's work is of value for feminists because it disrupts, through its refusal of the notions of transhistorical and stable categories of sexuality/sex, any analyses of the cultural relationships between women, bodies and sexuality based on the limitations of traditional understandings. Women have been, historically, identified in western culture with bodies – especially as sexualised bodies. Further, Foucault's suggestions about the new form of power, bio-power, or the disciplining of bodies and populations, have strong resonances with feminist theories, like Kim Chernin's, of women's bodies as the sites and expressions of power relations (Bordo 1988: 87–91).

FOUCAULT'S GENEALOGICAL METHOD AND ITS RELEVANCE TO FEMINISM

The terms of Foucault's approach to bodies are determined by the character of genealogy as a discursive production. 'Subjugated knowledges', be they scholarly or local, are excluded from official, authorised and authoritative histories because they disrupt the unity of history in its evolution towards claims of absolute truth and transparency. Genealogy does not seek to replace unitary histories with more authentic, more absolute and transcendent historical truths. Rather, Foucault's genealogies demonstrate the specific historical contextuality of, and the interests invested in, all truths. Genealogies, as much as authorised histories, are interested and partial. This characteristic of genealogy should be particularly appealing to some feminists because of the emphases on subjective experience and limited truth claims. This enables a more guerrilla-style attack, liquid and mobile, in the western tradition. Because the whole of western history cannot be rendered, explained, undermined and refuted, feminists are justified in practising limited interventions in areas of specific interest. Genealogical projects, further, are nothing new to feminists, though the name may be. 'Herstories', the reclamation of forgotten and overlooked women's histories, are a staple of feminist scholarship.

Foucault will not be looking for an essential self, an originary being, in bodies. Such an enterprise runs counter to genealogy's explicit rejection of ontological – fundamental and transcendent – truth. Genealogy, and thus Foucault as genealogist, is not concerned with the search for the origins of a system of truth or identity – this latter search is a hunt for the essential, the ultimate, the first and final nature. Feminist thought has been plagued by this sort of search.[5] Genealogy resists the search for an immutable truth of being. Having refused the quest for origins in tracking bodies through the discourse on sexuality and sex, Foucault's is a necessarily limited project. It is circumscribed, and enabled, by the self-proclaimed boundaries of genealogy.

Despite his dismissal of absolute, universal and univocal truth and knowledge, Foucault is intimately concerned with issues of truth and knowledge, but he attempts to redefine their character. He aims to show that they exist in a material world where power is brought to bear on all of their formulations. In his view, the role of the genealogist is to document the contingency of historical constructions of truth and identity through the construction of alternative truths and the explication of 'subjugated knowledges'. There are radical implications of this 'history of an error', the institutionalisation of accidental formations. It allows, for example, that present cultural arrangements and power relations need not be the logical heirs of a conscious and deliberate monolithic structure, like 'patriarchy'. This suggests that historically there may have been no universal fear and consequent oppression of women by men. Instead, the oppression and disciplining of women, like other relations of power, has taken different forms with different rationales – truths – at different times. Here, the notion of 'gender' is a perfect illustration; gender roles are different in different times, across various cultures. Only two things remain constant: the general relations of power (namely, that most women's life options are more constrained than most men's), and that these roles are tied to and justified by some notion of the truth, the absolute essence, of 'sex'.

Foucault's historical method is distinct from the discipline of history and the implication of the latter in the search for 'origins', the truths or essences which found and enable all knowledge, and thus the ways that knowledge is deployed. Foucault's method can have the effect of unsettling knowledge as absolute truth, or as the unavoidable consequence of a set of immutable events, as reflected in the material. For example, Sandra Bartky (1988: 77–83) has used Foucault's theoretical suggestions to demonstrate the twentieth century's cultural investment of female bodies with sexuality and libido, through and around the ideal of the 'feminine'. Women's very bodies are tailored, by women, to conform to social ideals which are historically specific. This is not an essential femininity with which women are 'getting in touch', but an expression of power–knowledge relations.

While genealogies, truth, knowledge are all cheerfully subjected to the label 'fiction', none the less genealogy is not solely the work of imagination, not the casual rewriting of existence: complete subjectivity could exist only in a plastic world furnished exclusively with ideas. Foucault's work is premised to a large extent on the porousness of materiality – for example, bodies and their pleasures – to the ideal. But this is not an absolute causal collapsibility. The materiality of the world is as undeniable as the power effects of ideas on it. And ideas are themselves dependent upon the material world for a jumping-off place. Ideas of the 'feminine' are the result of the interplay of previous historical understandings of femininity and the bodies these have produced (Bartky 1988; Bordo 1988). Ideas and materiality are intertwined in a spiral of mutually informed contingency. Materiality is not simply three-dimensional but, because of this complex relation of the material to the ideal and the nearly constant process of transformation, it is temporal as well. Historical research is thus very important in Foucault's conception of genealogy: by documenting the discontinuities of history, he dispels the shadow of a monolithic, transcendent culture from which marginalised groups and individuals must wrest the rights to their identities.

Though Foucault's approach to history has important empirical dimensions in the contributions of his own historical research (1970, 1972, 1977, 1978), it refuses the absolute truths claimed by science and metaphysics. This necessarily limits the degree of facticity to which his method can (or he would want to) lay claim. The conventional distinction between fact and fiction is based on a distinction between the subjective and objective world, a real material world and a false ideological one. It is premised on a belief in a 'real' and final truth. Genealogy acts, somewhat, to blur the boundary between 'fact' and 'fiction' by acknowledging its own interests, recognising the subjective process of its emphases. Foucault argues that the genealogist must interpret, must assign significance, must create truth from history with full knowledge that this truth is a fiction: but, paradoxically, it is truth. Genealogy cannot *prove* anything since Foucault rejects the idea that we can produce absolute truths. But genealogy can fabricate a discourse which can assume the role that is usually appropriated by the problematic claims of absolute truths.

> As to the problem of fiction, it seems to me to be a very important one; I am well aware that I have never written anything but fictions. I do not mean to say, however, that the truth is therefore absent. It seems to me that the possibility exists for fiction to function in truth, for a fictional discourse to induce effects of truth, and for bringing it about that a true discourse engenders or 'manufactures' something that does not as yet exist, that is, 'fictions' it. One 'fictions' history on the basis of a political reality that makes it true, one 'fictions' a politics not yet in existence on the basis of a historical truth.
>
> (Foucault 1980b: 193)

Genealogies of gender allow the partial truths of specific and historical differences in the lives of men and women, but disallow claims to an absolute truth about the 'nature' of men or women to justify or explain existing relations.

For Foucault, bodies are fabricated historically. Rather than revealing a complicity in transcendental, ahistorical structures, Foucault's genealogy of sexuality will fiction a truth of bodies as products of time, space and force, will attempt to construct bodies as foci in power–knowledge–truth struggles, a specific historical/ material construction. Radical feminisms, like the work of Mary Daly (1978) which depend on an embodied, transhistorical, female essence are insupportable in this context. Arguments like Susan Brownmiller's about the inherent and bodily vulnerability of women to men across time and culture are radically undercut by a genealogical account of bodies (Woodhull 1988: 170–1). In opposition to a continuity of expression of meanings, effects or subjection of bodies, this will highlight historical fractures and discontinuities of the signification and subjection of bodies. There will not be a transhistorical female body left as a reference for these arguments; instead, what is called 'the body' will be a site and expression of different, interested power relations in various times and places. This criticism of implicit or explicit essentialism in feminism need not be taken as negative since feminism can offer better resistance to the fragmented and diffuse, but undeniably interlocking, specific structures of masculinist power, than it can to the primordial monolith of 'patriarchy'.

> What is crucial is the capacity to shift the terms of the struggle, the ability to see our position within existing structures but to respond from somewhere else. What Leftists have criticised in the women's movement as fragmentation, lack of organisation, absence of a coherent and encompassing theory, and the inability to mount a frontal attack may very well represent fundamentally more radical and effective responses to the deployment of power in our society than the centralisation and abstraction that continue to plague Leftist thinking.
>
> (Martin 1988: 10)

FEMINISM AND FOUCAULT'S BODIES

Having framed Foucault, it remains to outline the possibilities enabled by his reading of bodies for tackling the issue of feminist identity and its relation to women's bodies. An exploration of *The History of Sexuality* illustrates Foucault's theory of the new forms of power – discipline, subjection, bio-power – and the ways in which this power both produces and limits identity. It also documents the historical contingency of 'sexuality' and 'sex', and the way in which bodies are subjected to the truth of these.

Foucault holds out the tantalising promise of bodies whose truth is not ultimately the truth of sexuality or sex. Bodies, women's bodies, with partial interested truths – as opposed to bodies read solely or primarily around the objective truth of a fixed sexuality – allow for fragmented identities, partial strategies and specific, interested resistances. Foucault offers a reformulation of power which facilitates intriguing possibilities for feminist identity. Because power is no longer only, or even primarily, legal-juridical, resistance to specific relations of power must take myriad and partial forms. Feminist scholarship is such a struggle. Grassroots political organisation is such a struggle. (I would also maintain that the seduction through, and subversion of, notions of the 'feminine' in the work of pop artists like Madonna is such a partial struggle.)

Foucault's conception of bodies in *The History of Sexuality*, his analysis of truth and knowledge as power which enables and limits identity, refuses the possibility of absolute and final cultural transformation. Instead, Foucault's readings of the history of our bodies as subject to the power relations of late twentieth-century post-industrial capitalist culture, allow us to win and lose battles without having an absolute war (for example, against patriarchy). Foucault's suggestion that resistances to these specific relations of power might start with a turn to bodies and their pleasures, embraces not only the partiality of identity, but consequently the partial knowledge which produced this identity.

This raises the problem of whether these bodies pre-exist the discursive power–knowledge practices which have figured them as the site of sex and a principal source of sexuality. Foucault suggests that women start resistance from 'bodies and pleasures', rather than from the hegemonic power–knowledge regimes of sexuality and sex. But is he then rejecting an historically problematic, ontological position for one which is seemingly more defensible by dint of its superior essentiality?

It is clear that bodies for/in which Foucault has fictioned this sexualised history do not yield the promise of a happy Utopia, a liberatory ground for identity. Foucault is not seeking recourse to a primary, pre-cultural body or sexuality. Rather, Foucault's bodies bear most profoundly the marks of the 'slings and arrows of outrageous fortune'. Bodies, and the discourses centred on understanding them, have been permanently altered by the power–knowledge machinery erected on, around and through human sexuality and sex. As a result, it is not possible to separate sexual identities from the cultural construction of bodies. This view is not a shift to a more essential material/biological, or psychoanalytic, or metaphysical truth to be unveiled in bodies, nor is it a plea to return to a golden age before bodies had been branded by sexuality and sex, as some of Freudian and post-Freudian theories of repression do. Bodies are so thoroughly understood according to the 'knowledge' about them – biological, psychoanalytic – that there is no 'outside', no access to bodies (and perhaps no bodies) external to these systems of truth.

But we must not refuse what might be afforded by this tattooed matter. Foucault offers up bodies as a source/site of resistance to colonisation by the crippling limitations to/for the existence of sexuality.[6] Bodies are multiply invested, by different and competing interests, but the subjection of bodies is never complete. The body has not been thoroughly subjected to 'sexuality', because the 'truth' of sexuality struggles with other competing truths, and because the deployments of sexuality are frequently partial and conflicting themselves.

Foucault is relying on some qualities of bodies which may exceed the explanatory capabilities of the discourse of sex and sexuality. But whether or not these bodily elements pre-exist, the hegemony of the discourse of sexuality is epistemologically indeterminate – there is no way to talk about it, think about it, write about it, know it – because there is no recourse to a language 'outside' of this *scientia sexualis*, the modern scientific study of sexuality. Foucault's bodies are not, then, essential, original, constant, facts; they are historical constructs, like sexuality and sex. Bodies are affected, altered, tattooed by historical circumstance – and they are indistinguishable from these effects, alterations, tattoos.

> the purpose of the present study is in fact to show how deployments of power are directly connected to the body – to bodies, functions, physiological processes, sensations, and pleasures; far from the body having to be effaced, what is needed is to make it visible through an analysis in which the

biological and the historical are not consecutive to one another, as in the evolutionism of the first sociologists, but are bound together in an increasingly complex fashion in accordance with the development of modern technologies of power that take life as their objective. Hence I do not envisage a 'history of mentalities' that would take account of bodies only through the manner in which they have been perceived and given meaning and value; but a 'history of bodies' and the manner in which what is most material and most vital in them has been invested.
(Foucault 1978: 151)

What is striking here is that Foucault refuses the distinction between 'mentalities' and 'bodies'; they are so thoroughly bound together that they are indistinguishable.

Bodies, power and the history of sexuality

In *The History of Sexuality*, Foucault traces the evolution of what we know as western sexuality from its inception as an issue of concern, to the present inadequate formulation of its character, which he terms the 'repressive hypothesis'. What Foucault terms the 'repressive hypothesis' is the major theoretical fundament of many psychoanalytic theories of sexuality – like those of Freud, Marcuse and some feminist psychoanalytic theorists. It posits that there is an original sexual energy (the id in babies for individuals, pre-cultural sexual relations for populations) which must be recovered to neutralise the crippling effects on the psyche (or self) of external and internalised repressions of this energy. There is a corollary desire to return to original, true sexuality in order to free ourselves.

Foucault emphasises in this genealogy that power is not at all as we have been given to understand it, at least not any more. It is not a restrictive, prohibitive, unidirectional relationship which manifests itself as the repression of subjects by an authority. Rather, Foucault understands power as a generative force, as well as a restrictive opportunity. It can create pleasures and dimensions to existence which had not previously existed. For example, there is a pleasure Foucault recounts in finding a name for one's 'self' – for example, 'homosexual' – and embracing the identity which is socially attached to this name. This is the pleasure of uncovering the 'truth' of self. Foucault also stresses that this evolution has been determined by specific historical circumstances – for example, the birth and growth of industry. Industry required human labour capital, so that the need for administration of the population could adopt the existence of sexuality as one of its techniques of control.

Foucault maintains that the traditional dualistic understanding of power is insufficient. The polarisation of the ruler and the ruled, the oppressor and the oppressed, the sovereign and the subjects are categories which fail to untangle the manifestations and potential of power. Power has changed its form/expression in accord with a shift in historical context. This shift must be understood if the effects of the hegemony of the project of the scientific normalisation of populations is to be subverted. Power is not a law which is, or can be, broken. It is, for example, a discipline which is cultivated, like the attachment to an 'appropriate' sexual object, or learning to sleep at night and eat at certain times. The appeal of the 'truth' discourse of the body and sexuality/sex is that they constitute identities and guide behaviours, even the 'abnormal' behaviours. The power in discourses of sexuality cannot be simply a power of repression, which subjects a society to the rule of a sovereign, or a class to domination at the hands of a wealthier class. 'It is a type of power which is constantly exercised by means of surveillance rather than in a discontinuous manner by means of a system of levies or obligations distributed over time' (Foucault 1980c: 104). Sexual power, like other forms of power, exists as a relation between all strands of a given social web, and does not necessarily take the form of a prohibition, refusal, denial.

The History of Sexuality articulates an alternative understanding of human sexuality and the power–knowledge relations constructing it. Foucault's insight in this genealogy consists not in positing that human sexual norms are social/cultural constructs; this is not a particularly original or perceptive revelation. Adrienne Rich, for example, has demonstrated the social construction and enforcement of compulsory heterosexuality (Eisenstein 1984: 55–6, 105). Rather, the underlying value of this analysis is Foucault's reading and understanding of the power relations involved in the creation of human sexuality in a specific historical context as an object of knowledge, a source of truth.

This perception of the forces involved in subjecting something to a body of knowledge, of making it knowable in terms of, and as, truth, necessitates a rethinking of how getting at the truth of (one's) sexuality is perceived to be personally/politically liberating.

Thus, feminist theories which seek to subvert or undermine masculinist power through recourse to a primary or essential sexuality will need to re-examine more closely what interests they are serving (Martin 1988: 11).

The History of Sexuality serves as an elaboration of the immanence of power in the construction and dispersion of truth, and of the specific construction of human sexuality as a subject of knowledge and truth, as well as a site for the power-play involved in defining the integral self. The way in which Foucault has challenged existing understandings of power, knowledge, truth and pleasure through his history of sexuality has implications for feminism. He demands that we take seriously the positive and generative, as well as the negative and coercive, possibilities of the 'will to knowledge' which is a contemporary expression of power. In the drive, the consumerist need for 'truth', most especially the drive for self-truth, identities are produced which simultaneously ground existence, and thus enable action, and also limit possibilities.

Foucault explicitly draws the connection between the growth of the study of sexuality and sex, and a set of very specific understandings of bodies. What is important for feminists – who have been enabled as feminists by their ability to unify partially and identify as women with specific interests produced by the discourses on sexuality and the truth of their bodily identity – is to recognise that there is no 'outside' to power. Thus there is no 'innocent' class of the purely oppressed, and feminists need to recognise the limits and dangers of identity-based politics.

It was in the course of the public administration innovation in the technology of sex that sexuality was constituted as an area of medical investigation, in the early nineteenth century: 'the flesh was brought down to the level of the organism' (Foucault 1978: 117). After this, modifications and mutations of the technologies of sex proliferated. The medical study of sexual normality/ deviation was wedded to a politics of eugenics, while the advent of the 'psyche' was linked to the 'talking cure' of psychotherapies. The body was somehow vital to realising, making factual and material, the subject sexuality. It was through the study of bodily behaviours and the excitations of the body that 'sexuality' was implanted and discovered. Bodies were indispensable as a topos, a site, at which this sexuality could be isolated, identified, interrogated, probed and, if need be (as in the case of 'aberrant' sexualities), modified. Discourse which focused attention on sexuality necessarily held a vigorous interest in bodies; knowledge about sex and sexuality was derived by contact with bodies (Foucault 1978: 44).

The advent of a new field of knowledge was the result of, and in turn had a profound influence on, a new kind of power. One of the effects was the conjunction, the joining, of bodies and sexuality/sex. This new power–knowledge regime seduced its subjects into participation, into confession and inspection and elaboration. Bourgeois wives, for example, were compelled to become better wives and mothers by submitting to analysis to uncover the origins – and thus the possible cure – for their 'hysteria'. In the search for knowledge and truth about sexuality, power and pleasure are inseparable and mutually reinforcing. Sexual truths are produced and, through the pleasure of, and the constructed need for their discovery, implanted and 'found'.

> The growth of perversions is not a moralising theme that obsessed the scrupulous minds of the Victorians. It is the real product of the encroachment of a type of power on bodies and their pleasures. It is possible that the west has not been capable of inventing any new pleasures, and it has doubtless not discovered any original vices. But it has defined new rules for the game of power and pleasures, the frozen countenance of the perversions is a fixture of this game.
>
> (Foucault 1978: 47–8)

Sexuality reproduced itself by creating a need for the truth it would deliver, and tying this truth of self to existent and new pleasures. Sexuality grew to be the dominant theoretical lens through which issues of individual and collective behaviours were analysed, and it made itself indispensable by offering access to pleasure and self. Sexuality became an institution unto itself, the modern science of sexuality, and increased the scope of power and pleasure through enumeration, classification, elaboration, specification.

It was the dispersal of the techniques of power which determined its current form. Ultimately, the realm of vested interest in sexuality primarily involved not the Church nor the much maligned state, but the truth quest of science (Foucault 1978: 12–13). None the less, many power relations were preserved intact, or further refined – for example, those of women to masculinist institutions – because they continued to serve specific interests.

The question of the history of sexuality as elaborated by Foucault has not involved identifying a guilty party who repressed sex or controlled it for whatever reasons. Rather, it has identified the construction of sexuality as an important issue in a particular historical period, and traced not only the tactics employed in order to administer sex, bodies, life, but also the interested parties in these discourses of sex. Foucault points out the interests of the eighteenth- and nineteenth-century European industrial bourgeoisie, and of the nascent scientific and medical communities, especially in the institutionalisation of the scientific knowledge of sex as truth. It is important to note, in the absence of such remarks by Foucault, that these interests were also masculinist. Foucault stresses that while the whole shift in the style of power he has theorised is important, it is only a dimension of the history of modern power relations. A distinction cannot really be drawn between the alteration in power's expression and the function of that expression.

Foucault acknowledges that sexuality, as it is understood through the repressive hypothesis, was the invention of bourgeois morality. However, the story does not go exactly as we have thought. The bourgeoisie did not originally set out to refuse, delete or deny the sexuality of humanity in order to channel libidinal energies into capitalist production, either directly (as labour), or on the long-term plan (by increasing the population/ labour pool). Sexuality was not initially employed to manipulate the working class, to multiply them as its primary industrial capital. Rather, it was introduced to define that which was unique and superior about the bourgeoisie, to serve the positive role of differentiating them favourably from the debauched, blue-blooded nobility and the naturally degenerate lower classes (Foucault 1978: 123–4).

Clearly, bodies were critical to the bourgeois project of creating a class sexual identity. Bodies were the product and location of that which thereafter defined these bodies – and so much more – bourgeois sexuality. Bodies, however, were not mere sites for the all-important sexuality and sex; they in turn were subjected to a process designed to differentiate and define, materially, the bourgeois body from that of the other classes. Bodies ensured – because this is how they were defined and constructed – the potency and the vitality of the bourgeoisie at the species as well as the cultural level. It was only in reaction to certain material historical conditions in Europe that the bourgeoisie's construction of its own pristine sexuality was put to the use of controlling people as populations.

Foucault's analysis provides feminists with much food for thought. For example, though the 'accidental' character of the institutionalisation of power relations undermines the notion of a 'patriarchy', it leaves open interpretations of power as masculinist in its expressions. Foucault also points to the dangers of turning to science for 'truth'; this has resonances with many feminist critiques of science and medicine. It also shows the intersection of various interests in the locus of women's bodies – the interested powers are not just masculinist, but also capitalist and bourgeois, and institutional, as in the case of medicine and science.

His analysis of power thus also tends to support the beliefs of feminists like Catherine MacKinnon who suggest that rape is not an anomaly nor an 'unsexual' act of violence but one extreme of existing power relations (MacKinnon 1987). However, his analysis of power allows for resistance, rather than the naïve rejection of power. This in turn allows for the tolerance of some expressions of these power relations, without necessarily rendering all expressions logical and acceptable conclusions, unlike MacKinnon's formulation. Finally, the constructed character of identity and its complicity in the discourses which enable it point to the limits of identity politics. Identities allow a certain fictional unity – a unity grouped around an historical identity, around specific relations of power. Though there is no universal category of women, there remain women whose interests are linked together by their similar positions in modern networks of power.

RESISTANCE AND IDENTITY

It is perhaps impossible to generalise about feminist resistance strategies – they are myriad, local, institutional political, scholarly, metatheoretical. Foucault's analysis of the partiality of truth, and his consequent turn to local, specific struggles, tend to render suspect the efficacy of certain strategies. For example, though legal and juridical institutional battles should by no means cease, they are just the tip of the resistance iceberg. Power is not expressed only or primarily through legal-juridical structures.

Jana Sawicki (1988: 186–90) points out that Foucault's notions of power are eminently compatible with feminist understandings of the personal as political. She also notes that Foucault's analyses of identity as historically constructed are compatible with analyses of identity by lesbian feminists which have been implemented in the reconstruction of identities. She points out that embracing a reconstructed identity based on its hierarchical distinction from other identities – for example, those of gay men – limits alliances which could strengthen local struggles around specific issues. The importance of the bodies in this history of sexuality is manifest. Bodies are produced, understood, deployed in the service of certain interests and relationships of power. Bodies, thus, are a battleground of interests and power, something feminists have long understood – though not in these terms. It is in helping to define the foci of these battles, then, that Foucault is of most service to feminist projects.

Perhaps it would be the case that there can be nothing hopeful/helpful in this body if the effects of power were not many and, some, entirely unpredictable. Foucault's understanding of bodies as the simultaneous source and product of a notion of self allows for strategic redeployment of these embattled bodies.

> In this view of the self, the relationship between the individual and society is not pictured as one of social determination – complete socialisation. Socialisation, rather, emerges as a project that is never fully realised in practice. Therefore, social constructionism does not imply social determinism. Foucault's certainly does not.
>
> (Sawicki 1988: 184)

Bodies as Foucault has described them *are* subjected to rigorous modification, solicitation, excitation. Yet Foucault has suggested that bodies and pleasures might be a source of resistance to the hegemonic self-truth of sex/sexuality. Socialisation is never complete, because competing interests and identities create conflicts. In arbitrating between identities, the power–knowledge of identity allows a limited self-definition and self-determination, which perhaps we could term 'agency', and so the possibility for new combinations and new understandings. Can Foucault possibly be referring to those *new* pleasures which have been an unintentional effect of the sexualisation of life?

No, Foucault is rather demonstrating in his description of these new pleasures – the pleasure of telling the truth of self – how it is that we truth-seekers have been complacently complicit in our own subjection to sexuality's unitary power–knowledge–truth dominion. Foucault is definitely not, however, suggesting a turn to these pleasures, or the truth that impregnated bodies with them. These pleasures are part and parcel of the systems of truths of identity which co-operate painfully to circumscribe the possibilities for human lives.

The theory that bodies are not biological essences, but are culturally constructed, just as much as sexuality and sex are cultural constructions, hobbles the possibility of a feminist identity grounded in any kind of 'natural' category of women. This means that women cannot share a universal, timeless identity based simply on being essentially, biologically women. But perhaps this is not such a sorry state of affairs for feminism. Foucault's own insistence on specific strategies for local struggles enables, perhaps, a careful and minimalist deployment of essentialism for concrete gains – for example, in women's struggles around health, abortion, maternity, rape. Foucault's suggestion that all discourses can give rise to resistance offers a more fluid, more partial 'identity' which could enable feminist politics without subjecting this politics to an absolute and eternal feminist identity. Foucault asserts that

> there is a plurality of resistances, each of them a special case: resistances that are possible, necessary, improbable; others that are spontaneous, savage, solitary, concerted, rampant, or violent; still others that are quick to compromise, interested, or sacrificial; by definition, they can only exist in the strategic field of power relations.

> (Foucault 1978: 96)

One possibility which comes to mind is the identification with certain characteristics and roles, without subjecting oneself to the truth of these as essence, as determinate identity. Foucault has pointed to the way that 'homosexuality' as an identity constructed through the hegemonic discourses on sexuality and sex has exploded the confines of this limited identity, constituted by, and enabling, a gay community which encompasses many other partial identities and differences. Similarly, Judith Butler (1990) has argued that the identification of gay men and lesbians with butch/femme roles can subvert notions of identity as essence.

Revolutions in the sense of traditional political opposition are ruled out as ineffective resistance because they are based on the assumption that power is an external force possessed by some ruling group and exercised through laws and prohibitions. Foucault suggests that the politics and political criticism which will resist and oppose disciplinary power have yet to be fabricated. This politics cannot reference the truth of a timeless identity – instead, it will be subject to various and changing interests of fragmented and partial identities.

> Political analysis and criticism have in a large measure still to be invented – so too have the strategies which will make it possible to modify the relations of force, to co-ordinate them in such a way that such a modification is possible and can be inscribed in reality. That is to say, the problem is not so much that of defining a political 'position' (which is to choose from a pre-existing set of possibilities) but to imagine and to bring into being new schemas of politicisation. If 'politicisation' means falling back on ready-made choices and institutions, then the effort of analysis involved in uncovering the relations of force and mechanisms of power is not worthwhile. To the vast new techniques of power correlated with multinational economies and bureaucratic States, one must oppose a politicisation which will take new forms.
>
> (Foucault 1980b: 190)

It should be kept in mind that this new politics will always be subject to co-option by other interests. This is perhaps the most compelling trap to be wary of in the deploying, even in limited ways, of strategic essentialisms.

Since Foucault sees truth, knowledge and power as entwined, it is necessary that a new feminist politics should embody a new understanding of self. This will mean a new truth and knowledge about one's 'identity' and its possibilities. Foucault's conception of resistance does not then resolve the problem of identity for feminism. Women's need for identity is produced by contemporary western relations of power as the need for truth, in which there is no 'outside' to power and no male possession of power. But as Foucault's theory does not give us truths which are absolute, it could also allow men and women to have identities which are not absolute. Conflicts, for example, over race, class and gender affiliations would no longer be subject to the need to choose and identify only with the 'true' and primary system of oppression, but could become sites of resistance to such exclusions and sources of possible new identifications. Sawicki points out the advantages of Foucauldian analyses which resist the ways in which unitary truth narratives and their unitary identities serve bourgeois and institutional, and masculinist, interests.

> this analysis enables us to think of difference as a resource rather than a threat. . . . In [a 'politics of difference'] one is not always attempting to overcome difference. Neither does one regard difference as an obstacle to effective resistance. Difference can be a resource insofar as it enables us to multiply the sources of resistance to the myriad of relations of domination that circulate through the social field. If there is no central locus of power, then neither is there a central locus of resistance.
>
> (Sawicki 1988: 187)

This theory that 'identity' is not a fixed essence, but is culturally constructed, is especially compatible with the loose, opportunistic coalitions which can embrace differences, described by Ernesto Laclau and Chantal Mouffe (1985: 193). With no absolute identity to determine the 'necessary' interests of a subject, there are no fundamental interests to be betrayed, and the dangers of 'coalition politics' – identified by Stokely Carmichael and Charles Hamilton (1967: 58–84) – are not quite so perilous.

CONCLUSION

In order to make fullest use of the radical potential of the theories of Michel Foucault, feminists will have to use their imaginations and fill the gaps left by Foucault, who was not especially interested in feminist issues. But this is not a very onerous chore, and it is well suited to Foucault's understanding of knowledge and truths as partial and interested. Genealogy is thus an excellent Foucauldian resource for feminist scholarship.

Foucault's understandings of sexuality and the body (the latter understood historically only through the context of the power–knowledge regime of the former) point to the limits and dangers of identity politics for feminists. Tying feminism to an essential female identity makes the differences between women a source of conflict rather than a source of strength. But these cautions are tempered by the specific context of masculinist power, and the possible need to invoke a strategic essentialism for immediate feminist gains. By 'strategic essentialism' I mean a fictional essence deployed within very specific institutional settings where the terms of debate are already circumscribed; the effort to change the terms of debate should not be abdicated.

Though Foucault's analysis of power undermines previous feminist understandings of a patriarchy as a monolithic power structure, it does not deny the possibility of understanding gender relations as serving specific, interlocking interests. Thus it allows an understanding of social formations as masculinist. The collapse of the concept of 'patriarchy' frees feminists to pursue specific, local struggles without justifying these with reference to an entirely male system of power and consequent oppositional female powerlessness.

Finally, Foucault's analysis of identities as plural and partial makes possible what Jana Sawicki (1991) calls a 'politics of difference', in which no system of classifying identity is taken as more primary than another, and different identities can intersect and be allied in individuals and over specific power struggles. All in all, though we feminists will have to do most of the 'leg-work' ourselves, there are many productive intersections of Foucauldian and feminist projects.

NOTES

1 The forms of radical feminism which emerged from the 1960s took feminism as a universal struggle of women against men's power, and this claim to universality has been much criticised. In this chapter I focus on western culture and sexuality in looking at what use feminists might make of Foucault's work.

2 In some versions of feminism, these gendered social roles are seen as psychological. In this view, western 'patriarchy' is conceived as a cultural monolith which has left its stamp indelibly on the psyches of both men and women. Men are raised to value themselves, in this model, only in so far as they can distinguish between themselves and some lesser other, whom they must dominate to enact and illustrate the distinction. Because women are raised and living in a culture in which the reference for humanity, for beings with value, is male, they suffer profound psychological damage – the effects of believing themselves, consciously or unconsciously, less than fully human. Transformation of the existing oppression of women, in these analyses of 'patriarchy', requires nothing less than a complete and constant re-orientation to culture. Either 'male' values must be

rejected entirely and the superior 'female' values proposed by Nancy Chodorow (Eisenstein 1984: 87–100) substituted, or the fundamental 'male' and 'female' cultural values suggested by Carol Gilligan (Eisenstein 1984: 160–1, n. 8) reconciled.

3 Genealogy is Foucault's analytic method. It relies heavily on history, but not the singular histories which have traditionally been rendered in academic history. Instead, Foucault seeks to displace the focus of these other, accepted histories by offering differing, historical, marginalised perspectives – the understandings of the subjects of knowledge rather than the experts (for example, 'lunatics' rather than psychiatrists), and the analyses of intellectuals with specific and acknowledged interests in a given field. This perspectivism of genealogy is based on Foucault's rejection of some notion that the interests involved in the truths and knowledges circulating in western post-industrial societies have been erased, allowing them to be presented as neutral.

4 *Herculine Barbin* (Foucault 1980a) deals more explicitly with the problematics of gender in its treatment of sexuality and bodies (both by Foucault and by the hermaphrodite Alexina, whose journals comprise the main body of the text of *Herculine Barbin*), by zooming in on the experiences of an individual whose life refused the reductive categorisations of the power–knowledge regime of sex fully to embody sex and gender possibilities. Judith Butler (1990) subjects Foucault's readings of Alexina's diaries to rigorous critique. She notes that Foucault's introduction is Utopian. Where Foucault wants to read Alexina's despair and suicide as the result of being forced to choose a singular sexual identity, Butler is not so ingenuous. She notes that there was no 'outside' of language and identity for Alexina, that the narrative of *Herculine Barbin* refers to a perpetual unease with and struggle for 'identity'. In Butler's reading, Alexina is not reduced to an identity at the time that s/he chose to be 'male', but that the problem of ambiguous sexual identity is the discourse which generates Alexina's sexual identity, plural or singular. While I could aspire no higher than to plagiarise or legitimately reproduce Judith Butler, her reading of Foucault's *Herculine Barbin* is critical and exhaustive. I consent to it. *The History of Sexuality*, volume I (Foucault 1978) offers a more wide-angle-lens view of the construction of sexuality.

5 Mary Daly (1978) for example, sought to embrace, as essence, the devalued characteristics associated in western culture with women, and to revalue them. In order to effect this revaluation, opposing 'patriarchal' values were devalued. For Daly, feminists must assume and enjoy their essential female nature or continue as men's pawns, victims and dupes of the patriarchy. Though the feminist goal of replacing the impossible male ideal with a woman-centred perspective was met by Daly's radical feminism, other needs – for example, the maintenance of certain forms of relationships with men and the struggles for political gains within existing 'patriarchal' society – were not. The essential identity suggested by Daly offers

some possibilities to women that have been denied them in western masculinist culture, but it refused them other options.

6   [T]here is a plurality of resistances, each of them a special case: resistances that are possible, necessary, improbable; others that are spontaneous, savage, solitary, concerted, rampant, or violent; still others that are quick to compromise, interested or sacrificial; by definition, they can only exist in a strategic field of power relations. . . . Just as the network of power relations ends by forming a dense web that passes through apparatuses and institutions, without being exactly localized in them, so too the swarm of points of resistance traverses social stratifications and individual unities. And it is doubtless the strategic codification of these points of resistance that makes a revolution possible, somewhat similar to the way in which the state relies on the institutional integration of power relations.

(Foucault 1978: 96).

BIBLIOGRAPHY

Bartky, S.L. (1988) 'Foucault, femininity and the modernization of patriarchal power', in I. Diamond and L. Quinby (eds) *Feminism and Foucault: Reflections on Resistance*, Boston: Northeastern University Press.

Bordo, S. (1988) 'Anorexia nervosa: psychopathology as the crystallization of culture', in I. Diamond and L. Quinby (eds) *Feminism and Foucault: Reflections on Resistance*, Boston: Northeastern University Press.

Butler, J. (1990) *Gender Trouble: Feminism and the Subversion of Identity*, London: Routledge.

Carmichael, S. and Hamilton, C. (1967) *Black Power: The Politics of Liberation in America*, New York: Vintage Books.

Daly, M. (1978) *Gyn/Ecology: The Metaethics of Radical Feminism*, Boston: Beacon Press.

Diamond, I. and Quinby, L. (eds) (1988) *Feminism and Foucault: Reflections on Resistance*, Boston: Northeastern University Press.

Eisenstein, H. (1984) *Contemporary Feminist Thought*, London: Allen & Unwin.

Elshtain, J. (1981) *Public Man, Private Woman: Women in Social and Political Thought*, Princeton, NJ: Princeton University Press.

Foucault, M. (1970) *The Order of Things: An Archaeology of the Human Sciences*, New York: Vintage Books.

—— (1972) *The Archaeology of Knowledge and the Discourse on Language*, New York: Pantheon Books.

—— (1977) *Discipline and Punish: The Birth of the Prison*, New York: Vintage Books.

—— (1978) *The History of Sexuality*, vol. I: *An Introduction*, New York: Vintage books.

—— (1980a) 'Introduction to Herculine Barbin', in *Herculine Barbin*, New York: Pantheon Books.

—— (1980b) 'The history of sexuality', in C. Gordon (ed.) *Power/Knowledge: Selected Interviews and Other Writings 1972–1977 by Michel Foucault*, New York: Pantheon Books.

—— (1980c) 'Two lectures', in C. Gordon (ed.) *Power/Knowledge: Selected Interviews and Other Writings 1972–1977 by Michel Foucault*, New York: Pantheon Books.

Gordon, C. (ed.) (1980) *Power/Knowledge: Selected Interviews and Other Writings 1972–1977 by Michel Foucault*, trans. C. Gordon *et al.*, New York: Pantheon Books.

Haraway, D.J. (1991) *Simians, Cyborgs, and Women: The Reinvention of Nature*, New York: Routledge.

Laclau, E. and Mouffe, C. (1985) *Hegemony and Socialist Strategy: Towards a Radical Democratic Politics*, London: Verso.

MacKinnon, C. (1987) *Feminism Unmodified: Discourses on Life and Law*, Cambridge, MA: Harvard University Press.

Martin, B. (1988) 'Feminism, criticism, and the question of rape' in I. Diamond and L. Quinby (eds) *Feminism and Foucault: Reflections on Resistance*, Boston: Northeastern University Press.

Okin, S. (1979) *Women in Western Political Thought*, Princeton, NJ: Princeton University Press.

Sawicki, J. (1988) 'Identity politics and sexual freedom: Foucault and feminism', in I. Diamond and L. Quinby (eds) *Feminism and Foucault: Reflections on Resistance*, Boston: Northeastern University Press.

—— (1991) *Disciplining Foucault: Feminism, Power and the Body*, New York: Routledge.

Woodhull, W. (1988) 'Sexuality, power, and the question of rape' in I. Diamond and L. Quinby (eds) *Feminism and Foucault: Reflections on Resistance*, Boston: Northeastern University Press.

Chapter 6

Feminism, difference and discourse
The limits of discursive analysis for feminism

Janet Ransom

INTRODUCTION

> What matter who is speaking; someone has said: what matter
> who is speaking.
>
> (Foucault 1991: 72)

When Foucault explains that his method of historical and
philosophical analysis focuses not on the speaker but on what is
said, he distances himself from the terms of modernist humanistic
thinking.[1] Modernist thinking, the foundations of which are set in
the Enlightenment, works with a conception of society as a
collection of rational beings and of the human agent as the source
of meaning and value. It assumes that the speaker or writer is
unified and coherent, the origin of what is spoken or written.
Foucault argues for a displacement of terms which is, for him, an
act of humility on the part of the theorist (Foucault 1991). For
Foucault, what matters is not the aspiration of the writer in
writing, the personal history or political or moral orientation
which makes 'me' want to write 'this'. Rather, he wants to develop
a method which proceeds from a different point of origin.

The focus of Foucault's work is discourse – the structured ways
of knowing which are both produced in, and the shapers of,
culture. Discourses are not merely linguistic phenomena, but are
always shot through with power and are institutionalised as
practices. So, for example, medical discourse is not simply a set of
terms or signifiers but also includes the power that the doctor's
presentation of the situation bears in relation to that of the patient,
as well as the institutional patterning of medical care.[2] It is, in part,
this recasting of the focus of historical understanding which plants
Foucault within a developing postmodernist tradition of thought,

and it is a move that might be felt to resonate with feminists' concern to study the ways that 'femininity' has historically been constituted.

A second feature of his work which locates it within postmodernism is his rejection of the idea of history as a process with a purpose, a story which attaches to the development of a historical subject, such as the proletariat, or a particular narrative, like 'class struggle'. Postmodernism offers an account of social reality in which the foci of political concern are conceived as fragmented, limitless and disparate, and no particular struggle is conceived as necessarily central. Foucault seems to allow for the integrity of feminist political struggle, and to provide a conceptual space that can accommodate the variety of feminist work. So it is that feminism, or feminisms, might be seen as part of this more general fragmentation, part of a loosely connected range of alternative voices drawing on a plurality of resources in the unanchored reality that is contemporary life.

Yet the relationship between feminism and the discourses of postmodernity is a contested one. Postmodernism may appear to account for, and potentially to subsume, feminism itself; but the relationship between Foucault's postmodernism and feminism can also be seen as part of an ongoing, complex and sometimes fraught dialogue between feminism and the mainstream or (more problematically) malestream production of ideas. In this chapter I want to address the question of whether, for feminists, it does matter who is speaking, whether feminism needs to retain the speaking subject whom Foucault methodologically abandons when he encourages us to focus on the spoken rather than on the speaker. The question is an important one because it bears upon whether feminism, or feminisms, can be best thought of as an aspect of postmodernism, or whether it is better seen as in tension with it. I shall argue that although Foucault's thought may at one level appear able to incorporate feminism, there is a more pressing level at which it undermines it, and that feminism needs to keep a critical distance from the recasting of the relationship between the human subject and the social world which Foucault proposes. Feminism is built on, and requires, the capacity to make certain sorts of statements which are not fully provided for in Foucault's theory so that the discursive mode of analysis which Foucault develops is not, finally, adequate to feminist concerns.

This is not to say that the reconstitution of social reality which has been characterised as postmodernity does not pose fundamental questions for feminist theory. On the contrary, the insight that relations of oppression cannot be accounted for in a single set of terms has been central to the development of feminist thought. New-wave feminism was distinguished by its claim that sexual or gender oppression was qualitatively distinct from more generally recognised forms of oppression – class, for example. So feminism entered the theoretical arena by posing the problems both of commonality – how we might conceptualise and explain the shared or common oppression of women as women – and of difference: how women's oppression is distinct from other forms, and the consequences of those other forms of power relationships as manifested in the differences between women. If there is a central difficulty in feminist debate today, it is still the problem of generating a theory which can articulate and explain both the commonalities and differences in women's experiences. The heterogeneity of women's lives, since women are divided by social differences, forms one major axis of the difficulty of providing for the coherence of feminism itself.[3]

Commonality and difference

The difficulty of identifying what women have in common across these different social experiences might be felt to threaten disintegration for feminism, or at least to call for a recon-ceptualisation of the kind of knowledge we see ourselves as producing. If the differences between women of race and sexuality have provided the main points of departure for the critique of 'feminism' conceived as a unitary body of theory, it is not the case that these differences, or for that matter class differences, can be taken to establish the boundaries of what needs to be rethought. The possible range of differences between women, on inspection, turns out to be infinite. The experienced reality of womanhood turns out to be, not unproblematically homogeneous, but internally differentiated in cross-cutting ways. Forms of differentiation which are analytically distinct, not only from gender but also from 'race' and class, stake their claims to the coherence of political agency. Women with disabilities, for example, campaign (with men) for better facilities and a social reconceptualisation of who they are; in recent years we have heard the voices of groups of survivors of child abuse, including (but not predominantly) men. The social construction of 'old age' has been called into question. This proliferation of difference is difficult to conceptualise in any patterned or coherent way, in part because the factors which make us different from one another as women often create commonalities between some women and some men, but also because each of these emergent collectivities is cut across by gender asymmetry. This makes it difficult to abstract, or constitute, a unitary female subject on which the coherence of feminism seems to depend. What threatens to disappear is the hook on which to hang our feminism.

Commonality in the sense of 'woman' as the subject of feminism, then, has been difficult to identify in terms of the experience of actual women. The need for historical and cultural specificity in grasping the qualitative differences in women's experiences of oppression has led Spelman (1990) to propose that we need a conception, not of two genders, but of a plurality of genders to accommodate the complexity. The bedrock of women's biological sameness as something which underpins or explains 'women's oppression' here disappears. From another direction, Foucault compounds the problem by recasting the terms in which we might think about the body. While women's biological difference from men might appear to provide the only distinction which can underpin the notion that women are oppressed 'as women', Foucault challenges this conception by focusing on the discourses which constitute the body. Here, our experiences of the body are seen as fundamentally socially constructed. Foucault brings essentialist assumptions about women's bodies into question by querying the body's status as something given in nature and existing outside the operations of power. In his view the body itself is not helpfully regarded as 'natural' but becomes thoroughly socialised. The coherence of any distinction between nature as fixed and culture as variable, sex as biological and gender as social, is undermined. For Foucault, the categories within which we think about the body do not derive from transparent necessity, but rather are seen to be fundamentally culturally embedded and imbued with the workings of power. 'Sex', or 'sexuality', for example, is not self-explanatory; rather, we become eroticised within the discourses of sex and sexuality, and it is within discourse that we learn the coherence of an identity as 'straight', 'lesbian', 'sado-masochistic' or 'sexually healthy'.[4] If the body is thus deployed upon and constituted at the experiential level, its status as a binding factor across the historical experiences of 'being female' becomes problematic.

How, then, is it possible to retain the coherence of a feminist theory focused on 'women' if 'women' is not a fixed category? The biological body no longer provides us with brute matter which merely requires classification. Philosophically, the possibility of a correspondence relationship between theory and the world is displaced. Sociologically, the social differentiation of women's experience itself means that 'women' are not in any sense a uniform social category.

It has seemed to some feminists that Foucauldian theory can provide a framework for the recasting of feminist theory in a way that can under-cut the problems we face in identifying our commonality (Weedon 1987; Flax 1990). The differences between different traditions of, or impulses within, feminism, become less pressing, it is argued, if 'feminism' becomes 'feminisms'. Feminisms then become one set of subversive discursive strategies amongst others – forms of counter-science, events in the 'insurrection of subjugated knowledges' (Foucault 1980: 81). These provide, according to Foucault, the only form of potentially radical knowledge or political action in the contemporary world (Hartsock 1990). The implication is that feminism can lose its attachment to the constitution of a unitary female subject based in the brute biological condition of femaleness or the cultural relationships in which that condition has been embedded. Rather, difference, the challenge of counter discourse, provides the movement of resistance.

In the following sections I consider whether Foucault's discursive analysis helps us as feminists in meeting the clearly signalled need for a kind of theory which can accommodate the plurality of women's experiential realities. Foucault's work is pluralistic in orientation, but is it a pluralism that can help sustain the force of feminist insight? To begin to provide an answer to this question, it is important first to look at Foucault's own account of his method. In the second and third sections of the chapter I discuss some of the ways this can be argued to be problematic for feminism.

DISCOURSE AND PLURALISM

Foucault's work is difficult to characterise in any over-arching way, but if there is a point that he emphasises more forcefully than any other in his lectures and interviews, it is the significance for him of his pluralism. It is on the basis of his conception of discourse that he develops a pluralistic form of theory which opposes itself to humanistic thinking. His work, he says, is an attempt to establish that 'discourse is not nothing or almost nothing' (1991: 63). It is through focusing on discourse that Foucault seeks both to subvert the problems of humanistic thinking and to develop a pluralistic methodology adequate to its critique.

As Hekman (1990) has pointed out, whilst Foucault in general did not like being labelled as a particular kind of theorist, the label of anti-humanist was one he did not dispute. Foucault wanted to generate a critique of humanism because he rejected a notion of an essential humanity which could inform a programme of social and political transformation, and because he rejected a theory of history as the process of development of a particular collective subject. There is some tension in Foucault's work because his broader claims, about the inadequacies of a humanistic conception of social reality and of the human subject, are often tempered by the specific ways in which he discusses his method. For the most part, he restricts himself to very specific claims. He explains that in his work he has posed himself particular problems and that his method is developed to respond to them (Foucault 1980, 1991). The question we are left with as feminists is whether the method which Foucault develops can simply be seen as a specific set of tools suitable for a particular intellectual project, as he sometimes wants to do, or whether the anti-humanism intrinsic to the pluralistic method that he develops is incompatible with feminism. Foucault's pluralism is distinct from a liberal-humanistic pluralism in several ways. Most importantly, it is premised on a distinct theory of power.

Power and truth

For Foucault, negotiations or struggles within society are not essentially about the possession of power, but rather about the contested terms of the deployment of power. He argues that power is both limitless and productive, and that it is coextensive with knowledge: where there is one, there is the other (Foucault 1980). Because power is not primarily something possessed by people or groups of people, it cannot be thought about as something that can be distributed between people or finally 'taken' on a zero-sum model. Power is not finite like a cake; it does not follow that if I have more, you have less. Neither is it something that attaches to a particular person; so, for example, Foucault implicitly contests a notion of men's possession of power over women. For these reasons, Foucault's pluralism is radically distinct from liberal forms of pluralism which would see power as something for possession of which competing interest groups battle. In Foucault's conception there is no point outside power from which a 'fair' decision about who should 'have' it can be made. Knowledge, then, cannot be neutral in the sense of existing outside the sphere of power.

This theory of power underpins Foucault's pluralism. Because power 'comes from everywhere' (1981: 93), he can claim that where there is power there is resistance. Radical movements are not best understood as seeking to seize or take power, but rather as producing alternative power-saturated knowledges. So power is itself a plural matter; it does not operate on a single trajectory, or with reference to a single core question, but is conceived as capillary, spreading through discourses, bodies and relationships, in the metaphor of a network (Foucault 1980). There are many knowledges, and political struggle is the struggle of these knowledges. There is not, however, a single truth.

Foucault's pluralism is distanced from humanistic thinking in that the latter implies that there can be a point of certainty in knowledge, an Archimedean point from which it is possible to access truth-as-such, to distinguish truth from falsity. Foucault's thought is pluralistic in that it emphatically rejects such a position and argues that to propose it necessarily poses a threat of tyranny, of imposing one particular view of the world on to others. Pluralism for Foucault actually requires that truth be seen as a thing produced and not revealed (Foucault 1991). On this methodological model, then, we can focus on the ways that 'femininity' is produced in the culture, the ways, for example, that conceptions of woman have been conceived in terms of a distinction between the virgin and the whore.[5]

So it is that Foucault locates himself within a Nietzschean tradition of thought in that he displaces a substantive conception of truth – that is, a conception of truth as something that can be known directly and distinguished from untruth – in favour of a conception of truth as emergent, a matter of identifiable categories (Foucault 1980). The strength of this move is in part that it might be argued to help us attend to the cultural specificity of the 'feminine' or the 'sexual'; we cannot assume that these are fixed, timeless truths, but are rather encouraged to study them in terms of the ways they are contrasted with other social and ideological phenomena in the context of a particular power-saturated meaning system. For Foucault, however, this is tied to an argument that it becomes illegitimate to refer to truth as having an existence beyond that which counts as truth within a given context or discourse:

> Since Nietzsche this question of truth has been transformed. It is no longer, 'What is the surest path to Truth?', but, 'What is the hazardous career that Truth has followed? . . . What is the history of this 'will to truth'? What are its effects?
>
> (Foucault 1980: 66)

Foucault recognises that this methodological and theoretical move makes the production of knowledge problematic. The question becomes: 'what historical knowledge is possible of a history which itself produces the true/false distinction on which such knowledge depends?' (1991: 82). For the historian or the philosopher (and Foucault's work is itself a testimony to the spuriousness of any clear distinction between them) the task cannot be one of identifying 'the truth'. This is part of the importance for Foucault of distinguishing his work from the conceptual structure of humanistic thought which expresses a sovereign aspiration to knowledge by proposing an external point from which there is access to truth. For Foucault this means that the task of the theorist cannot be prescriptive. He has to recast the relationship between the theorist and her or his object of study in terms which are consistent with his conception of truth as 'a thing of this world' (1980: 131). Theorists are not people who have privileged knowledge in the sense of knowing better than people engaged in resistance; theory is not something for people to refer to for correct political strategy. Rather, Foucault's pluralism requires that the political question is a problem for the 'subject who acts – the subject of action through which the real is transformed' (1991: 84).

It is at this point that the conception of discourse becomes crucial, because it provides Foucault with a method for generating a kind of knowledge which does not, on his account, prescribe or presuppose a particular moral or political reality.

Discourse

Foucault is insistent that discourse is not merely a concept. Discourses exist in reality: they have an objective actuality. Discourses are not ideal types or, in a more phenomenological rendering, merely grids through which the theorist sees the world: 'the fact that . . . real life isn't the same thing as the theoreticians' schema doesn't entail that these schemas are therefore utopian, imaginary etc.' (1991: 81). Rather, discourses present a distinct object of study, rather like Durkheimian social facts, except that they exist in a state of fluidity and are coextensive, as knowledge, with movements of power. Foucault explains that 'in discourse something is formed according to clearly definable rules; alongside everything a society can produce (alongside: that is to say, in a determinate relationship with) there is the formation and transformation of "things said" ' (1991: 63).

So for Foucault discourses have a quality of 'exteriority' (1991: 60). On this conception of the methodology appropriate to the theorist, it becomes possible to study, for example, 'things said' about women within the discourse of sexology and to generate a detailed historical analysis. It is not, however, legitimate to see this knowledge as a recommendation for a particular sort of action. The task of the theorist is not to correct an erroneous discourse. We could not make the statement that the discourses of sexology have misrepresented women's sexuality, or that the language of frigidity or the instrumentalisation of sex have constituted some sort of negation of women's sexuality. The focus of Foucault's method would be to identify the subject position which the discourse constitutes – the 'problematic frigid wife', for example, – and to see how that subject position is discursively located in relation to other categories. It would also allow for seeing that the label 'frigid' is immediately shot through with power; it is not a matter of unproblematic description. But the woman herself is curiously absent from the theorist's concern. If the accuracy of the label is to be challenged, she must do this herself – perhaps with other women so labelled – but when she does so, she is not acting as a theorist but as a political agent.

For Foucault the distinction is important. It is because discourse exists in a 'neutral' sense that the work of the theorist can become a matter of accuracy rather than interpretation, and the temptation to install an Archimedean point of access to 'truth' can be avoided 'The discursive field deploys a "neutral" domain in which speech and writing may vary the system of their opposition and the difference of their functioning' (Foucault 1991: 63). The exteriority of discourse and the neutral domain that it deploys make it possible 'to avoid mixing up . . . [historical] analysis with a procedure of psychological diagnosis' (1991: 58).

Foucault argues that if we analyse history through the procedure of identifying discourses and transformations in discourses, we can thereby free ourselves of the habit of approaching the analysis of history through the filter of our preconceptions of the kind of process that it is. We can, as it were, turn the process around, and interrogate these preconceptions themselves as phenomena of discourse. Rather than making the methodologically illegitimate assumption that history is the history of men's oppression of women, for example, we would identify the emergence of feminist discourses, the moment at which it became possible for it to make sense to claim that women are oppressed 'as women'. This yields a sense of history as 'the play of specific modifications' (1991: 58). Put simply, history cannot be assumed to be, for example, 'essentially' the history of class struggle or progress or scientific illumination or, by implication, patriarchy. The point, however, is a methodological one: 'I don't say that humanity doesn't progress. I say that it is bad method to pose the problem as "How is it that we have progressed?" The problem is: how do things happen?' (Foucault 1980: 50). This is not then to argue that there is no determinate or intelligible pattern in historical material, but that that intelligibility is provided for, not by any inner or teleological necessity, but in that-which-went-before, in the logic of the spaces that temporally precede it, which allow for particular statements to acquire the quality of self-evidence or coherence. Foucault is enquiring into what he calls 'the law of existence of statements, that which rendered them possible – them and none other in their place' (1991: 59). History here is not 'a' process at all: 'My problem is to substitute the analysis of *different types of transformation* for the abstract, general and monotonous form of "change" which so easily serves as our means of conceptualizing succession' (1991: 55–6).

Discourse, then, underpins a further facet of Foucault's pluralism. History here is a matrix of phenomena constituted through an open-ended productivity. It does not prioritise any one set of phenomena over any other by virtue of some property internal to itself, so that we cannot know a priori the shape of social reality. History is not to be thought of on the model of a development or a continuity in which some phenomena are essentially reflective of others, or of an inner purpose; it can be studied only in its actual manifestations, and the task, methodologically, is to develop adequate tools.

But what is the relationship between discourse and the human subject implied here? Is it one in which the human agent exists in some sort of tension with discourse, as Foucault's theory of power and resistance might imply? The question is one which Foucault systematically refuses. He is clear that it is not the task of the theorist to address the complexity of the world as experienced by the human subject. His methodological pluralism stops here. When he discusses the place of the experiencing subject, he tends to do so in terms of the constraints which he places on himself. He seeks to answer his own historical questions:

> without referring the facts of discourse to the will – perhaps involuntary – of their authors; without having recourse to that intention of saying which always goes beyond what is actually said; without trying to capture the fugitive unheard subtlety of a word which has no text.
>
> (Foucault 1991: 59)

Discourse 'is a space of differentiated subject positions and subject functions' (1991: 58) and so, Foucault claims, is identifiable without reference to subjective experience, intentionality or personal aspiration. This has the effect, as Hartsock has noted, of generating a language which constitutes 'a world in which things move rather than people' (1990: 167). Foucault's methodology clearly provides for the possibility of a plurality of political concerns, and may at some level be in tune with the attempts of feminists to create more democratic forms of knowledge production in recognising the dangers of hierarchical conceptions of knowledge. But Foucault's democratisation of knowledge is the outcome of a method which severs the moral link between the theorist and the theorised. It effects a closure on the epistemological resources of empathy or identification upon which a great deal of feminist work has been built.

It might however be argued that this is a matter of methodological self-discipline on Foucault's part, and that a theory of agency is not necessarily precluded by Foucauldian theory. It is to the issues raised here that I now want to turn.

FEMINISM AND THE LIMITS OF DISCOURSE ANALYSIS

Subjectivity, agency and resistance

Feminists who have been drawn to Foucault's work have been concerned to extricate him from the charge that in his development of a constitutive conception of discourse, necessarily linked to power, he dissolves the agency of the human subject and replaces it with a passive conception. Broadly, this charge sees Foucault's work as problematic in focusing on discourses and the production of subject positions, viewing it as unable to account for the place of human experience and consciousness in acting to change the world. It might be argued that the prime mover here is discourse and the human agent simply a *tabula rasa* on which society writes its order. Feminists sympathetic to Foucault's work have resisted the force of this critique: 'Although the subject . . . is socially constructed in discursive practices, she none the less exists as a thinking, feeling and social subject and agent, capable of resistance and innovations produced out of the clash between contradictory subject positions and practices' (Weedon 1987: 125). On this argument, Foucault does not undermine women's ability to act for themselves but centralises subjectivity by seeing it as a site contested in discourse. So, for example, discursive constructions of the perfect mother exist, but are challenged by competing feminist conceptions of what women can be or of the ways in which women can be mothers. Women's identity as mothers is contested; a woman can resist the traditional discourse of motherhood by refusing to be a mother, by setting up alternative parenting arrangements, by taking her children on 'reclaim the night' marches or doing an evening course in roofing. By discarding the simplistic liberal conception of the subject as timeless brute personality, it is argued, it becomes possible better to conceptualise the ways in which subjectivity is contested and experience transformed.

In a similar vein, Hekman (1990) argues that the critique that would see discursive analysis as disempowering the subject is itself caught up in a polarity of humanistic thought. For her, Foucault's strength lies in the fact that he refuses the false alternatives of the free individual on the one hand or the conditioned, passive subject on the other: 'In Foucault's conception the constituted subject is a subject that resists' (Hekman 1990: 73). In other words, the social and historical constitution of the subject is not a limit on women's agency but the precondition for women taking action. It is because, and not in spite of, our embeddedness in discursive practices that political action is possible.

What Foucault is trying to under-cut, in Hekman's view, is not the agency of the subject, but the liberal essentialist conception of the subject which provides the centre of humanistic thought. Where thinkers of the Enlightenment proposed a polarity between a knowing subject and a known-about world, Foucault proposes a relationship between the subject and the world in which each implies and is implicated in the other. For Hekman, Foucault's method – his displacement of focus from the speaking subject to the neutral domain of subject positions and subject functions which discourse deploys – is important for feminism, because it offers a method and a theory of social reality which 'serves as an important corrective to the tendency among some feminists to define the essentially female' (1990: 72). It becomes possible to generate a form of feminism which does not proceed from the assumption that women's biological condition delimits a fixed nature.

So here, to conceive of the deployment of subject positions and subject functions does not mean that human experience or political resistance is in any way unreal, and the fact that power is all-pervasive does not mean that resistance is always already beaten: 'To say that one can never be "outside" power does not mean that one is trapped and condemned to defeat no matter what' (Foucault 1980: 141–2).

Arguably, then, it is not the agency of people as such which is undermined in Foucault's work. Foucauldian subjects are like Marx's subjects in being able to act and resist within, and in relation to, the constraints of historical context. Foucault departs from Marx in taking the deployment of power as his central notion, but he retains a form of theory in which human agency can have effects.

For Foucault it is important to decentre subjectivity in this way, because he challenges the belief in the subject of Enlightenment humanism who is assumed to have a consciousness governed by reason and so to have access to a universal and atemporal form of truth. Foucault did not accept that reason could exist beyond the limits of a socially embedded and partisan vision. To claim this form of reason is a form of conceptual and interpretative imperialism, because it entails a claim that knowledge can be true in a sense that is final and impartial. It lays the ground for the (dangerous) legitimation of closure in knowledge.[6]

But we need to think carefully about what it is we lose if we decide to adopt an anti-essentialist feminism consistent with Foucault's position. This is not just a question about whether biology mechanically determines women's experience of femininity, but also about the coherence of any notion of human limit or capacity, of the emotional realities of human life, and of the possibility of a language which can make qualitative distinctions.

Emotion, reason and subjectivity

Where feminists have warmed to Foucauldian theory, it has often been because they have seen an affinity between it and the feminist challenge to universality and value-neutral, impartial, objective knowledge. Yet the terms of feminist engagement with, and critique of, Enlightenment thinking have often shown marked and important dissimilarities from a Foucauldian form of critique, in a way that exceeds that critique and affects what we can take to be the legitimate range of epistemological resources.

The women's liberation movement of the late 1960s was not simply concerned with the negative task of dethroning reason. It also recast the whole question of how we make sense of the world through a critical engagement with the terms of the Enlightenment dichotomy between reason and emotion. Feminism can challenge the terms of this dichotomy by a different route from Foucault, and it is a difference reflected in the development of a feminist practice of consciousness-raising. Whatever its difficulties, it proceeded by asking how it feels to be subjugated, and by attempting to provide the context in which it would be possible to develop the critical and reflexive relationship to experience that the beginnings of a response to that question required. Feminists were interested in how it was that particular versions of reality were privileged over others, and in how accounts of the world which could present themselves as impartial and having nothing to do with the particularities of personal experience, carried more weight than those which could be seen as 'merely' personal or emotional. The point was not to create a language exterior to the dualism, but to transcend it by developing a transformed sense of what was epistemologically admissible. By challenging not reason *per se* but a form of reason which defined itself in opposition to the particular and the emotional, feminists sought to generate a different vision of sexual and social justice.

This is not just a question of what we take as our object of study, but is a matter of recognising that if a whole facet of human experience is disregarded, the overall picture becomes skewed. It was crucial to feminism to recognise that the conception of the human subject which characterised Enlightenment thinking was not simply flawed in the sense that it installed an illusory point from which objectivity could be claimed, but that that objectivity was provided for in the denial of particular realms of experience crucial to the processes of making sense of the world. So, for example, Miller (1976) sought to explain both women's intuitive skill and its denigration when she argued that it developed as part of a process in which dominant conceptions reflected the difficulty of acknowledging these realms of experience. If these kinds of explanation are still problematic in terms of biological determinism and cultural specificity, we should nevertheless be wary of adopting a theory which leaves the association of women with the particular and the emotional unremarked or unexplained.

In Foucault's work the dichotomy between reason and emotion appears in a recast form. The question of how it feels to be subjugated is left to the political agent, and that agent is seen as set in a separate sphere from the theorist who generates knowledge of a neutral domain. The actions of political agents are left at some level as arbitrary.

What is at issue here is the sense in which people's emotional experience impinges on their material reality. The relationship between feminism and Foucault depends on whether this relationship between experience and reality can best be understood in terms of a discursive analysis which refuses to engage with the terms of political agents' experience. The common experience of domestic violence can provide an important example here. To understand women's experiences of domestic violence requires a sensitivity to complexity. It is not that emotional life is straightforwardly transparent, but even to begin an analysis involves a conception of the human condition as intrinsically limited, albeit in complex ways. So it might be that a woman stays in a violent relationship for many reasons, that a lack of self-worth or even a feeling that she deserves some sort of punishment are contributory factors, but we cannot imagine a limitless range of responses here. She will not feel joy or refreshment when she is attacked. Her experience of violence cannot be adequately expressed in the terms of the deployment of a subject position which can be interrogated externally.

Foucault felt it important that his work should be able to account for the intrinsic intelligibility of conflict; but from a feminist point of view it is not clear that we can adequately generate a theory of conflict without also assuming the intrinsic intelligibility of care or distress. Domestic violence resists an analysis cast in terms of an external relationship to discourse because the theoretical questions which arise necessarily concern the experience and anguish involved, as well as the statements of police, judges and women's magazines. What is horrific in sexual and domestic violence is precisely that it *is* sexual and domestic violence, that the violence is a property of the actual situation. The study of things said by its apologists may be important for feminists, but it can never exhaust feminist concern or provide the basis for a fully fledged feminist methodology.

The connection between oppression, emotion and knowledge is particularly stark in the example of domestic violence, but I shall argue in the next section that it is also relevant in the context of textual analysis. Foucault tries to resolve the tension between the social embeddedness of the subject who experiences oppression, and the generation of knowledge by the historical theorist, by positing a distance between the theorist and the object of study, which he tends to discuss simply as a matter of method. He thereby raises in a new way a problem which is fundamental to the social sciences: the problem of neutrality.

FOUCAULT'S METHODOLOGY AND THE PROBLEM OF NEUTRALITY

Foucault's work is difficult to place in relation to feminism in part because he wants to democratise knowledge, but claims that his focus on the neutral domain of discourse is part of that effort. From a feminist vantage point this methodology can have some paradoxical consequences. Whereas for some, Foucault's claim that difference is the very stuff of history and social reality means that his theory can accommodate the different impulses within feminism, and the different experiences of womanhood they seek to embrace, it can also be argued that Foucauldian theory is marked precisely by its incapacity to voice the ever-present asymmetry which gender difference determines. Braidotti argues along these lines that 'Foucault elaborates a new ethics that remains within the confines of sexual sameness' (1990: 38). Here the notion of the exteriority of discourse is problematic precisely *because* power, as Foucault puts it, 'reaches into the very grain of individuals, touches their bodies and inserts itself into their actions and attitudes, their discourses, learning processes and everyday lives' (1980: 39). There is no position outside gender power from which to identify 'things said' in discourse. Foucault may be right to challenge the metaphor of power as something that can finally be possessed, but the challenge is valid partly because gender power is linked to subjectivity.

The issue is most clearly illustrated in Foucault's work on sexuality. He is concerned to challenge the notion that sex is some sort of timeless essence or given instinct which society represses.

> The question I would like to pose is not, Why are we repressed? but rather, Why do we say, with so much passion and so much resentment against our most recent past, against our present, and against ourselves, that we are repressed? By what spiral did we come to affirm that sex is negated?
>
> (Foucault 1981: 8–9)

Here Foucault seems to depart from his own methodological rigour which requires that any 'we' be the outcome of historical investigation and not its point of origin. It is not at all self-evident that the self-castigation to which he refers is a shared phenomenon. We need to ask whether men and women are, and whether they have historically been, talking about the 'same thing' in this discourse of sex and sexuality, and whether 'things said' in this discourse, the subject positions and subject functions which the discourse of sexuality deploys, can in any sense be thought about as a 'neutral' domain. Although it may be of value to study the language in which sex is offered to us as pleasure, Foucault does not give us a framework in which it is possible to recognise any systematic gender asymmetry in relation to the masculinist discourses of sex and sexuality. As Braidotti argues, 'Whatever the female "use of pleasure" might have been like, with its truth-effects and production of knowledge about the female subject, remains a matter for speculation' (1990: 42).

The domain of sex and sexuality for women is not properly thought about as a constituted object at all but rather exists as a confusing range of contradictory experiences. Not just pleasure is involved here, but fear, violence, and for many women a whole range of everyday accommodations to masculinist constructions of what is at issue in sexuality (including the notion that it exists as a discrete field).

When Foucault describes discourse as 'neutral' he is not, of course, claiming that the deployment of subject positions is not itself a function of the dominant positions of dominant groups. He is not claiming a power- or a value-neutrality in this sense, since on his own premises all social situations are power-saturated. But we need a methodology which is pluralistic not only in recognising a variety of struggles, but in articulating their different levels and moments. We need, in other words, a theory that can grasp that the gender of the social agent determines an asymmetry in relationship to the categories in which 'sex' is presented to us.

If power is, as Foucault claims, necessarily implicated in the constitution of subjectivity, then the relationship of the theorist to 'things said' cannot itself be located outside the terms of power. This means that what is heard in what is said will itself be determined in its very coherence in part by the ways in which gender and power are interwoven. For example, Foucault uses the label 'the hysterization of women's bodies' to characterise the sexual discourse of a specific period, but there is a problem if we take his labelling as neutral (Foucault 1981: 104). The neutrality of the language itself contributes to the political constitution of the label. Neutrality here might be seen less as an expression of methodological rigour than of Foucault's personal distance from the experience of this particular discourse. This distance enables him to perceive the discourse as neutral when from a feminist position we might argue that the label is itself a function of sexual privilege. As MacKinnon has argued, 'Reification is not just an illusion to the reified; it is also their reality' (1982: 28). In this instance we can question the appropriateness of Foucault's method since its claims to instrumental purity in practice yields a form of knowledge which can operate as a political resource against women by positing an illusory symmetry.

We have seen that Foucault's method is in part an attempt to provide for the possibility of historical work which undercuts the notion of the theorist as the occupier of a particular, special, all-seeing vantage point. But this is an effort heavily reliant on a notion of neutrality which is necessarily problematic for feminism. As Bordo (1990) has argued, there is a paradoxical sense in which the Archimedean point returns when theory becomes pre-occupied with the rejection of essentialist premises. The theorist proceeds as if it is possible equally to attend to all possible realities. One consequence is that what threatens to disappear in discourse analysis is any possibility of recognition of the consequences of a shared relationship to oppression. It becomes hard to make any reference to the 'difference gender makes' (Bordo 1990: 137).

It was a feature of early new-wave feminism to insist that the theorist account for him or herself reflexively. This insistence was based on the link between the production of feminist knowledge and the political commitment to feminism, and feminist scholarship as praxis (Stanley and Wise 1983; Du Bois 1983; Mies 1983). Through focusing on the contradictory experience of being subjugated, and incorporating how it 'felt' as a valid epistemological resource, early new-wave feminism represented a systematic refusal to pose the question of the historical oppression of women without recourse to the actual experiences of the oppressed. New-wave feminism challenged the Enlightenment's conception of an external point from which truth can be distinguished from falsity, but it did so, not by seeking to locate neutrality on new theoretical ground, but by pointing to the ways in which the notion of a point from which truth could objectively be discerned were tied into the social construction of a dominant form of masculinity.[7] Speaking and hearing themselves become activities which have a gendered content. As Gilligan argued in her study of the differences between men's and women's perceptions of moral dilemmas:

men and women may speak different languages that they assume are the same using similar words to encode disparate experiences of self and social relationships. Because these languages share an overlapping . . . vocabulary, they contain a propensity for systematic mistranslation.

(Gilligan 1982: 173)[8]

Reason, impartiality and objectivity were never gender-neutral. As Bordo has put it:

Feminism . . . was a cultural moment of revelation and relief. The category of the 'human' – a standard against which all difference translates to lack, insufficiency – was brought down to earth, given a pair of pants and reminded that it was not the only player in town.

(Bordo 1990: 137)

This allowed feminists to develop a fuller sense of the way that power penetrates subjectivity. It has been an important part of feminist work, not merely to reject the truth claims of reason to impartiality, but also to account for their plausibility.

It is a fundamental characteristic of Enlightenment thinking to set the relationship between reason and emotion in a hierarchy. The marginalised work of Griffin (1981) is important here. Griffin explored the dichotomous relationship between reason and emotion as the key characteristic of a form of subjectivity which was fundamentally threatened by its place in nature, by the fact of existing as a being with natural limits – a being having a particular emotional constitution and natural needs. She showed how the attempt to escape from the threat that human limit posed to a subject whose dignity could be felt to be guaranteed only in the escape from determination, permeated western culture. This, Griffin argued, led to the constitution of the 'other', a space where the fears generated by being out of control could be projected. Subjugated groups – women, people of colour, Jews – are made to carry and represent the fear of those who take themselves to represent impartiality and neutrality – the freedom, that is, from natural limit. So the subject for whom emotion opposes freedom as an ongoing inner struggle becomes not a mere fiction, but a form of self which institutionalises power relationships in specific and substantive forms. Impartiality represents a form of power, but it is a form which is not intelligible without reference to that to which it is opposed.

Griffin notes, for example, that it is often the case that subjugated groups, in the minds of dominant groups, are seen as highly sexualised as well as infantile and lacking proper control over themselves. This key fissure between a form of subjectivity which conceives its freedom as a freedom from determination, and the 'nature' which it projects elsewhere, is important then in understanding the coherence of the subjugated knowledges which Foucault sees as holding the potential for resistance; subjugated groups have to challenge these images of themselves. The point is important because the need for some conception of what it is that is shared by a subjugated group provides a point of friction rather than continuity in the relationship between feminism and Foucauldian thought.

None of this, of course, is to suggest that there is no sense in which Foucault's vast range of work can provide a resource for feminists; it is, however, to contest the view that feminism can be subsumed within the categories which it, to use a Foucauldian term, deploys, or within which it moves. The tension between commonality and difference in feminism cannot be resolved through a method which distances the theorist from the terms of women's experience.

This is not to suggest either that we can proceed unproblematically from a conception of experience as transparent, or from an ontologically grounded conception of women's 'otherness'. We need to stay focused on the actual complexity of the dualisms which structure both Enlightenment thinking and common-sense perception, and see that they deploy a contradictory matrix of constraint and possibility. Feminism has shown how emotional knowledge, for example, can be explored and reclaimed, and how intuitive skills which may have their source in subordination can be reconceptualised, not as the inexplicable and merely personal knowledge of a group of people who lack the fullness of culture, but as a positive source of strength.

CONCLUSION

The adoption of a pluralism purged of any sense of human capacity or limit, and guaranteed in the distance between the theorist and the object of study, does not offer feminism an adequate theory for accommodating either what it is that we have in common, or the ways in which we are different. Foucault's work may seem to resonate with feminism in its open-endedness, but he does not offer a theoretical framework which can distinguish between the kinds of differences which cut across women's lives. So it may be that we want to celebrate the rich diversity of women's culture, but we need to retain the capacity to identify the structural contradictions of our differences. If the difference between two women is that one can buy cheap tea while the other works long hours in impoverished conditions to produce it, then that difference has to be grasped as located in a contradictory social reality. There is no position of moral purity – or neutrality – to which the tea-buyer can withdraw. Most significantly, this is not a difference that can be captured in the terms of discursive analysis.

Foucault's theory can be applauded for the capacity of discourse analysis to accommodate difference but at the same time castigated for his perpetuation of sameness. The tension exposed here goes to the heart of the contradictory relationship between feminism and discourse theory. Feminism struggles within the parameters of the problems of sameness and difference, and these are problems which do not yield in any final sense to a purely theoretical resolution. Yet in terms both of what women share and the cultural and structural factors which divide or distinguish us from one another, feminism requires the development of a methodology which acknowledges the presence of the speaker in what is spoken. Feminism is premised on a particular sort of effort of attention to the experience of other women, which is why it *does* matter 'who is speaking'. This effort of attention to what we share and to the ways in which we differ, brings the speaker, her world, her knowledge and her contemporary or historical silences into connection with the theorist's experience and knowledge production. It is in part because feminism is concerned not just with 'difference' but with the variable moral and political weight, and the different dynamics, of difference, that it both exceeds the terms of modernist thinking and resists absorption into the discourses of postmodernity.

NOTES

1 For a detailed discussion and critique of the foundations of modernist humanistic thought, see MacIntyre (1981).
2 For Foucault's account of the development of medical discourse and practice, see his *The Birth of the Clinic* (1973).

3 A discussion of the problems of differences between women and the consequences for feminist theory is given in Ramazanoğlu (1989) and Spelman (1990).

4 Weeks (1985) provides an interesting account of modern sexual identities using a discursively based analytic framework.

5 For an interesting radical feminist discussion of the ways that femininity is produced within discourses of sexology, see Jeffries (1990).

6 These themes come together in Foucault's *The Order of Things* (1971), where he used a discursively based methodology to enquire into the historical constitution of the category 'man' or 'humanity', the production of the contradictory entity which is at once constituted as an object of knowledge and as the subjective ground of inner dignity, reason and freedom.

7 For an exploration of the relationship between reason and dominant forms of masculinity, see Seidler (1989).

8 Gilligan is not proposing a form of biological determinism to explain differences in men's and women's perceptions, but rather notes an empirical correlation between gender and the different terms in which men and women think about moral dilemmas.

BIBLIOGRAPHY

Du Bois, B. (1983) 'Passionate scholarship: notes on values, knowing and method in feminist social science', in G. Bowles and R.D. Klein (eds) *Theories of Women's Studies*, London: Routledge & Kegan Paul.

Bordo, S. (1990) 'Feminism, postmodernism and gender scepticism', in L. Nicholson (ed.) *Feminism/Postmodernism*, London: Routledge.

Braidotti, R. (1990) 'The problematic of "the feminine" in contemporary French philosophy: Foucault and Irigaray', in T. Threadgold and A. Cranny-Francis (eds) *Feminine, Masculine and Representation*, Sydney: Allen & Unwin.

Flax, J. (1990) 'Postmodernism and gender relations in feminist theory', in L. Nicholson (ed.) *Feminism/Postmodernism*, London: Routledge.

Foucault, M. (1971) *The Order of Things: An Archaeology of the Human Sciences*, New York: Random House.

—— (1973) *The Birth of the Clinic*, New York: Pantheon.

—— (1980) *Power/Knowledge*, C. Gordon (ed.), New York: Pantheon.

—— (1981) *The History of Sexuality*, vol. I: *An Introduction*, Harmondsworth: Penguin.

—— (1991) 'Politics and the study of discourse', in G. Burchell, C. Gordon and P. Miller (eds) *The Foucault Effect: Studies in Governmentality*, Hemel Hempstead: Harvester Wheatsheaf.

Gilligan, C. (1982) *In a Different Voice: Psychological Theory and Women's Development*, Cambridge, MA: Harvard University Press.

Griffin, S. (1981) *Pornography and Silence*, London: The Women's Press.

Hartsock, N. (1990) 'Foucault on power: a theory for women?', in L. Nicholson (ed.) *Feminism/Postmodernism*, London: Routledge.

146 Identity, difference and power

Hekman, S.J. (1990) *Gender and Knowledge: Elements of a Postmodern Feminism*, Cambridge: Polity Press.
Jeffries, S. (1990) *Anticlimax: a Feminist Perspective on the Sexual Revolution*, London: The Women's Press.
MacIntyre, A. (1981) *After Virtue: A Study in Moral Theory*, London: Duckworth.
MacKinnon, C.A. (1982) 'Feminism, Marxism, method and the state: an agenda for theory', in N.O. Keohane, M.Z. Rosaldo and B.C. Gelpi (eds) *Feminist Theory: A Critique of Ideology*, Brighton: The Harvester Press Ltd.
Mies, M. (1983) 'Towards a methodology for feminist research', in G. Bowles and R.D. Klein (eds) *Theories of Women's Studies*, London: Routledge & Kegan Paul.
Miller, J.B. (1976) *Toward a New Psychology of Women*, Boston: Beacon Press.
Ramazanoğlu, C. (1989) *Feminism and the Contradictions of Oppression*, London: Routledge.
Seidler, V.J. (1989) *Rediscovering Masculinity: Reason, Language and Sexuality*, London: Routledge.
Spelman, E. (1990) *Inessential Woman: Problems of Exclusion in Feminist Thought*, London: The Women's Press.
Stanley, L. and Wise, S. (1983) *Breaking Out: Feminist Consciousness and Feminist Research*, London: Routledge & Kegan Paul.
Weedon, C. (1987) *Feminist Practice and Poststructuralist Theory*, Oxford: Basil Blackwell.
Weeks, J. (1985) *Sexuality and its Discontents: Meanings, Myths and Modern Sexualities*, London: Routledge & Kegan Paul.

Chapter 7

Dancing with Foucault
Feminism and power–knowledge[1]
Maureen McNeil

> I do not conclude from this that one may say just anything
> within the order of theory, but, on the contrary, that a
> demanding, prudent, 'experimental' attitude is neces[s]ary; at
> every moment, step by step, one must confront what one is
> thinking and saying with what one is doing, with what one is . . .
> but, on the other hand, I have always been concerned with
> linking together as tightly as possible the historical and theor-
> etical analysis of power relations, institutions, and knowledge,
> to the movements, critiques, and experiences that call them
> into question in reality.
>
> (Foucault 1991a: 374)

The title of this chapter was inspired by a poster from the
Women's Studies Centre at the University of Utrecht which shows
a group of men and women disco-dancing under the title
'Foucault-a-go-go' with the caption: 'She loved him in theory. But
how could she find a place for him in practice?'[2] The image of
dancing seems an appropriate representation of the interaction
between Foucault and feminism: constant movement – now
coming together, then moving apart, coming together at other
moments, moving apart – and so on. It signals my intention to
de-centre Foucault as the subject of my chapter and to make
feminism the equal subject/partner, perhaps the leading partner?
The imagery also implies the absence of a prescriptive tone in my
approach to yet another male theorist: my intention is not to cast
my vote for or against. It is *how* feminists dance with Foucault and
the implications of their engagement with his ideas that concern
me. Foucault is one of many possible partners and it is 'women's
[rather than 'ladies'] choice'. In short, feminism does not require

Foucault and women do not need him. Yet, feminists have expressed and may continue to express interest in Foucault's ideas.[3] As I shall show, some feminists have been influenced by him and some of his ideas could be used as aids in reflecting about the emergence of, the changes within, and the current state of feminism.

In this chapter, I take my lead from Foucault in several ways. I reflect about the history of recent feminist thought and of the power–knowledge relations developed therein. These reflections are in the fashion of a critical analysis in which, as Foucault described, 'one tries to see how the different solutions to a problem have been constructed; but also how these different solutions result from a specific form of problematisation' (Foucault 1991a: 389). Like Foucault, I do not propose 'a methodological examination in order to reject all possible solutions except for the one valid one'; rather, what follows is more in the spirit of his 'order of "problematisation" – which is to say, the development of a domain of acts, practices, and thought that seem to me to pose problems for politics' (Foucault 1991a: 384). So the spirit of the venture is itself Foucauldian. In addition, at the level of its explicit content the chapter considers how Foucault *has influenced* feminist thought and practice and how his ideas *might be used* to reflect on developments within feminism. Because of the limits of my own knowledge and experience, I shall be exploring this occasional partnership from within, and in the context of, Anglo-American feminism.

SO THE MUSIC STARTS TO PLAY . . . POWER AND KNOWLEDGE FOR FOUCAULT

I begin by noting that both feminism and Foucault have danced to, or played, the same tune. At the centre of all of Foucault's enquiries was the concern with the power–knowledge relationship. This began with his early methodological texts – most notably, *The Archaeology of Knowledge* (1972), carried on in his study of the general characteristics of the modern age in *The Order of Things* (1973) through to his specific historical studies. The latter were case-studies on madness, criminality and sexuality which, as he described them, were concerned with

the relations between experiences (like madness, illness,

transgression of laws, sexuality, self-identity), knowledge (like psychiatry, medicine, criminology, sexology, psychology) and power (such as the power which is wielded in psychiatric and penal institutions and in all other institutions which deal with individual control).

(Foucault 1991a: 71; see also 387)

These were the focuses of his mode of critical enquiry, eventually labelled *genealogy*[4] which he defined as

a form of history which can account for the constitution of knowledges, discourses, domains of objects etc. without having to make reference to a subject which is either transcendental in relation to the field of events or runs in its empty sameness throughout the course of history.

(Foucault 1980: 117; see also 83–4)

Genealogical investigation revolved around not the history of thought in general, but around 'all that "contains thought" in a culture' (Foucault 1989: 9) beginning 'from a question posed in the present' (Foucault 1990c: 262). It was designed to excavate patterns of power: not who had power but rather the patterns of the exercise of power.[5] Foucault's genealogy was a method and project which rejected the search for origins and took as its object and subject the relations between knowledge and power: 'The exercise of power perpetually creates knowledge and, conversely, knowledge constantly induces effects of power' (Foucault 1980: 52). In fact, the fused appellation 'knowledge/power' (Foucault 1980) has become associated with Foucault. Despite this association, he insisted that 'studying their relation' was 'precisely my problem' (Foucault 1991a: 43; see also Foucault 1990c: 263).

MEANWHILE, ON THE OTHER SIDE OF THE ROOM . . . POWER AND KNOWLEDGE WITHIN FEMINISM

The women who gave birth to second-wave feminism can be thought of as daughters of the Enlightenment in that they seemed to have inherited some Enlightenment assumptions.[6] In its early, heady days of the late 1960s and 1970s, they created a movement which held out the promise of increased and better knowledge of gender relationships and, through this knowledge, women's liberation. Knowledge and liberation were regarded as incremental and interrelated goals: as women gained more knowledge of their position in the world it was presumed that their power to transform it would increase accordingly. The methods by which liberatory knowledge was to be gained were two-fold: diverse investigations of the patriarchal order and consciousness-raising. Most feminists of this period presumed that the two methods shared a common orientation around the revelation of the features of the patriarchal order: both were to shed light on the structures of oppression in which women were enmeshed.

Nevertheless, consciousness-raising was a distinctive and, for critics of feminism, a controversial method. Juliet Mitchell described it as 'the process of transforming the hidden, individual fears of women into a shared awareness of the meaning of them as social problems' (Mitchell 1974a: 61). Although claimed as *the* unique method of their movement, they had borrowed and adapted its form from other political movements, most notably from the Chinese Revolution (Mitchell 1974a: 62). Moreover, questions could be raised about its Enlightenment pedigree in that consciousness-raising seemed to imply an unconscious which was the depository of forms of knowledge not generally accessible through conventional modes of rational investigation.[7] The practice of consciousness-raising encouraged the creation of unique women-only spaces and new forms of relationships amongst women. Indeed, some feminists – most notably, Catharine MacKinnon (1982) – regarded it as the linchpin of feminism and the foundation of a distinctive feminist epistemology.

However unique consciousness-raising was as a method, it fitted into a larger picture of feminism unveiling and transforming the patterns of women's oppression. In the supposedly 'safe' spaces of consciousness-raising groups individual women would begin 'to see the light', while the larger, more public picture was being revealed by feminist polemicists and scholars. Many of the texts of this early period of the movement had a no-nonsense and excited tone, basking in the light of fresh revelations culled from these two kinds of activities. The feminist express was moving with speed and there was little room for hesitation: jump on and leave your patriarchal past behind! Indeed, who would want to stay behind with the confused, down-trodden and 'duped' women, blinded by patriarchal ideology, once they had seen the feminist light and truth?

WERE THEY SUITED AS PARTNERS? FEMINISM AND FOUCAULT

At first sight the encounter of new-wave feminists with the work of the rebellious son of the Enlightenment, Michel Foucault, seemed unpropitious. Foucault never presented himself as a champion of feminism although he regarded it as a 'revolutionary movement' (Foucault 1977: 216) and did express admiration for what he considered to be its strengths.[8] There are few references to feminist authors or activities within his opus.[9] However, he does give some attention to the position of women in his major project on the history of sexuality, particularly to 'all the fuss about hysterical women' (Foucault 1990c: 9). Despite this, the neglect of gender divisions, or what Judith Butler has described as 'a problematic indifference to sexual difference', is a much noted feature of his work (Butler 1990: xii; see also Bland 1981).

More generally, it would seem that in challenging many of the traditions and presumptions of the Enlightenment, Foucault was at odds with the initial orientation of new-wave feminism. However, as some feminists have argued, Foucault never totally abandoned Enlightenment parameters.[10] Rather, there is a way in which, to use his own words, 'The question of *Aufklärung*, or of reason, as a historical problem' haunted all of his work, as he claimed it had 'traversed the whole of philosophical thought' (Foucault 1990c: 95).[11] Indeed, it is striking that for both early new-wave feminism and Foucault, power–knowledge were of central importance. Feminism was clearly the legitimate child of the Enlightenment in that it mobilised notions of liberatory knowledge. Foucault, the rebellious illegitimate offspring, in contrast, disavowed claims about this emancipatory impulse within any discourse (including, by implication, feminism), rejecting the Enlightenment presumption that knowledge and freedom went hand-in-hand. Yet, his preoccupation with the power–knowledge relationship bespoke his lingering Enlightenment pedigree.

AND THE BAND PLAYED ON . . . TRANSFORMATIONS OF THE POWER–KNOWLEDGE PROJECT WITHIN FEMINISM

My observations about the current wave of feminism as an Enlightenment project focused on knowledge and power is a significant starting point in understanding the relationship between Foucault's ideas and feminism. However, the story does not end there. What follows are some reflections on what has happened to this project during the last twenty to twenty-five years in the Anglo-American context and on some dilemmas now facing feminists. Along the way Foucault's ideas will be the recurring reference point suggesting: (1) some ways they have been drawn on during the changes that have occurred within feminism, and (2) how they might be used in analysing the features of these transformations. So, the questions which will percolate to the surface will include: what has Foucault meant for women within feminism? How have his ideas been used and are they still useful?

Twenty-something years after the re-launch of the women's movement in the west, understanding patriarchy – that is, the knowledge project within feminism – has become far more complex and diversified.[12] Over the last twenty-five years feminists have developed sophisticated tools for analysing gender relations. Publishers' catalogues and book shops evidence the veritable explosion of knowledge about gender relations. It may not be too far-fetched to suggest that this has been one of the most rapidly expanding analytical fields in the western world during the last twenty years. And it is not just that there is more of it: there have been observable qualitative dimensions to this explosion. Returning to many of the early feminist texts, it is easy to admire their rhetoric, but much of it seems shallow and limited compared to the systematic development of theory in recent feminist output.

This quantitative explosion notwithstanding, it is the diversification of this knowledge project which is now so striking. I noted above that the methods employed in the early stages of the movement were two-fold: consciousness-raising and diverse, mainly empirical, investigations of the features of patriarchy by feminist scholars and polemicists. Although consciousness-raising has not disappeared, it is much less widely practised. It has either been replaced by, or incorporated within, various forms of individual or group therapy (see Ernst and Goodison 1981; Eichenbaum and Orbach 1983; Ernst and Maguire 1987). Empirical work on gender relations has continued. However, more theoretical research, much of it utilising psychoanalytic and/or poststructuralist theories (including Foucauldian discourse analysis) now has a prominent profile within feminism.[13] In short, the knowledge project of feminism has been transformed in and through diverse therapeutic and theoretical modes.

The therapeutic turn is a much-observed feature of late twentieth-century feminism. Hence, the expansion of feminist knowledge is registered not only in published material, but also in the detailed self-knowledge of body, emotions and psyche that so many women in the western world now cultivate (although feminism is by no means the only factor here). Obviously there are crucial distinctions within these methods, most notably perhaps between psychoanalysis, on the one hand, and, on the other, popular psychology of diverse kinds, self-help, and the variety of counselling methods that have increasingly flourished in the western world during the past twenty years. It is impossible in this synoptic essay to provide a detailed consideration of this range of developments, so I shall approach these in these two groupings. First, I shall briefly discuss psychoanalysis, which has become important in both its directly therapeutic moment and as a more general set of analytical tools within feminism. Then, I shall consider as a second grouping other specifically therapeutic developments.[14]

The publication of Juliet Mitchell's *Psychoanalysis and Feminism* (1974b) was something of a watershed for feminism in the English-speaking world. Mitchell proposed that feminism turn to psychoanalysis to provide a deeper understanding of how male power was continually reproduced within contemporary capitalist societies. Mitchell's advocacy of psychoanalysis was not because of its therapeutic potential, but rather because it provided a more adequate account of how patriarchy 'worked'. Since then, there has been an ongoing debate within feminism about the benefits and dangers of psychoanalysis (Wilson 1981; Gallop 1982; Sayers 1982; Mitchell and Rose 1982; Rose 1983; Sayers 1986; Rose 1986; Brennan 1990). This debate about the analytical potential of psychoanalysis raged in the background as more and more feminists turned to psychotherapy as a therapeutic practice. In Britain, a specific adaptation of psychoanalytic theory and practice has been developed under the label of 'feminist therapy' (see Eichenbaum and Orbach 1983, esp. ch.1; Ernst and Maguire 1987).

While some feminists sought support in psychoanalysis, others sampled one or more of the other kinds of therapy and counselling that were gaining popularity in the western world from the 1970s onwards. The American feminist Gloria Steinem (1992) is one of the latest to declare her involvement with these techniques. Steinem and many other women (feminists and non-feminists) have sampled a range of practices in which, as one commentator has put it, they use a 'mixture of therapy and mysticism' in the search for their 'true sel[ves]' (Sternhell 1992: 6).

It is difficult to generalise about such a wide and diverse range of practices and theories, but they can be seen as an extension of the original feminist liberatory knowledge project. In any one form, they are more or less feminist (that is, orientated around challenging women's oppression), and differences in evaluation are likely to abound in any assessment of the 'feminist potential' of any particular practice. In so far as they are represented in terms of the power–knowledge project of feminism, they are often explained in terms of women's need for deeper knowledge, particularly of themselves and of how they are implicated in patriarchy. The result of this turn has been an enormous investment (both emotional and financial) in techniques of self-knowledge amongst feminists.

These developments within feminism have transformed the original knowledge project. The diverse investigations of the patriarchal order and consciousness-raising of the early move-ment were means to acquire knowledge of and, thereby, change the patriarchal order. Clearly, particularly within consciousness-raising, self-knowledge was part, *but only part*, of this process. In its current forms, self-knowledge is more likely to become an end in itself. Indeed, it would appear that contemporary feminism has become a pre-eminent torch-bearer of the humanist imperative to 'know thyself'. In addition, as I shall discuss below, therapeutic modes have carried feminism more and more on to the terrain of professional expertise.

A FOUCAULDIAN TAKE ON FEMINISM'S NEW PARTNERS

Foucault and many of his followers have been deeply suspicious of the new human sciences that emerged in nineteenth-century Europe, and of the therapies orientated around self-knowledge which have been cultivated in the twentieth century. Foucault insisted that the assumption of an autonomous, self-determining subject was one of the great illusions of the Enlightenment, which has been carried by humanist traditions and related disciplinary practices. He proposed, instead, that 'subjects' are created in and through discourses and discursive practices, and developed what has been characterised as 'the most sustained critique of the notion of the subject' (Hekman 1990: 68).[15]

So within a Foucauldian perspective the development and elaboration of the human sciences and their techniques were by no means harbingers of freedom: 'the birth of the human sciences goes hand in hand with the installation of new mechanisms of power' (Foucault 1990c: 106). For Foucault the techniques associated with these sciences comprised distinctively modern fetters on freedom. They could be described, in a modified version of Sandra Lee Bartky's terms, as involving 'a finer control of the body's [and mind's] time and its movements–a control that cannot be achieved without ceaseless surveillance and a better understanding of the specific person' (Bartky 1990: 79, my addition). In particular, Foucault considered any presumption of an essential self as an illusion (see Foucault 1977: 221–2). The confessional mode in its secular adaptations, utilised in most contemporary self-help and therapy regimes, was a further object of Foucault's critical scrutiny.[16]

Despite these critiques, Foucault's relationship to psychoanalysis was somewhat more equivocal. He regarded psychoanalysis as one of the human sciences and, as such, a characteristically modern form of social regulation. As noted above, he also called attention to the secularised confessional mode which is the core of psychoanalytic practice, one of the mechanisms 'which invite, incite and force us to speak about sex' (Foucault 1989: 138). He recognised in psychoanalysis 'the institution and functioning of an organised scientific discourse' embodied in what he called 'a theoretical-commercial institution' (Foucault 1980: 84). Moreover, psychoanalysis can revolve around notions of the 'true self' and reinforce the belief that sexual identity constitutes its core – a notion which Foucault sought to problematise and to locate as historically specific. In an interview in 1983, he reflected that he had 'never been a Freudian' (Foucault 1990c: 22).[17]

Yet Foucault was influenced by psychoanalysis. In fact he aligned his own genealogical project with psychoanalysis, explaining that he was 'trying to discover in the history of science and of human knowledge (*des connaissances et du savoir humain*) something that would be like its unconscious' (Foucault 1989: 39).

Although he recognised that the 'still rudimentary elaborations of psychoanalysis on the positions of the subject and object in the context of desire and knowledge' could not be easily applied to the study of history, this evaluation was something of a back-handed compliment to its potential (Foucault 1977: 201). It would seem that the macro-project of psychoanalysis, and Freud's ideas, were an important resource for Foucault, although he was wary of the many features of psychoanalysis which made it a modern science of self-regulation and control.[18]

FOUCAULT AND FEMINISM – TOGETHER AND APART: THE CASE OF EATING DISORDERS

Perhaps there is no better case to illustrate the dilemmas that Foucauldian analysis might pose about the therapeutic orient-ation within contemporary feminism. There is now an extensive feminist literature about this worrying social problem which some have argued has taken on epidemic proportions in the western industrial world (see Orbach 1984; Diamond 1985; Wolf 1991). Feminists have tried to challenge the monopoly of medical discourses in tackling this problem. These challenges have often drawn on psychoanalytic or self-help therapies which depend on notions of an essential subject, the restoration of identity or self-esteem. The success of these strategies has varied from case to case but it is clear that they have by no means 'solved' this social problem.

Anorexia nervosa (to take one instance of eating disorders) seems to exemplify Foucault's judgement that contemporary conditions require that 'We should try to grasp subjection in its material instance as a constitution of subjects' (Foucault 1980: 97). It seems a very sensitive and acute instance of the impossibility of sifting 'the subject' from 'the social' (see Henriques *et al.* 1984). For this reason, some feminist analysts have used Foucauldian approaches in tackling this problem (Diamond 1985; Bordo 1990b) and in more general work on body politics (Bartky 1990; Bordo 1990a; Jacobus *et al.* 1990; Sawicki 1991). Furthermore, Foucault's insights about the regimes of the human sciences could be taken as a warning about the dangers of strategies which are built around self-knowledge and regulation in the treatment of eating disorders. Although she does not take up the specific issue of eating disorders, Sandra Lee Bartky's Foucauldian analysis of the 'disciplinary practices' around feminine bodies which have proliferated in the contemporary western world is very apposite to this problem (1990: 63–82). She sketches some of these practices, which she sees as characteristic of the 'modernisation of patriarchal power'. In many respects, eating disorders are extreme versions of these practices.

It would appear that Bartky and Foucault can be drawn on as warning that, far from liberating women, therapeutic strategies can reinforce and proliferate the mechanisms of self-regulation and self-control which are precisely the heart of the problem. My point is not to condemn the feminist turn towards psychoanalysis or other therapies, but to suggest that Foucauldian work does highlight some of the dangers of the preoccupation with personal development and 'growth' within recent feminism. The analyses of patterns of 'normalising' self-regulation that Foucault and his followers have provided underscore the difficulty of relying on self-knowledge *in and for itself* as *the* vehicle to women's freedom.[19]

LET'S STROLL ACROSS THE DANCE FLOOR...
FEMINIST THEORY

As outlined above, psychoanalysis has been sought by feminists both as individual clinical practice and as an analytical repertoire which can inform feminist theory. This brings me to the third strand of the contemporary feminist power–knowledge project. This could be characterised as the emergence of a more complex and highly theoretical body of knowledge about patriarchy. The early texts of the women's movement were widely circulated and many feminists drew on specialist academic skills, while writing accessibly for a wide audience. Germaine Greer, Sheila Rowbotham, Juliet Mitchell, Kate Millett and Ann Oakley were some of the authors whose early texts exposed the nature of women's oppression to a broad readership. Since then, feminist analysis has become more specialised. To some degree this has resulted from the entry into the academy of feminists who have had to perform within fairly rigid academic boundaries and who want to challenge and transform practices within those niches. The result is that we now have feminist literary criticism, feminist philosophy, feminist history and so on.

This diversification and specialisation of feminist knowledge was perhaps predictable. What was less predictable has been the emergence of a distinctive form and, some would say, level of knowledge designated as 'feminist theory'. Some of this material is not accessible to much of the feminist movement, let alone to the majority of literate women. Although diverse, it is characterised by a move away from (and sometimes disdain for) empirical investigations of gender relations and patriarchy.[20] Moreover, within this literature it is common to find expressions of ambiguity about how such investigations relate to the project of liberating women or disavowals of such concerns. This trajectory is illustrated in Tania Modleski's recent comments that

> the once exhilarating proposition that there is no 'essential' female nature has been elaborated to the point where it is now often used to scare 'women' away from making *any* generalisations about or political claims on behalf of a group called 'women'.
>
> (Modleski 1991: 15)

The mode of analysis in this body of material is more or less abstract, as exemplified in Modleski's assessment of Judith Butler's (1990) recent publication: 'Her book becomes a highly abstract Foucauldian meditation on theories of sexuality and sexual difference' (Modleski 1991: 18).

Foucault has been a major, though by no means the only, influential figure in this turn within the feminist power–knowledge project. In many respects, feminists are explicitly or implicitly adhering to Foucault's vision of critical intellectual work which he saw as involving the investigation of the conditions of the possibilities of particular systems of knowledge. They are engaged in Foucauldian forms of critique which are not matters 'of saying that things are not right as they are. It is a matter of pointing out on what kinds of assumptions, what kinds of familiar, unchallenged, unconsidered modes of thought the practices we accept rest' (Foucault 1990c: 155). The investigations of the categories of 'woman' and of 'gender' are recent exemplary feminist forays involving the interrogation of feminism's own discourse, inspired by poststructuralism, in general, and often Foucault, in particular (see, for example, Riley 1988; Butler 1990). Such investigations constitute, as Judith Butler has labelled it, 'a feminist genealogy of the category women' (Butler 1990: 5).

The world of 'feminist theory' is often identified with the term 'theoretical practice' associated with Foucault's mentor Louis

Althusser, and echoed by Foucault in his comment that 'theory is practice' (Foucault 1977: 208). These are amongst the touchstones for forms of intellectual work in which references to any wider movement or to the goal of women's liberation tend to fade into the background or disappear (see Stuart 1990; Modleski 1991; Campbell 1992). Foucault can be taken as one of the sponsors of these trends within feminism and other radical work, in that he does seem to call for some standing back from the immediate political fray and for forms of thought that reflect this distancing. On the other hand, his call for intellectuals to be involved in 'constituting a new politics of truth' could be carried in rather different directions (Foucault 1980: 132). Certainly his notion of theory as 'a tool kit' involves a stress on local, specific and reflective knowledge (Foucault 1980: 145). These differences in the readings of Foucault on theory bring us to the larger issue of the role of intellectuals.

'PUBLIC DANCERS': FOUCAULDIAN INTELLECTUALS[21]

The extended channelling of the feminist emancipatory drive for knowledge into diverse forms of therapy (including psycho-analysis) and into an intensified feminist theory (drawing most notably on poststructuralism and psychoanalysis) has transformed feminism. One important off-shoot of these developments has been the increasing role of professionals – therapists, counsellors and academics within and around feminism. Many women (including some feminists) have taken up this work, in the wake of increased female access to higher education realised through post-Second World War social reforms and encouraged by the women's movement in Britain and North America. In this respect, this cadre is, in part, a welcomed product of the achievements of feminist struggles.

However, the increasing importance of professional work within and for feminism has not been without its own problems. To begin with, the 'equality' trajectory of feminism is by no means progressively realising its goals.[22] Moreover, there are still strong gender divisions within the hierarchies of many of these professions, with men generally occupying the more powerful positions. The opening of this world has also exposed inequalities amongst women: particularly differences of class, race, sexual orientation, physical ability. Beyond this, the forms of labour which women have taken on in these positions could be interpreted as yet another version of the traditional sexual division of labour, involving women, once again, in caring and often, under-valued, work. Perhaps most worrying of all has been the tendency which Andrea Stuart (1990) has traced of the splitting of 'professional feminism' from 'popular feminism'.

In turning to Foucault I find a social analyst who was very much interested in contemporary professions and professionals. His historical work on psychiatry, medicine, psychology and other fields of the human sciences carried him in this direction. Partly because of this and because of his celebrated status within French and broader western intellectual circles, he was often called upon to reflect about the role of intellectuals. As in other facets of his thought, there is no gender dimension to Foucault's reflections on this topic. Nevertheless, Foucault has provided a series of reflections which have had much currency and have provoked controversy within feminist and other radical intellectual circles (see Weedon 1987; Hartsock 1990; West 1992). A thorough review of the interaction between Foucault and feminism on the topic of intellectuals is beyond my scope at this point. What I shall offer instead are some reflections about this sometimes realised, sometimes potential coming together.

I would begin by advocating that, if we are to use Foucault's ideas on this topic, we must place them in their full historical context. My own grasp on this context is limited, but I feel that it is significant that he was writing as a prestigious university professor, in a country and at a time in which high status accrued to such a position and in which there has been a tradition of philosophers as public figures (from Sartre to the *Nouveau Philosophes*). He was also situated within a political setting in which the role of intellectuals as party agents (most notably in the PCF – French Communist Party) had often been taken for granted.

My reading of Foucault would highlight his critical advocacy of modesty and withdrawal for intellectuals but would see this against his very specific historical and political context. There is a recurrent move within Foucault's comments towards divesting the intellectual of many potential roles. He deplored the 'call for prophetism' and insisted that 'the role of an intellectual is not to tell others what they have to do' (Foucault 1990c: 16, 265). He was not sanguine about 'all the prophecies, promises, injunctions, and programs that intellectuals have managed to formulate over the last two centuries and whose effects we can now see' (Foucault 1990c: 265).

I find these reflections double-edged. On the one hand, as Nancy Hartsock has argued more generally, on this topic as on so many others, Foucault speaks from a position of power. As a white, male member of the intellectual elite he is, to use Hartsock's borrowing from Albert Memmi (1967), 'the colonizer who refuses and thus exists in a painful ambiguity ... the colonizer who refuses to become a part of his group' (Hartsock 1990: 164). Acknowledging from where Foucault speaks on this and other topics leads Hartsock and others to question the value of his ideas for feminists.

My own position is rather more equivocal. I do find much that is useful in Foucault's disclaimers about intellectuals. I agree with him (*although he does not put it in these terms and this in itself is important*) that the world would be a better place if white, mainly middle-class, western European men had not realised their own 'will to power' as intellectuals in 'prophecies, promises, injunctions, and programs'. Beyond this, contemporary feminist professionals might do well to heed his counsel about the need for modesty, for caution in prophecies and promises, and for the dangers in *our* injunctions and programmes. On the other hand, I want to go even further with Hartsock's line of critique. There is something ironic about Foucault's disavowals in that, although challenging the expectations of and about intellectuals, the role is always taken for granted.

Feminists, and indeed female intellectuals and professionals more generally, are not the 'natural' heirs (heiresses?!) of knowledge and power. Thus, we cannot slot ourselves into Foucault's position as the 'colonizer who refuses'. Moreover, as he himself advises, his reflections must not be taken prescriptively, particularly without regard to their specific context. This was a setting in which intellectuals have been revered and in which they have wielded extraordinary power on the left (particularly within the PCF). In short, we have to work out our own politics of professions and of intellectual labour; Foucault cannot provide it.

Nevertheless, many have been attracted to Foucault's notion of 'the specific intellectual'. He spoke as an analyst and an advocate in presenting this category, tracing the emergence of this role as a feature of developments (including science and technology) within capitalism since the Second World War. He also posed it as a desirable alternative to that of the 'universal' intellectual who presents himself [*sic*] as the 'bearer of universal values' and as 'the genius absolute savant' (Foucault 1980: 132, 129). In his estimation 'specific' intellectuals should distance themselves from the direct moral or political mission associated with 'the universal intellectual'. Through this concept Foucault emphasised that 'it was quite possible, to do one's job as a psychiatrist, lawyer, engineer, or technician, and on the other hand to carry on work that may properly be called intellectual, an essentially critical work' (Foucault 1990c: 107). Hence he called for work in specific niches, effectively accepting and working within the existing division of labour.

The Foucauldian model of the 'specific intellectual' has much resonance for late-twentieth-century professionals. His comments register important changes in the division of labour, especially amongst what others have called 'the professional middle classes' (Walker 1979). He also gives due attention to the fragmentation and proliferation of knowledge identified with distinctive expertises. Moreover, extolling the modesty referred to previously, he saw the need for re-evaluations of political aspirations on the left in the light of these developments.

There is no doubt that some feminists have embraced the model of the 'specific intellectual'. For others, the pressures on intellectual workers in the contemporary west have pushed them in this direction, and Foucault's formulation can provide solace about the political potential in their current situation. So there are positive dimensions to the acceptance of this role. However, as Toril Moi (1989), Andrea Stuart (1990), Tania Modleski (1991) and Kate Campbell (1992) have warned, there have been tendencies towards feminist intellectuals becoming ever more distanced from the mass of women whom feminism set out to liberate and towards a body of feminist knowledge which circulates more or less exclusively within the academy. As they warn, in these circumstances the relationship between this knowledge and the emancipatory goals of feminism can easily drop off the agenda.

I have concentrated on what Foucault might have to offer feminist professionals reflecting about their own position in the world. My tentative evaluation is that Foucault's work has been extremely valuable in highlighting aspects of that position and in proposing a re-evaluation of the role of the intellectual. However,

I have some reservations as well. I would suggest that Foucault's proposal that professionals should effectively 'dig where they stand' can be a conservative injunction. In effect the Foucauldian injunction leaves the current sexual (and racial) division of labour intact, and it is no coincidence that he never discusses this.[23] Furthermore, his modesty merges into, and is often hard to distinguish from, withdrawal and distancing. Ironically, the Enlightenment seems to come back to haunt and direct Foucault. This can result in a figure who is remarkably like the Enlightenment heroic scientific knower, characterised by detachment, value-neutrality and the wielding of technical tools: 'What the intellectual can do is to provide instruments of analysis . . . a topographical and geological survey of the battlefield' (Foucault 1980: 62). Being an intellectual involves for him the 'work of examination that consists of suspending as far as possible the system of values to which one refers when testing and assessing it' (Foucault 1990c: 107). At some moments, the intellectual appears as a neutral observer, standing outside and above the fray. As both Cornell West (1992) and Nancy Hartsock (1990) have commented, the analyst/intellectual becomes distanced from political movements in Foucault's version of critical intellectual work.[24]

However, there are other strands within Foucault's work. In his later years, perhaps tiring of the constant pressure to discuss this topic, Foucault problematised the very notion of intellectuals: 'The word intellectual strikes me as odd. Personally, I've never met any intellectuals. I've met people who write novels, others who treat the sick. . . . But intellectuals never.' He protested that 'the right to knowledge must not be reserved to a particular age-group or to certain categories of people' (Foucault 1990c: 324, 329). At these moments, Foucault was more challenging of divisions of labour, and close to Antonio Gramsci's vision that everyone is a potential intellectual (Gramsci 1971: 3–23, esp. p. 9). So some have found in him a patron for the 'decentered, pluralistic, non-hierarchical and hermeneutic' models of knowledge associated with feminism (Hekman 1990: 126). Moreover, he did not always detach himself; rather, he became involved in specific political campaigns (in prisons, in asylums, and within the gay community) and recognised the need for 'some kind of involvement' if 'historical work were to have political meaning, utility and effectiveness' (Foucault 1980: 65).

Clearly there is need for more reflection about the patterns and impact of professionalisation within feminism and about the nature of feminist intellectual labour. In observing the emergence of feminist professional caucuses, the development of feminist therapy and so on, we might be witnessing sites of 'specific intellectuals'. This is one of many potential Foucauldian reference points on which feminists might draw. Nevertheless, in turning to Foucault we need to be aware of the dangers, as well as the gains, in taking up with this particular partner.

IS THE DANCING COMING TO AN END? FEMINISM IN THE 1990S

In the early 1990s, there is considerable pessimism about feminism. The causes of this are legion and they might include: the backlash against it, particularly from the mass media (see Faludi 1992); the power of the now not-so-new right; the dominance of conservative governments in Britain, the United States, Canada and other western countries; economic recession; and so on. So, somewhat ironically, the explosion of feminist knowledge in the three areas described above (self-help therapies, psychoanalysis and feminist theory) has occurred in this negative setting.

It is not clear what, if any, relationship there might be between this loss of confidence and the transformation of the knowledge project within feminism. Nevertheless, I would offer two observations about the meshing of these two features of the contemporary movement. First, I would suggest that there has emerged a common-sense proviso which runs along the following lines: the more we know about patriarchy, the harder it seems to change it. Secondly, it would seem that knowledge and power are less obviously melded in contemporary feminist frameworks. In short, feminist knowledge has become somewhat detached from the goal of women's liberation.[25] My comments about the investment in forms of self-knowledge and in a particular form of abstract theory are indicative of this. The current situation is certainly a far cry from the optimistic early days of the movement when the expectation was that consciousness-raising accompanied by empirical exposition would be universal and democratic methods of generating liberatory knowledge.

It would seem, returning to my starting point, that feminism's dance with Foucault around power–knowledge is coming to an end. Although this seems to be the case, this is not quite the whole picture. How can we make sense of the proliferations of feminist therapy, of feminists training as therapists, of the flood of feminist publications in the present circumstances? I want to propose two different (but possibly not incompatible) analyses of these developments. Through both accounts I am speculating that feminists continue to be attracted to the vision of that fused notion of power–knowledge referred to previously.

The current state of the feminist power–knowledge project can be illustrated by considering two rather different recent books – Gloria Steinem's *The Revolution from Within: A Book of Self-esteem* (1992) and Tania Modleski's *Feminism without Women* (1991). Steinem's is an autobiographical exploration of various forms of popular psychology and new-age self-help which she feels women (at least, in the western world) need today.[26] This book has been given considerable media coverage and, amongst feminists, it has sparked much controversy and sometimes condemnation. In a respectful, but critical, review, Carol Sternhell asks: 'How can it be, after so many years of trying to change the world, that one of our best-known feminists is suddenly advising women to change ourselves instead?' (1992: 5). Steinem's book can be taken as a celebrated and personalised testimonial to the therapeutic turn of feminism associated with the first two knowledge frameworks discussed above (therapeutic/counselling practices, more than psychoanalysis). In Sternhell's assessment this particular transformation of the power–knowledge project (which may be associated with the first two strands I analysed) is displayed and condemned. As I have suggested above, Foucault's ideas have sometimes been used to bolster protests about this trend within feminism.

My second reference point is a rather differently controversial recent feminist text, Tania Modleski's *Feminism without Women* (1991). Modleski's attack is aimed primarily at the third strand in the contemporary feminist knowledge project outlined above, associated with what she calls 'theoretical discourse' particularly linked to poststructuralism (1991: ix). Her argument is that feminism has turned in on itself, most notably in some of the questioning of categories 'woman' and 'gender'. Although she does not pose it in this way, Modleski's book can be read as protest against the breaking down of the power–knowledge project which was feminism in a different way and in a different set of developments from those represented in Steinem's book. In the various parts of her study Modleski is effectively posing over and over again the question: what is the relationship between the elaborate development of knowledge associated with feminist theory and women's power in the world?

Taking a clue from Foucault, and with these two texts in mind, it might be appropriate to see the expansion and proliferation of the feminist knowledge project not in terms of a loss of power, but in terms of new circuits of power, in these rather unpropitious times. The first two elaborations of the power–knowledge project I sketched in this chapter have been orientated around self-knowledge. In many respects Steinem's book is one of the more controversial testimonials to the power many women (including feminists) have realised in going down these roads.

However, drawing on Modleski's critique and learning from Foucault's power–knowledge studies, I would maintain that there is also a micro-politics of power within the third strand of the contemporary feminist knowledge project described in this chapter. There are different circuits of power in the world of the feminist theorist which revolve around the power of claiming to be '*the* knower', '*the* theorist'. This is manifested in claims of knowledge for knowledge's sake and in the hermetic sealing of intellectual labour which can result. I would venture to suggest that there are signs of this in some recent feminist literature: inscrutable texts, a form of analysis which presents and celebrates itself (the text) as the only imaginable political intervention. This brings us full circle to the dangers in Foucault's vision of the 'specific intellectual'.

Indeed, I would speculate that the Foucauldian power/ knowledge logo has itself reinforced these patterns within feminist and some other radical work. I have sometimes thought that the distortion and simplification of Foucault's project into the formula of power–knowledge was suspiciously attractive as the powers of academics waned in the last decades of the twentieth century. This has been a time when our economic and social status has fallen, when our ideas have been dismissed by those in power in the formal political structure, and when the relationship between our production (critical knowledge) and feminism outside the academy is not clear. In these circumstances, we quite clearly and wilfully wanted to believe in and reassert the power/knowledge formula. Yet there is a very dangerous side to this reassuring logo.

As Foucault protested, the formulation of power/knowledge denies not only his own historical work but also the wider need to investigate the relationship between knowledge and power in every specific context. More immediately, it can discourage and, as Modleski and others have suggested, *has* discouraged feminists from assessing their role in a wider struggle to change in the world. The appeal of the power of being *'the* knower' (however circumscribed the sphere) can be very attractive in these times.

Moreover, both of these circuits of power are embedded in institutions and settings which have their own power relations and which are enmeshed in patriarchy. Hence, women *have* realised power in marriage, in the traditional nuclear family through cultivating forms of self-knowledge – ironically, sometimes even in the name of feminism. In short, in acquiring self-knowledge women can become locked into the circuits of traditional motherhood or femininity. Likewise, feminist theory can and has helped some women realise power in, and often *not against*, patriarchal institutions. Hence, Kate Campbell writes of the academy 'harbouring feminism: building it up and replenishing it in some ways, yes; but at the same time given to running it dry, keeping it within walls, seeing to its overall containment' (Campbell 1992: 2)

The highlighting of these positive circuits around power–knowledge shows that women have not been victims in these processes. Even if we see these patterns as a form of short-circuiting of feminism, it seems important to acknowledge that these have been means through which women have realised power. The problem is that, particularly in the context of institutions which remain fundamentally patriarchal, there can be conservative dimensions to the realisation of power.

My second take on the new forms of the feminist knowledge project would highlight the differences, rather than the similarities, in the trajectories. Sternhell and other critics of Steinem's book have responded with a range of reactions from concern to condemnation. These reactions are not just to one text but to a whole move within feminism which they see represented in Steinem's book and in the popular take-up of it.[27] The question can be posed: what is the appeal of these techniques to Steinem and countless other women (feminists or not)? Undoubtedly there are many answers, but going back to power–knowledge, I would propose that Steinem and others are attracted by precisely the promise of change, of a form of knowledge which promises this. It is predominantly the power to change oneself which is on offer. Indeed, the turn to forms of self-knowledge could be interpreted as a return to some of the appealing features of the early recent feminist movement – a rekindling of its democratic impulse (we can all know) and the seeking of change. The complexification of feminist theory, on the other hand, promises a deeper, more profound understanding of the patriarchal order. However, it also seems to proclaim that very few women can understand the workings of patriarchy and that the prospects for change are remote and largely removed from the realms of most women's everyday lives.[28]

'Perhaps feminism is facing and living the emptiness of the Enlightenment dream,' Foucault might whisper in my ear. Others would protest that it is poststructuralism and postmodernism (with which Foucault can be identified) which have helped to shape the nightmares of contemporary feminism. Still others would smirk at the fracturing of a feminism which claimed it could know and speak for 'women' universally, without due regard to the diversity encompassed by that label.[29]

Amidst this cacophony I scarcely dare raise my voice. Have we been dancing in circles? Foucault has been a challenging yet teasing partner. He has made us self-conscious about our steps. More than anything else, Foucault has called our attention to our own entanglements in the power–knowledge tango. As 'alternative' intellectuals, as feminist professionals, as oppressed women using self-help techniques, we are as fully caught up in these patterns as the scientists of 'man' and as the Marxist intellectuals whom Foucault criticised. Awareness of this could make us better dancers: less naïve about the truth making us free, more tentative about our theories and analyses, less prophetic and triumphalist in our pronouncements and more aware of the specific patterns of power in which we are ensnared. In this sense this chapter is an invitation to take our potential partner (Foucault) more seriously and to look more carefully at these patterns within and around feminism. In these respects my invitation echoes, but is somewhat different from, that of Peggy Kamuf (1990), who advocated more open forms of feminist analyses.[30] Yet Foucault is not a discriminating partner: he makes us mindful of patterns of power–knowledge but he provides few (if any) tools for shifting those patterns. In this respect he is yet another Enlightenment man and there is still a lot of dancing to that old tune. For me, *this* is the 'conservative' (Fraser 1989) or pessimistic aspect of his work.

Some feminists have danced with Foucault and found that a stimulating experience. Others have rejected this would-be partner, impatient with his steps and his side-stepping. Whatever we decide about Foucault, the power–knowledge relationship remains at the centre of recent feminist uncertainties. The knowledge project of feminism has proliferated and changed, but it has not transformed the world. The hope that it still might keeps some of us dancing.

NOTES

1 I have used 'power–knowledge', rather than the more familiar 'power/knowledge' formulation, to highlight the need to investigate the specific relations between power and knowledge in any particular context. This will be discussed below.
2 Thanks to Rosi Braidotti from the Anna Maria Van Schuurman Centrum: Graduate School for Advanced Research on Women's Studies, University of Utrecht, for the poster. After I had decided on this title I was amused to find that in discussing the role of intellectuals in France, Foucault refers to the origins of existentialism in academic philosophy, and to the figures of Husserl and Heidegger who, as he puts it 'were hardly public dancers' (Foucault 1990c: 44). For Foucault's reflections on his own titles and on the accusation that he was 'playing a double game of surprise and deception' through them (see Foucault 1990c: 251).
3 By now there have been various assessments of the significance and value of Foucault's work for feminism. Amongst these are Bland 1981; Diamond and Quinby 1988; Weedon 1987; Hartsock 1990; Butler 1990; Bartky 1990: 63–82; Hekman 1990; Flax 1991: esp. 187–221; Barrett 1991: 150–2; Brodribb 1992: esp. 39–60. It is fascinating to compare the different terms and criteria of these assessments.
4 Foucault borrows this term from Nietzsche (see Foucault 1991a: 76–100). The outlining of the genealogical project was a modification of Foucault's earlier conception of archaeological projects. The former was most fully realised in *Discipline and Punish* and *The History of Sexuality*.
5 Foucault distinguished between the history of ideas and his 'history of thought': 'The history of thought – that means not simply a history of ideas or of representation, but also the attempt to respond to this question: How is that thought, in so far as it has a relationship with truth, can also have a history?' (Foucault 1989: 294).
6 The term 'Enlightenment' refers to the movement which emerged in eighteenth-century Europe and which sought to apply the methods

of the natural sciences (associated with the Scientific Revolution) to the organisation of social and political life. This was expressed as a faith in a universal reason. The continuing influence of this movement and its expectations have been traced into the contemporary world and identified with the belief that there is a unified reason which can light the way to progress in social and political domains. In a discussion of Kant's text, *Was ist Aufklärung?* (What is Enlightenment?), Foucault described the significance of the Enlightenment:

> After all it seems to me that the *Aufklärung* both as singular event inaugurating European modernity and as permanent process manifested in the history of reason, in the development and establishment of forms of rationality and technology, the autonomy and authority of knowledge, is for us not just an episode in the history of ideas. It is a philosophical question, inscribed since the eighteenth century in our thoughts . . . What we need to preserve is not what is left of the *Aufklärung* in terms of fragments; it is the very question of the event and its meaning . . . that must now be kept present in our minds as what must be thought.
>
> (Foucault 1990c: 94–5)

7 Of course, the question of whether psychoanalysis is continuous with, or marks a break from, the Enlightenment is itself a large topic.

8 He commented:

> The real strength of women's liberation movements is not that of having laid claim to the specificity of their sexuality and the rights pertaining to it, but that they have actually departed from the discourses conducted within the apparatuses of sexuality.
>
> (Foucault 1980: 219; see also Foucault 1989: 144;
> Foucault 1990c: 115–16)

9 For an unusual example, see Foucault's discussion of Lillian Faderman, *Surpassing the Love of Men* in Foucault 1989: 208.

10 Susan J. Hekman maintains that Foucault 'rejects humanism not Enlightenment' in that he seems to retain the latter's 'call to critique' (1990: 183).

11 It is interesting to consider how Eurocentric this assessment is. For further discussion of Foucault's Eurocentric views, see Said 1984: 222, and Said 1988.

12 Despite the difficulties with the term 'patriarchy', and recognising the problems in its use, I have used it as a short-hand in this essay to refer to the social and political dominance of men over women.

13 It is difficult to provide a definition of poststructuralism. Indeed, some commentators, such as Robert Young, have claimed that 'the premises of post-structuralism disallow any denominative, unified, or "proper" definition of itself'. Despite his disavowals, Young offers the following definition: 'Broadly . . . it involves a critique of metaphysics (of the concepts of causality, of identity, of the subject, and of truth), of the theory of the sign, and the acknowledgement and incorporation of psychoanalytic modes of thought' (1981: 8).

Poststructuralism has been identified with the work of three main figures: Foucault, Lacan and Derrida. The allusion to 'psychoanalytic modes of thought' in Young's definition indicates both that Foucault is uneasily accommodated under this label and the diversity of positions referred to by this term. Foucault himself bristled about labelling and often protested about being characterised as a 'structuralist', a 'poststructuralist' or a 'postmodernist' (see Foucault 1973: xiv; 1990c: 22). Nevertheless, his identification with poststructuralism has become fairly well established by now (see Weedon 1987; Hekman 1990).

Psychoanalytic theory originates with Freud, but there are now a number of different 'schools' of psychoanalytic theory. The most influential groupings within recent feminism have been object-relations theory and Lacanian theory. For an account of the different schools of psychoanalysis from a feminist perspective, see Sayers 1986.

14 Obviously there are problems in lumping these together. However, this is justified by my interest in the form rather than in the precise content of these therapies. Also, they differ from psychoanalysis in that they have not been so widely used for more general analytical purposes by feminists.

15 As Michèle Barrett explains, Foucault's use of the term 'discourse' is distinctive and not narrowly associated with statements in texts: 'In direct contrast to the concerns associated with "textuality", Foucault's use of the concept of discourse, and what we could call *discursivity* in general, is very much related to *context*' (1991: 126).

16 Foucault acknowledged that his use of the term 'confession' 'may be a little annoying' and then defined it as 'all those procedures by which the subject is incited to produce a discourse of truth about his [*sic*] sexuality which is capable of having effects on the subject himself' (Foucault 1980: 216).

17 He continued his disavowals: 'I have never been a Marxist and I have never been a structuralist.'

18 Parallels could be drawn with the influence of Marx and Marxism here. However, for Foucault, psychoanalysis was not associated as negatively as Marxism was with an elaborated political apparatus (particularly and most locally in the form of the PCF – the French Communist Party).

19 Foucault uses the term 'normalisation', together with 'discipline', to refer to 'the mechanisms of power which have invested human bodies, acts, and forms of behaviour' since the nineteenth century. See Foucault 1980: 61.

20 I recognise that there is a theoretical dimension which is more or less explicit in every form of knowledge. Nevertheless, I do think that the designation of a specific realm of 'Feminist Theory' (capital F and capital T, possibly) represents a very particular development.

21 This is Foucault's term (see note 2 above). I am also mindful of Tina Turner's hit single 'Private Dancer'.

22 See Phillips (1987). For a very interesting reflection on the neglect of

this dimension of feminist aspirations within recent feminism literary criticism, see Campbell 1992.

23 This absence is part of a more general rejection by Foucault of 'the conception of social structure so powerfully present in Marxism', as Michèle Barrett has pointed out (1991: 131).

24 Herbert Dreyfus and Paul Rabinow argue that there is a shift between Foucault's earlier and later work on the issue of the detachment of the analyst. They claim that in his later work, particularly in *Discipline and Punish* and *The History of Sexuality*, the analyst is no longer regarded as a detached observer (Dreyfus and Rabinow 1982: ch.4). See also Barrett 1991: 134–51.

25 This also ties in with the pattern, traced above, of the generation of feminist knowledge that is accessible only to a relatively small circle of intellectual women. I am grateful to Caroline Ramazanoğlu for pointing out that I am side-stepping arguments about what constitutes 'feminist knowledge' here. It can be argued that 'feminist knowledge' must be *grounded in women's lived experience* and that such knowledge continues to be devalued. The corollary to this is that any other claims that present themselves as 'feminist' are not truly feminist. However, this begs the question about what it means to be 'grounded in women's lived experience', and about how we *know* this experience, and about *which* women's experiences provide the basis for these claims. There are also problems about who decides what is and what is not 'feminist knowledge'. However, I do think that the abandonment of *any* attempt to make women's experience *a* or *the* reference point in feminist theory is a very significant shift.

26 It would seem to me that not only are her recommendations specific to and only available to western women, they are only available to the more privileged amongst these.

27 I would expect feminist academics, in general, to be rather more critical of the self-help, counselling and other modes of counselling (the first strand considered in this chapter) partly because of the intellectual stature of psychoanalysis. It is precisely its double appeal as mentioned previously, in its therapeutic and theoretical dimensions which are crucial here. Moreover, it should be said that psychoanalysis has had much appeal amongst feminist academics in the form of individual therapy, and so on.

28 See Butler 1990.

29 In this respect the daughters of the Enlightenment re-created many of the illusions of the sons of the Enlightenment in speaking in a unified voice about the 'liberation of woman', in a mode not dissimilar to the aspirations of men of the Enlightenment when they spoke of the 'freedom of man'.

30 I have been struck by how feminists easily abandon traditional political prescriptions, yet continue to carry the powerful trappings of 'the knower' and 'the theorist'. Hence, there are many dimensions to triumphalism. Kamuf's appeal focuses on the form of feminist theories. I would place more emphasis on the need to consider the sorts of social relations that revolve around feminist knowledge.

BIBLIOGRAPHY

Barrett, M. (1991) *The Politics of Truth*, Cambridge: Polity Press.

—— (1992) 'Words and things: materialism and method in contemporary feminist analysis', in M. Barrett and A. Phillips (eds) *Destabilizing Theory and Contemporary Feminist Debates*, Cambridge: Polity Press.

Bartky, S.L. (1990) *Femininity and Domination: Studies in the Phenomenology of Oppression*, London: Routledge.

Bland, L. (1981) 'The domain of the sexual: a response', *Screen Education*, 39: 56–67.

Bordo, S. (1990a) 'The body and the reproduction of femininity: a feminist appropriation of Foucault', in A.M. Jaggar and S.R. Bordo (eds) *Gender/Body/Knowledge: Feminist Reconstructions of Being and Knowing*, London: Rutgers University Press.

—— (1990b) 'Reading the slender body', in M. Jacobus, E.F. Keller and S. Shuttleworth (eds) *Body/Politics: Women and the Discourses of Science*, London: Routledge.

Brennan, T. (ed.) (1990) *Between Feminism and Psychoanalysis*, London: Routledge.

Brodribb, S. (1992) *Nothing Mat(t)ers: A Feminist Critique of Postmodernism*, North Melbourne, Australia: Spinifex Press.

Butler, J. (1990) *Gender Trouble: Feminism and the Subversion of Identity*, London: Routledge.

Campbell, K. (1992) 'Introduction: matters of theory and practice – or, we'll be coming out the harbour', in K. Campbell (ed.) *Critical Feminism: Argument in the Disciplines*, Milton Keynes: Open University Press.

Diamond, I. and Quinby, L. (eds) (1988) *Feminism and Foucault*, Boston: Northeastern University Press.

Diamond, N. (1985) 'Thin is the feminist issue', *Feminist Review*, 19: 45-64.

Dreyfus, H. and Rabinow, P. (1982) *Michel Foucault: Beyond Structuralism and Hermeneutics*, Brighton: Harvester.

Eichenbaum, L. and Orbach, S. (1983) *Understanding Women*, London: Penguin.

Ernst, S. and Goodison, L. (1981) *In Our Own Hands: A Book of Self-Help Therapy*, London: The Women's Press.

Ernst, S. and Maguire, M. (eds) (1987) *Living with the Sphinx: Papers from the Women's Therapy Centre*, London: The Women's Press.

Faludi, S. (1992) *Backlash: The Undeclared War against Women*, London: Chatto & Windus.

Flax, J. (1991) *Thinking Fragments: Psychoanalysis, Feminism and Postmodernism in the Contemporary West*, Berkeley, LA: UCLA Press.

Foucault, M. (1972) *The Archaeology of Knowledge*, A.M. Sheridan Smith (trans.), London: Routledge.

—— (1973) *The Order of Things: An Archaeology of the Human Sciences*, (*Les Mots et les choses*, 1966), New York: Vintage Books.

—— (1977) *Language, Counter-Memory, Practice: Selected Essays and Interviews*, D.F. Bouchard (ed. with intro.) and D.F. Bouchard and S. Simon (trans.), Oxford: Basil Blackwell.

—— (1979) *Discipline and Punish: The Birth of the Prison*, (*Surveiller et punir: naissance de la prison*, 1975), Harmondsworth: Penguin.

—— (1980) *Power/Knowledge: Selected Interviews and Other Writings 1972–1977*, C. Gordon (ed.) and C. Gordon, L. Marshall, J. Mepham, K. Soper (trans.), New York: Pantheon Books.

—— (1981) 'The order of discourse', in R. Young (ed.) *Untying the Text: A Post-Structuralist Reader*, London: Routledge.

—— (1987) *The History of Sexuality*, vol. II: *The Use of Pleasure*, (*L'Usage des plaisirs*, 1984) R. Hurley (trans.) , London: Penguin.

—— (1989) *Foucault Live (Interviews, 1966–84)*, S. Lotringer (ed.) and J. Johnson (trans.), New York: Semiotext (e).

—— (1990a) *The History of Sexuality*, vol. III: *The Care of the Self*, (*Le souci de soi*, 1988) R. Hurley (trans.), London: Penguin.

—— (1990b) *The History of Sexuality*, vol. I: *An Introduction*, (*La volonté de savoir*, 1976) R. Hurley (trans.), London: Penguin.

—— (1990c) *Michel Foucault: Politics, Philosophy, Culture: Interviews and Other Writings 1977–1984*, L. Kritzman (ed.) and A. Sheridan *et al.* (trans.), London: Routledge.

—— (1991a) *The Foucault Reader: An Introduction to Foucault's Thought*, P. Rabinow (ed.), London: Penguin.

—— (1991b) *Madness and Civilization: A History of Insanity in the Age of Reason*, (*Histoire de la folie*, 1961) R. Howard (trans.), London: Routledge.

Fraser, N. (1989) *Unruly Practices: Power, Discourse and Gender in Contemporary Social Theory*, Cambridge: Polity Press.

Gallop, J. (1982) *Feminism and Psychoanalysis: The Daughter's Seduction*, London: Macmillan.

Gramsci, A. (1971) *Selections from the Prison Notebooks of Antonio Gramsci*, Q. Hoare and G. Nowell-Smith (eds) , London: Lawrence & Wishart.

Hartsock, N. (1990) 'Foucault on power: a theory for women?', in L. Nicholson (ed.) *Feminism/Postmodernism*, London: Routledge.

Hekman, Susan J. (1990) *Gender and Knowledge: Elements of a Postmodern Feminism*, Cambridge: Polity Press.

Henriques, J., Hollway, W., Urwin, C., Venn, C. and Walkerdine, V. (1984) *Changing the Subject: Psychology, Social Regulation and Subjectivity*, London: Methuen.

Jacobus, M., Keller, E.F. and Shuttleworth, S. (eds) (1990) *Body/Politics: Women and the Discourses of Science*, London: Routledge.

Kamuf, P. (1990) 'Replacing feminist criticism', in M. Hirsch and E.F. Keller (eds) *Conflicts in Feminism*, London: Routledge.

de Lauretis, T. (1987) 'The technology of gender', in T. de Lauretis (ed.), *Technologies of Gender: Essays on Theory, Film and Fiction*, London: Macmillan.

—— (1989) 'The essence of the triangle or, taking the risk of essentialism seriously: feminist theory in Italy, the US and Britain', in *differences: A Journal of Feminist Cultural Studies*, 1 (3): 3–37.

MacKinnon, C.A. (1982) 'Feminism, Marxism, method and the state: an agenda for theory', in N.O. Keohane, M.Z. Rosaldo and B.C. Gelpi (eds) *Feminist Theory: A Critique of Ideology*, Brighton: Harvester Press.

Memmi, A. (1967) *The Colonizer and the Colonized*, Boston: Beacon Press.
Mitchell, Juliet (1974a) *Woman's Estate* (1971), Harmondsworth: Penguin.
—— (1974b) *Psychoanalysis and Feminism*, Harmondsworth: Penguin.
Mitchell, J. and Rose, J. (eds) (1982) *Jacques Lacan and the Ecole Freudien*, J. Rose (trans.), London: Macmillan.
Modleski, Tania (1991) *Feminism without Women: Culture and Criticism in a 'Postfeminist Age'*, London: Routledge.
Moi, T. (1989) 'Men against patriarchy', in L. Kauffman (ed.) *Gender and Theory: Dialogues on Feminist Criticism*, Oxford: Blackwell.
Orbach, S. (1984) *Fat is a Feminist Issue*, rev. edn, London: Hamlyn.
Phillips, A. (1987) *Feminism and Equality*, Oxford: Blackwell.
Riley, D. (1988) *'Am I that Name?' Feminism and the Category of 'Women' in History*, Basingstoke: Macmillan.
Rose, J. (1983) 'Femininity and its discontents', *Feminist Review*, 14: 5–21.
—— (1986) *Sexuality and the Field of Vision*, London: Verso.
Said, E. (1984) *The World, the Text and the Critic*, London: Faber & Faber.
—— (1988) 'Michel Foucault, 1926–1984', in J. Arac (ed.) *After Foucault*, New Brunswick, NJ: Rutgers University Press.
Sawicki, J. (1991) *Disciplining Foucault: Feminism, Power and the Body*, London: Routledge.
Sayers, J. (1982) 'Psychoanalysis and personal politics: a response to Elizabeth Wilson', *Feminist Review*, 10: 91–5.
—— (1986) *Sexual Contradictions: Psychology, Psychoanalysis and Feminism*, London: Tavistock.
Steinem, G. (1992) *The Revolution from Within: A Book of Self-esteem*, London: Bloomsbury.
Sternhell, C. (1992) 'Sic transit Gloria (review of G. Steinem, *The Revolution from Within: A Book of Self-esteem*)', *Women's Review of Books* (June): 5–6.
Stuart, A. (1990) 'Feminism: dead or alive?', in J. Rutherford (ed.) *Identity: Community, Culture, Difference*, London: Lawrence & Wishart.
Walker, P. (ed.) (1979) *Between Labour and Capital*, Hassocks: Harvester Press.
Weedon, C. (1987) *Feminist Practice and Poststructuralist Theory*, Oxford: Basil Blackwell.
West, C. (1992) 'The dilemma of the black intellectual', first published in *Cultural Critique*, 1 (1) (1985), reprinted in b. hooks and C. West, *Breaking Bread: Insurgent Black Intellectual Life*, Boston: Southend Books.
Wilson, E. (1981) 'Psychoanalysis: psychic law and order', *Feminist Review*, 8: 63–78.
Wolf, N. (1991) *The Beauty Myth: How Images of Beauty are Used against Women*, London: Vintage.
Young, R. (1981) 'Post-structuralism: an introduction', in R. Young (ed.) *Untying the Text: A Post-structuralist Reader*, London: Routledge.

Part III

Bodies and pleasures
Power and resistance

Chapter 8

Feminism, Foucault and the politics of the body[1]
Susan Bordo

A PERSONAL PROLOGUE

Sitting down to consider the unusually strong attraction that Foucauldian thought has held for contemporary feminism, it occurred to me that I might learn something from consulting personal history. What did *I* think when I first encountered the work of Michel Foucault? I can remember, when I was a graduate student in the late seventies, rebelling against the infatuation with poststructuralist thought which was then beginning to simmer in the 'continental wing' of my department. I had not the slightest knowledge of the *substance* of Derrida's or Foucault's ideas. My aversion was based solely on what I felt to be the aestheticised and elitist accoutrements of poststructuralism. I had tried one of the most popular of the early courses and found the conversations pretentious and the atmosphere cultish. The language was too self-conscious, too eroticised for my tastes; I felt instinctively that I could never wear such *haute couture* with comfort and conviction. My prejudice (against poststructuralist ideas; I never did learn to wear the clothes) was challenged in 1980 when I finally read Foucault, on assignment for a book review of *The History of Sexuality: An Introduction* which had just been published. I had been asked to do the review by my dissertation adviser, who was the book review editor of the journal, and who apparently (and correctly) had recognised a deep intellectual affinity that I had yet to discover.

That affinity was based on Foucault's historicism – the intellectual orientation which insists that ideas neither descend from a timeless heaven nor are grounded in the necessities of 'nature', but develop out of the imaginations and intellects of historical human beings. As a philosopher and a feminist, historicism was for me the great liberator of thought, challenging both the most stubborn pretensions of my discipline (to the possession of eternal truths, atemporal foundations, universal reason) and enduring social myths about human nature and gender by showing them to be, in Nietzsche's words, 'human, all too human'. Like works of art and literature, like styles of architecture and forms of governance, such notions are products of a temporal imagination negotiating its embodied experience; the point, therefore, is not to refute such notions, but to demystify them, to excavate their concrete human (psychological, social, political) origins. 'Because they are made they can be unmade', as Foucault said in an interview late in his life, 'assuming we know how they were made' (Foucault 1989: 252).

As an undergraduate, all my male heroes had been philosophers of historical consciousness: Nietzsche, Marx, Marcuse; in graduate school, I added John Dewey and later Richard Rorty (for *Philosophy and the Mirror of Nature*); after graduate school, Foucault. But with the possible exception of Marx, whose influence on my thought goes back very far, none of these thinkers opened my eyes or converted me to historicism or the social construction of reality. Rather, they inspired, instructed and delighted me with the intelligence, knowledge and insight which they brought to bear on the objects of their exploration, with the elegance and persuasiveness of their arguments, and with the legitimacy they conferred on what was already the way I looked at the world. How affirming and exciting it was for me to have that way of looking at things confirmed, to put all those enthusiastic 'yes!' marks in the margins! (This was before 'the new historical consciousness' hit philosophy and literary studies.) Where my historicism 'came from' in my life is, of course, a complex mix of personality, gender, culture and the times within which I developed the rudiments of my intellectual and social world view. But certainly, feminism had a great deal to do with it. I do not mean the academic feminism of the 1980s (within which I place my own work), which has produced an enormous feminist/historicist scholarly literature. I mean the more general challenge to cultural consciousness which began in the late 1960s – the demonstrations, the manifestos, the consciousness-raising sessions, the early writings – which first raised for so many of us the startling and potentially life-altering idea that 'man' (and

'Man') and 'woman' (and 'Woman') and all that we had been taught to believe about them were human inventions.

The feminist demystification of the naturalness and political innocence of gender was not 'owned' or articulated by any one person. It was more like a collective 'click', to invoke the metaphor of one early piece, which many different people spoke and wrote about in different ways, most of them 'popular' rather than scholarly. Here is Germaine Greer in *The Female Eunuch*:

> It is impossible to argue a case for female liberation if there is no certainty about the degree of inferiority or natural dependence which is unalterably female. . . . We know what we are, but know not what we may be, or what we might have been. . . . [W]omen must learn how to question the most basic assumptions about feminine normality in order to reopen the possibilities for development which have been successively locked off by conditioning . . . . [F]rom the outset our observation of the female is consciously and unconsciously biased by assumptions that we cannot help making and cannot always identify when they have been made. The new assumption behind the discussion of the body is that everything that we may observe *could be otherwise*.
>
> (Greer 1970: 4; Greer's emphasis)

As feminists explored and elaborated such ideas, they put intellectual suspicion of the 'natural' and a radical social constructionism in the cultural air. (Greer's conclusion about the body now seems to me quite extreme.) They did not make much ado about the meta-implications of their work or spend much time elaborating the theoretical presuppositions or consequences involved. We did not see ourselves as developing a new intellectual paradigm; nor, indeed, did we primarily locate ourselves in *intellectual* history. Rather, we saw ourselves first and foremost as participating in a political movement, and as such went straight for the concrete social and political analysis and critique. For these, and for other less benign reasons, feminism's contribution to the major theoretical shifts of the last twenty years is rarely credited.

A striking example of this is the paradigm which re-conceptualised the body from a purely biological form to an historical construction and medium of social control: the 'politics of the body'. Such a view of the body was central to the 'personal politics' articulated by Anglo-American feminists in the late sixties and seventies. Yet almost everyone today claims Foucault (perhaps with a backward nod to Marx) as its founding father and guiding light:

> Another major deconstruction [of the old notion of 'the body'] is in the area of sociopolitical thought. Although Karl Marx initiated this movement in the middle of the 19th century, it did not gain momentum until the last 20 years due to the work of the late Michel Foucault. Marx argued that a person's economic class affected his or her experience and definition of 'the body'. . . . Foucault carried on these seminal arguments in his analysis of the body as the focal point for struggles over the shape of power. Population size, gender formation, the control of children and of those thought to be deviant from the society's ethics are major concerns of political organisation – and all concentrate on the definition and shaping of the body. Moreover, the cultivation of the body is essential to the establishment of one's social role.
>
> (Johnson 1989: 6)

Not a few feminists, too, appear to accept this view of things. While honouring French feminists Irigaray, Wittig, Cixous and Kristeva for their work on the body, 'as the site of the production of new modes of subjectivity', and Beauvoir for the 'understanding of the body as a situation', Linda Zerilli (1991: 2–3) credits Foucault with having 'showed us how the body has been historically disciplined'; to Anglo-American feminism she simply attributes the 'essentialist' view of the body as an 'archaic natural'.

One of my goals in this chapter is to help restore feminism's rightful parentage of the 'politics of the body'. My point here is not only 'to set the record straight' out of some feminist chauvinism (although I admit frustration at the continual misunderstandings and caricatures of Anglo-American feminism, both from within and outside feminist scholarly circles). Rather, I think that we can learn something here from history and from the ways that we have re-membered and re-presented that history to ourselves; reflecting on my own participation in such representations, I certainly learned a great deal. In the next section I discuss the original feminist construction of the politics of the body. I then go on to describe what I view as the two key Foucauldian contributions to the further development of that construction, contributions which have significantly deepened, and (rightly) complicated, our understandings of both social 'normalisation' and social resistance.[2] But despite the fact that I view both these contributions as valuable, I am concerned about the recent theoretical *over*-appropriation (as it seems to me) of some of Foucault's more 'postmodern' ideas about resistance.[3] These ideas have been argued to represent more adequately the fragmented and unstable nature of contemporary power relations; my argument in the final section of this chapter is that 'normalisation' is still the *dominant* order of the day, even in a postmodern context, and especially with regard to the politics of *women's* bodies. Looking at contemporary commercials and advertisements, I will also show how the rhetoric of resistance has itself been pressed into the service of such normalisation.[4]

FEMINISM AND THE POLITICS OF THE BODY

In my review of *The History of Sexuality* (Bordo 1980), I acknowledged what I felt to be truly innovative about Foucault's critique of the scientisation of sexuality. But I also pointed out that his notion of a power that works not through negative prohibition and restraint of impulse but proliferatively, at the level of the *production* of 'bodies and their materiality, their forces, energies, sensations and pleasures' was not itself new. I had in mind here Marcuse's notion, in *One-Dimensional Man* of the 'mobilisation and administration of libido', whose similarities and differences from Foucault's notion of the 'deployment of sexuality' I discussed in some detail in the review. Not for a moment did I consider the relevance of the extensive feminist literature (from the 1960s and 1970s) on the social construction and 'deployment' of female sexuality, beauty and 'femininity'. I was thoroughly familiar with that literature; I simply did not credit it with a *theoretical* perspective on power and the body. How could this have been? How could I have read Andrea Dworkin, for example, and failed to recognise the 'theory' in the following passage?

> Standards of beauty describe in precise terms the relationship that an individual will have to her own body. They prescribe her motility, spontaneity, posture, gait, the uses to which she can put her body. *They define precisely the dimensions of her physical*

freedom. And of course, the relationship between physical freedom and psychological development, intellectual possibility, and creative potential is an umbilical one.

In our culture, not one part of a woman's body is left untouched, unaltered. No feature or extremity is spared the art, or pain, of improvement. . . . From head to toe, every feature of a woman's face, every section of her body, is subject to modification, alteration. This alteration is an ongoing, repetitive process. It is vital to the economy, the major substance of male–female differentiation, the most immediate physical and psychological reality of being a woman. From the age of 11 or 12 until she dies, a woman will spend a large part of her time, money, and energy on binding, plucking, painting and deodorising herself. It is commonly and wrongly said that male transvestites through the use of makeup and costuming caricature the women they would become, but any real knowledge of the romantic ethos makes clear that these men have penetrated to the core experience of being a woman, a romanticised construct.

(Dworkin 1974: 113–14; emphasis Dworkin's)

The answer to my question is complex. My failure to recognise the theoretical insight and authority of such work, as I suggested earlier, is in part attributable to the paucity of philosophical scaffolding and scholarly discussion in the works themselves. For the most part, these were not politically motivated academics (at least, not at that point in their lives), but writer/activists; their driving concern was *exposing* oppression, not elaborating the *ideas* most adequate to exposing that oppression (as was the case with Marcuse and Foucault and is arguably the case with much academic feminism today). Moreover, the way 'political writing' was conceived by feminists in those days was aimed at actually effecting *change* in readers' lives. This put a priority on clarity and immediacy, on startling and convincing argument and example, a shunning of obscurity and jargon. And yet: I cannot let myself entirely off the hook here (and of course I am hardly alone on that hook). In 1980, despite the fact that I was writing a dissertation historically critiquing the duality of male mind/female body, I still expected 'theory' only from men. Moreover – and here my inability to 'transcend' these dualisms reveals itself more subtly – I was unable to recognise *embodied* theory when it was staring me in the face. For it is hardly the case that these early feminist works were not theoretical, but rather that their theory never drew attention to *itself*, never made an appearance except as it shaped the 'matter' of their argument. That is, theory was rarely abstracted, objectified and elaborated as of interest in itself. Works that perform such abstraction and elaboration get taken much more seriously than works which do not. This is as true or truer in 1992 as it was in 1980.

Let me clarify here that I am *not* denying the value of such abstraction, or claiming that Foucault's complex theoretical contribution to the 'politics of the body' is contained or even anticipated in the work of Andrea Dworkin or any other feminist writer. Indeed, the next generation of feminist writers on the body often were drawn to Foucault precisely because his theoretical apparatus highlighted the inadequacies of the prevailing feminist discourse and was useful in reconstructing it. I will discuss these issues in more detail in the next section of this chapter. For now I only wish to point out, contrary to current narratives, that neither Foucault nor any other poststructuralist thinker discovered or invented the 'seminal' idea (to refer back to Johnson's account) that the 'definition and shaping' of the body is 'the focal point for struggles over the shape of power'. *That* was discovered by feminism, and long before it entered into its recent marriage with poststructuralist thought – as far back, indeed, as Mary Wollstonecraft's 1792 description of the production of the 'docile body' of the domesticated woman of privilege:

> To preserve personal beauty, woman's glory! the limbs and faculties are cramped with worse than Chinese bands, and the sedentary life which they are condemned to live, whilst boys frolic in the open air, weakens the muscles and relaxes the nerves. As for Rousseau's remarks, which have since been echoed by several writers, that they have naturally, that is since birth, independent of education, a fondness for dolls, dressing, and talking – they are so puerile as not to merit a serious refutation. That a girl, condemned to sit for hours together listening to the idle chat of weak nurses, or to attend to her mother's toilet, will endeavour to join the conversation, is, indeed, very natural; and that she will imitate her mother and aunts, and amuse herself by adorning her lifeless doll, as they do in dressing her, poor innocent babe! is undoubtedly a most natural consequence . . . genteel women are, literally speaking,

slaves to their bodies, and glory in their subjection. . . . Women
are everywhere in this deplorable state. . . . Taught from their
infancy that beauty is woman's sceptre, the mind shapes itself
to the body and, roaming round its gilt cage, only seeks to
adorn its prison.

(Wollstonecraft 1988: 55–7)

A more activist generation urged escape from the gilt prison,
arguing that the most mundane, 'trivial' aspects of women's bodily
existence were in fact significant elements in the social construction of an oppressive feminine norm. In 1914, the first
Feminist Mass Meeting in America – whose subject was 'Breaking
into the Human Race' – poignantly listed, among the various
social and political rights demanded, 'the right to ignore fashion'
(Cott 1987: 12). Here already, the material 'micro-practices' of
everyday life – which would be extended by later feminists to
include not only what one wears, but who cooks and cleans and,
more recently, what one eats or does not eat – have been taken out
of the realm of the purely personal and brought into the domain
of the political. Here, for example, is a trenchant 1971 analysis,
presented by way of a set of 'consciousness-raising' exercises for
men, of how female subjectivity is normalised and subordinated by
the everyday bodily requirements and vulnerabilities of 'femininity':

Sit down in a straight chair. Cross your legs at the ankles and
keep your knees pressed together. Try to do this while you're
having a conversation with someone, but pay attention at all
times to keeping your knees pressed tightly together.

Run a short distance, keeping your knees together. You'll find
you have to take short, high steps if you run this way. Women
have been taught it is unfeminine to run like a man with long,
free strides. See how far you get running this way for 30
seconds.

Walk down a city street. Pay a lot of attention to your clothing:
make sure your pants are zipped, shirt tucked in, buttons done.
Look straight ahead. Every time a man walks past you, avert
your eyes and make your face expressionless. Most women
learn to go through this act each time we leave our houses. It's
a way to avoid at least some of the encounters we've all had with
strange men who decided we looked available.

(Willamette Bridge Liberation News Service 1971)

Until I taught a course in the history of feminism several years ago, I had forgotten that the very first public act of second-wave feminist protest in the United States was the 'No More Miss America' demonstration in August 1968. The critique presented at that demonstration was far from the theoretically crude, essentialising programme that recent caricatures of that era's feminism would suggest. Rather, the position paper handed out at the demonstration outlined a complex, non-reductionist analysis of the intersection of sexism, conformism, competition, ageism, racism, militarism and consumer culture as they are constellated and crystallised in the pageant.[5] The 'No More Miss America' demonstration was the event which earned 'Women's Libbers' the reputation for being 'bra-burners', an epithet many feminists have been trying to shed ever since. In fact, no bras *were* burned at the demonstration, although there was a huge 'Freedom Trash Can' into which were thrown bras, as well as girdles, curlers, false eyelashes, wigs, copies of *The Ladies' Home Journal*, *Cosmopolitan*, *Family Circle*, and so on. The media, sensationalising the event, and also no doubt influenced by the paradigm of draft-card burning as the act of political resistance *par excellence*, misreported or invented the burning of the bras. It stuck like crazy glue to the popular imagination; indeed, many of my students today still refer to feminists as 'bra-burners'. But whether or not bras were actually burned, the uneasy public with whom the image stuck surely had it right in recognising the deep political meaning of women's refusal to 'discipline' our breasts – culturally required to be so completely 'for' the other – whether as symbol of maternal love, wet-nurse for the children of the master's house, or erotic fetish.

'Whither the bra in the '90s?' asks Amy Collins, writing for *Lear's* magazine. She answers:

> Women are again playing up their bust lines with a little artifice. To give the breasts the solid, rounded shape that is currently desirable, La Perla is offering a Lycra bra with pre-formed, pressed-cotton cups. To provide a deeper cleavage, a number of lingerie companies are selling side-panel bras that gently nudge the breasts together. Perhaps exercising has made the idea of altering body contours acceptable once more. In any case, if anatomy is destiny, women are discovering new ways to reshape both.

> (Collins 1991: 80)

Indeed. In 1992, with the dangers of silicone implants on public trial, the media emphasis was on the irresponsibility of Dow, and the personal sufferings of women who became ill from their implants. To my mind, however, the most depressing aspect of the disclosures was the *cultural* spectacle: the large numbers of women who are having implants purely to enlarge or re-shape their breasts, and who consider any health risk worth the resulting boon to their 'self-esteem' and market value. These women are not 'cultural dopes'; usually, they are all too conscious of the system of values and rewards that they are responding to and perpetuating. They know that Bally Matrix Fitness is telling the *truth* about our culture when it tells them that 'You don't just shape your body. You shape your life'. They may even recognise that Bally Matrix is also *creating* that culture. But they insist on their right to be happy on its terms. In the dominant ethos, that right is the bottom line; proposals to ban or even regulate silicone breast implants are thus often viewed as totalitarian interference with self-determination and choice. Many who argue in this way consider themselves feminists, and many feminist scholars today theorise explicitly *as* feminists on their 'behalf'. A recent article in the feminist philosophy journal *Hypatia* for example, defends cosmetic surgery as '*first and foremost. . .* about taking one's life into one's own hands' (Davis 1991: 23).

I will return to this contemporary construction later. For now, I would only highlight how very different it is from the dominant feminist discourse on the body in the late sixties and seventies. *That* imagination of the female body was of a *socially* shaped and historically 'colonised' territory, not a site of individual self-determination. Here, feminism inverted and converted the old metaphor of the 'body politic', found in Plato, Aristotle, Cicero, Seneca, Macchiavelli, Hobbes and many others, to a new metaphor: 'the politics of the body'. In the old metaphor of the body politic, the state or society was imagined as a human body, with different organs and parts symbolising different functions, needs, social constituents, forces and so forth – the head or soul for the sovereign, the blood for the will of the people, the nerves for the system of reward and punishments, and so forth. Now, feminism imagined the human *body* as itself a politically inscribed entity, its physiology and morphology shaped and marked by histories and practices of containment and control – from foot-binding and corseting to rape and battering, to compulsory heterosexuality, forced sterilisation, unwanted pregnancy and (in the case of the African-American slave woman) explicit commodification:[6]

> Her head and her heart were separated from her back and her hands and divided from her womb and vagina. Her back and muscle were pressed into field labour where she was forced to work with men and work like men. Her hands were demanded to nurse and nurture the white man and his family as domestic servant whether she was technically enslaved or legally free. Her vagina, used for his sexual pleasure, was the gateway to the womb, which was his place of capital investment – the capital investment being the sex act and the resulting child the accumulated surplus, worth money on the slave market.
>
> (Omolade 1983: 354)

One might rightly object that the body's actual bondage in slavery is not to be compared to the metaphorical bondage of privileged nineteenth-century women to the corset, much less to twentieth-century women's 'bondage' to the obsession with slenderness and youth. I think it is crucial, however, to recognise that a staple of the prevailing sexist ideology against which the new feminist model protested was the notion that, in matters of beauty and femininity, it is *women* who are responsible for whatever 'enslavement' they suffer from the whims and bodily tyrannies of 'fashion'. According to that ideology, men's desires have no responsibility to bear, nor does the culture which subordinates women's desires to those of men, sexualises and commodifies women's bodies, and offers them little other opportunity for social or personal power. Rather, it is in our essential feminine nature to be (delightfully if incomprehensibly) drawn to such trivialities, and to be willing to endure whatever physical inconvenience is required. In such matters, whether having our feet broken and shaped into 4–inch 'lotuses', or our waists strait-laced to 14 inches, or our breasts surgically stuffed with plastic, we 'do it to ourselves', are our 'own worst enemies'. Set in cultural relief against this 'thesis', the feminist 'anti-thesis' was the insistence that women are the *done to* not the *doers* here, that *men* and *their* desires (not ours) are the 'enemy', and that our obedience to the dictates of 'fashion' is better conceptualised as bondage than choice. This was a crucial historical moment in the developing articulation of a new understanding of the sexual politics of the body. The limitations of that understanding at this early stage are undeniable. But a new and generative paradigm had been put in place, for later feminist thinkers to develop and critique. It is to this criticism that I now turn in the next section of this chapter.

FOUCAULT'S RE-CONCEPTUALISATION OF THE POLITICS OF THE BODY: NORMALISATION AND RESISTANCE

The initial feminist model of body politics presented various problems for later feminist thought. The 'old' feminist model, for one thing, had tended (although not invariably) to subsume all patriarchal institutions and practices under an oppressor/ oppressed model which theorised men as 'possessing' and wielding power over women, who are viewed correspondingly as being utterly power-*less*. Given this model, the woman who has a breast enlargement operation 'to please her man' is as much the victim of his 'power' over her as the slave woman who submits to her owner's desires. Moreover, the oppressor/oppressed model provides no way in which to theorise adequately the complexities of the situations of men, who frequently find themselves implicated in practices and institutions which they (as individuals) did not create, do not control and may feel tyrannised by. Nor does this model acknowledge the degree to which women may 'collude' in sustaining sexism – for example, in our willing (and often eager) participation in cultural practices which objectify and sexualise us.

When I first read Foucault, I remember thinking: 'finally, a male theorist who understands western culture as neither a conversation among talking heads nor a series of military adventures, but as a history of the body!' What fascinated me most about Foucault's work were the historical genealogies themselves. But what I ultimately found most useful to my own work was Foucault's re-conceptualisation of modern 'power'. For Foucault, modern power (as opposed to sovereign power) is non-authoritarian, non-conspiratorial, and indeed non-orchestrated; yet it none the less produces and normalises bodies to serve prevailing relations of dominance and subordination. The key 'moments' of this conception (as Foucault initially theorised it and which I will now attempt to characterise) are found in 'The eye of power' (1977), *Discipline and Punish* (1979), and *The History of Sexuality*, vol. I (1980); later revisions concerning resistance are discussed in 'The subject and power' (1983). Understanding how modern power operates requires, according to Foucault: first, that we cease to imagine 'power' as the *possession* of individuals or groups – as something people 'have' – and instead as a dynamic or network of non-centralised forces. Secondly, we recognise that these forces are *not* random or haphazard, but configure to assume particular historical forms (for example, the mechanisation and later scientisation of 'man'). The dominance of those forms is achieved, however, not from magisterial decree or design 'from above' but through multiple 'processes, of different origin and scattered location', regulating the most intimate and minute elements of the construction of space, time, desire, embodiment (Foucault 1979: 138). Thirdly, (and this element became central to later feminist appropriations of Foucault) prevailing forms of selfhood and subjectivity are maintained not through physical restraint and coercion, but through individual self-surveillance and self-correction to norms. Thus, as Foucault writes,

> there is no need for arms, physical violence, material constraints. Just a gaze. An inspecting gaze, a gaze which each individual under its weight will end by interiorising to the point that he is his own overseer, each individual thus exercising this surveillance over, and against himself.
>
> (Foucault 1977: 155)

I would also argue (not all feminists would agree[7]) that this 'impersonal' conception of power does *not* entail that there are no dominant positions, social structures or ideologies emerging from the play of forces; the fact that power is not held by any*one* does not entail that it is equally held by *all*. It is 'held' by no one; but people and groups *are* positioned differently within it. No one may control the rules of the game. But not all players on the field are equal. (I base my interpretation here less on Foucault's explicitly theoretical statements than on his historical genealogies themselves.)

Such a model seemed to many of us particularly useful to the analysis of male dominance and female subordination, so much of which, in a modern western context, is reproduced 'voluntarily', through self-normalisation to everyday habits of masculinity and femininity.[8] In my own work, Foucault's ideas were extremely

helpful both to my analysis of the contemporary disciplines of diet
and exercise (1990a) and to my understanding of eating disorders
as arising out of and reproducing normative feminine practices of
our culture. These are practices which train the female body in
docility and obedience to cultural demands while at the same time
being *experienced* in terms of 'power' and 'control' (Bordo 1985,
1990a).

Within a Foucauldian framework, power and pleasure do not
cancel each other. Thus, the heady experience of feeling
powerful, or 'in control', far from being a necessarily accurate
reflection of one's actual social position, is always suspect as itself
the product of power relations whose shape may be very different.
Within such a framework, too, one can acknowledge that women
are not always passive 'victims' of sexism, but that we may
contribute to the perpetuation of female subordination, for
example, by participating in industries and cultural practices
which represent women as sexual enticements and rewards for
men – without this entailing that we have 'power' (or are equally
positioned with men) in sexist culture. While men cease to be
constructed as 'the enemy' and their often helpless enmeshment
in patriarchal culture can be acknowledged by a Foucauldian
model, this does not mitigate the fact that they often may have a
higher stake in maintaining institutions within which they have
historically occupied dominant positions *vis-à-vis* women. That is
why they have often *felt* (and behaved) like 'the enemy' to women
struggling to change those institutions. (Such a dual recognition
seems essential, in particular, to theorising the situation of men
who have been historically subordinated *vis-à-vis* their 'race', class
and sexuality.)

Foucault also emphasised, later in his life, that power relations
are never seamless, but always spawning new forms of culture and
subjectivity, new openings for potential resistance to emerge.
Where there is power, he came to see, there is also resistance
(1983). I would add to this that prevailing norms themselves have
transformative potential. While it is true that we may experience
the illusion of 'power' while actually performing as 'docile bodies'
(for example, my analysis of the situation of the anorectic), it is also
true that our very 'docility' can have consequences that are
personally liberating and/or culturally transforming. So, for
example, (to construct some illustrations not found in Foucault),
the woman who goes on a rigorous weight-training programme in

order to achieve a currently stylish look may discover that her new muscles also enable her to assert herself more forcefully at work. Or – a different sort of example – 'feminine' decorativeness may function 'subversively' in professional contexts which are dominated by highly masculinist norms (such as academia). Modern power relations are thus unstable; resistance is perpetual and hegemony precarious.

The 'old' feminist discourse, whose cultural work was to expose the oppressiveness of femininity, could not be expected to give much due to the *pleasures* of shaping and decorating the body or their subversive potential. That was left to a later generation of feminist theorists, who have found both Foucault and deconstructionism to be useful in elaborating such ideas. Deconstructionism has been helpful in pointing to the many-sided nature of meaning; for every interpretation, there is always a reading 'against the grain'. Foucault has been attractive to feminists for his later insistence that cultural resistance is ubiquitous and perpetual. While an initial wave of Foucauldian-influenced feminism had seized on concepts such as 'discipline', 'docility', 'normalisation' and 'bio-power', a second, more 'postmodern'[9] wave has emphasised 'intervention', 'contestation', 'subversion'. The first wave, while retaining the 'old' feminist conception of the 'colonised' female body, sought to complicate that discourse's insufficiently textured, good guys/bad guys conception of social control. Postmodern feminism, on the other hand, criticises *both* the 'old' discourse *and* its reconstruction for over-emphasising such control, for failing to acknowledge adequately the creative and resistant responses that continually challenge and disrupt it.

From this postmodern perspective, both the earlier emphasis on women's bodies as subject to 'social conditioning', and the later move to 'normalisation', under-estimate the unstable nature of subjectivity and the creative agency of individuals – 'the cultural work' (as one theorist puts it) 'by which nomadic, fragmented, active subjects confound dominant discourse.[10] In this view the dominant discourses which define femininity are continually allowing for the eruption of 'difference', and even the most subordinated subjects are therefore continually confronted with opportunities for resistance, for making meanings that 'oppose or evade the dominant ideology'. There is power and pleasure in this culture, television critic John Fiske insists, 'in being different'. (He then goes on to produce examples of how *Dallas, Hart to Hart* and other shows have been read by various sub-cultures to make their own empowering meanings out of the 'semiotic resources' provided by television (Fiske 1987: 11).) In a similar vein, Judith Butler (1990: 137–8) suggests that by presenting a mocking enactment of how gender is artificially constructed and 'performed', drag and other 'parodic practices' (such as cross-dressing and lesbian 'butch/femme' identities) that are proliferated *from within* gender-essentialist culture effectively expose and subvert that culture and its belief in 'the notion of a true gender identity'.

In terms of the very general overview presented in this section, there are thus 'two' Foucaults for feminism, and in some ways they are the mirror-image of one another. The 'first' Foucault, less a product of postmodern culture than a direct descendant of Marx, and sibling to 1960s and 1970s feminism, has attracted feminists with his deep and complex understanding of the 'grip' of systemic power on the body. The appeal of the 'second' Foucault, in contrast, has been his later, postmodern appreciation, for the creative 'powers' of bodies to *resist* that grip. Both perspectives, I would argue, are essential to a fully adequate *theoretical* understanding of power and the body. Yet the question remains as to which emphasis (for we are always and of necessity selective in our attention and emphases) provides the greater insight into the specific historical situations of women today. In the next section of this chapter, focusing on the politics of appearance, I will consider this question.

WHICH FOUCAULT FOR FEMINISM TODAY? NORMALISATION AND RESISTANCE IN THE ERA OF THE IMAGE[11]

In general, I find the 'postmodern' inclination to emphasise and celebrate 'resistance' – the creative agency of individuals, and the instabilities of systems rather than their recuperative tendencies – to be highly problematic. In other pieces, I discuss Fiske's and Butler's proposals in some detail (Bordo 1990b, 1991); here, I will critique the resistance-orientation as a more general intellectual tendency. I acknowledge that power relations are neither static nor seamless, and that resistance and transformation are indeed continual. These elements deserve their recognition in cultural analysis. The degree to which they deserve emphasis, however, must vary according to the historical realities being explored. Just how helpful, for example, is an emphasis on creative agency in describing the relation of women and their bodies to the image industry of post-industrial capitalism, a context in which eating disorders and exercise compulsions are flourishing? Does the USA have a multi-million-dollar business in corrective, cosmetic surgery because women are asserting their racial and ethnic identities in resistance to prevailing norms, or because they are so vulnerable to the normalising power of those norms? Does an intellectual emphasis on 'resistance' really help us to describe and diagnose the politics of the body within the culture in which we live? Or, rather, does it participate in key mystifications of that culture? I will close this chapter by briefly addressing these questions.

Jean Baudrillard (1983) has suggested that a key characteristic of incessantly self-recreating, postmodern culture is the disappearance of the distinction between reality and appearance. Today, all that is meaningful to us are our simulations. I think that Baudrillard is exactly right here. We all 'know' that Cher and virtually every other female star over the age of 25 is the plastic product of numerous cosmetic surgeries on face and body. Some of us can even remember what Cher *used* to look like. But in the era of the 'hyperreal' (as Baudrillard calls simulations) such historical 'knowledge' becomes faded and indistinct, unable to cast the merest shadow of doubt over the dazzling, compelling, utterly authoritative new images of Cher. Like the 'knowledge' of our own mortality when we are young and healthy, the knowledge that Cher as we see her today is a fabricated product is an empty abstraction; it simply does not compute. It is the present image that has the hold on our most vibrant sense of what is, what matters. In so far as the history of Cher's body has meaning at all, it has meaning not as the 'original' over which a false copy has been laid, but as a *defect* which has been corrected. It becomes constructed as 'defect' precisely because the new image is the dominant reality, the normalising standard against which all else is judged. This has tremendous implications for our relationship to physical appearance, which more and more has come to be understood not as a biological 'given' which we have to learn to accept, but as a plastic potentiality to be pressed into the service of image – to be arranged, re-arranged, constructed and deconstructed as we choose (Bordo 1990b). Cosmetic surgery is now a $1.75 billion-a-year industry in the United States, with almost 1.5 million people a year undergoing surgery of some kind, from face-lifts to calf implants. These operations have become more and more affordable to the middle class (the average cost of a nose job is $2,500), and almost all can be done on an outpatient basis – some during the lunch hour. Lest it be imagined that most of these surgeries are to correct disfiguring accidents or birth defects, it should be noted that liposuction (vacuum extraction of 'surplus' fat) is the most frequently requested operation (average cost $1,500), with breast enlargement (average cost $2,000) a close second. More than two million women have received breast implants since they have been on the market.

Advocates of cosmetic surgery, as I noted earlier, argue that it is 'about' self-determination and choice, about 'taking one's life into one's hands'. But do we really choose the appearances that we reconstruct for ourselves? The images of beauty, power and success which dominate in US culture are generated out of Anglo-Saxon identifications and preferences and are images which, with some variations, are globally influential through the mass media. These images are still strongly racially, ethnically and heterosexually inflected – a reality that is continually effaced by the postmodern emphasis on resistant elements rather than dominant cultural forms. Products still promote 'hair that moves' and 'faded beauty' for black women; the slender-hipped, long-legged bodies of fashion models are infrequently produced by the Eastern European gene pool. Certainly, high-fashion images may contain touches of exotica: collagen-plumped lips or corn rows on white models, Barbra Streisand noses, 'butch' styles of dress. Consumer capitalism depends on the continual production of novelty, of fresh images to stimulate desire, and it frequently drops into marginalised neighbourhoods in order to find them. But such elements will be either explicitly *framed* as exotica, or, within the overall system of meaning, they will not be permitted to overwhelm the representation to establish a truly alternative or 'subversive' model of beauty or success. White models may collagen their lips, but black models are usually light-skinned and anglo-featured (unless, of course, their 'blackness' is being ideologically exploited, as in the many advertisments which code dark-skinned women with lust and animal desire). A definite (albeit not always fixed or determinate) system of normalising boundaries sets limits on the validation of cultural 'difference'. This system is reflected in the sorts of surgery people request; does anyone in this culture have her nose re-shaped to look more 'African' or 'Jewish'?

Popular culture offers few models of resistance to all this. Cher's public-relations image emphasises her individuality, honesty and defiance against norms. In the minds of many people, she (like Madonna) stands for female power, for rebellion against convention. Yet if we look past the 'discursive' hype to the message conveyed by her *body* we see that Cher's operations have gradually replaced a strong, decidedly 'ethnic' look with a more symmetrical, delicate, 'conventional' (i.e. Anglo-Saxon) and ever-youthful version of female beauty. Cher admits to having had her breasts 'done', her nose bobbed and her teeth straightened; reportedly she has also had a rib removed, her buttocks re-shaped, and cheek implants. But whatever she has or has not done, the transformation from 1965 to 1992 is striking: in Foucauldian terminology, Cher has gradually 'normalised' herself. Her normalised image (the only 'reality' which counts) now acts as a standard against which other women will measure, judge, discipline and 'correct' themselves.

Such normalisation, to be sure, is continually mystified and effaced in our culture by the rhetoric of 'choice' and 'self-determination' which plays such a key role in commercial representations of diet, exercise, hair and eye-colouring and so forth. 'You get better or worse every day,' cautions Glen Frye on behalf of Bally Matrix Fitness, *'The choice is yours.'* (Yes, you are free to choose to be a lazy, self-indulgent slob?) 'The body you have is the body you inherited, but you must decide what to do with it,' instructs Nike, offering glamorous shots of lean, muscled athletes to help us 'decide'. 'Now, choosing your very own eye colour is the most natural thing in the world,' claims Durosoft (who does not market dark brown lenses). A recent television advertisment (featuring the 'new' Cher) even yokes the discourse on agency and self-determination to the selection of *Equal* over *Sweet 'N Low*; 'When I sit down to make a choice', explains Cher, 'I choose *Equal.'*

Rendered utterly invisible in the spa and exercise equipment advertisments, of course, is the coerciveness of the slenderness and fitness aesthetic (and ethic) itself. Rather, a nearly total inversion is effected, and the normalised body becomes *the* body of creative self-fashioning, even the body of cultural resistance. 'I believe' is the theme of a recent series of Reebok commercials, each of which features muscled, energetic women declaring their feminist rebellion as they exercise: 'I believe that babe is a four letter word', 'I believe in baying at the moon', 'I believe that sweat *is* sexy'. The last declaration – which 'answers' the man in a Secret deodorant advertisement who claims that, 'a woman just isn't sexy when she sweats' – not only rebels against gender ideology, but suggests resistance to the world of commercials itself (nice trick for a commercial!). Perhaps the most insidious of the series is a magazine advertisement which pictures a lean, highly toned, extremely attractive young woman, leaning against a wall, post-workout; 'I believe', the copy reads, 'that if you look at yourself and see what is right instead of what is wrong, that is the true mark of a healthy individual'. Now, those convinced that 'resistance is everywhere' might see this advertisment as offering a trans-gressive, subversive model of femininity: a women who is strong, fit and (unlike most women) *not* insecure about her body. What this reading neglects is that we have a visual message here as well: her body *itself* – probably the most potent 'representation' in the advertisment – is precisely the sort of perfected icon which women compare themselves to and of course see 'what is wrong'. The advertisment thus puts 'real' women in a painful double-bind. On the one hand, it encourages them to view themselves as defective; on the other hand, it chastises them for their insecurities. The offered resolution to this bind, of course, is to buy Reebok and become like the woman in the advertisment.

One might argue that an adequate analysis of advertisments such as those I have been discussing would take into account both their resistant elements and their normalising messages. (Weight-training and exercise, after all, often do have socially empowering results for women.) I have no problem granting this, so long as the normalising thrust of these advertisments *vis-à-vis* the politics of appearance is not obscured. In connection with this, we need to recognise that the symbols of resistance in these advertisments are included by advertisers in the profoundest of cynical bad faith; they pretend to reject the objectification of women and value female assertiveness, while attempting to convince women who *fail* to embody dominant ideas of (slender, youthful) beauty that they need to bring themselves into line. To resist *this* normalising directive is *truly* to 'go against the grain' of our culture, not merely in textual 'play', but at great personal risk – as the many women who have been sexually rejected for being 'too fat' and fired from their jobs for looking 'too old' know all too well. Subversion of dominant cultural forms, as bell hooks has said (1990: 22), 'happens much more easily in the realm of "texts" than in the world of human interaction . . . in which such moves challenge, disrupt, threaten, where repression is real'. The pleasure and power of 'difference' is hard-won; it does not freely bloom, insistently nudging its way through the cracks of dominant forms. Sexism, racism and 'ageism', while they do not determine human value and choices, while they do not deprive us of 'agency', remain strongly normalising within our culture.

The commercial texts that I have been examining, in contrast, participate in the illusion (which they share with other postmodern texts) that our 'differences' are already flourishing in the culture *as it is*, without need for personal struggle and social change – that we are already self-determining, already empowered to look in the mirror and see what is right, instead of what is wrong. The exposure of such mystifications, which should not be impeded by too facile a celebration of resistance, must remain central to a feminist politics of the body.

NOTES

1 Portions of this chapter are based on material from the introduction and conclusion to my book, *Unbearable Weight: Feminism, Western Culture and the Body* (Bordo 1993). Other portions were taken from talks that I delivered at the University of Rochester and Hobart and William Smith Colleges. I offer my thanks to all those who participated in discussions at those presentations.

2 By social 'normalisation' I refer to all those modes of acculturation which work by setting up standards or 'norms' against which individuals continually measure, judge, 'discipline' and 'correct' their behaviour and presentation of self. By social 'resistance' I refer to all behaviours, events and social formations that challenge or disrupt prevailing power relations and the norms that sustain and reproduce them.

3 The postmodern has been described and re-described with many different emphases and points of departure, some critical and some celebratory of the 'postmodern condition' (see Bordo 1991). Without entering into a lengthy and diverting discussion, for my purposes here I employ the term 'postmodern' in the most general cultural sense, as referring to the contemporary inclination towards the

unstable, fluid, fragmented, indeterminate, ironic and hetero-geneous, for that which resists definition, closure and fixity. Within this general categorisation, ideas that have developed out of poststructuralist thought – the emphasis on semiotic indeterminacy, the critique of unified conceptions of subjectivity, fascination with the instabilities of systems, and the ability to focus on cultural resistance rather than dominant forms – are decidedly 'postmodern' intellectual developments. But not all poststructuralist thought is 'postmodern'. Foucault, as I read him, has both 'modern' and 'postmodern' moments. In his discussions of the discipline, normalisation and creation of 'docile bodies' he is very much the descendant of Marx; later revisions to his conception of power emphasise the ubiquity of resistance – a characteristic 'postmodern' theme.

4 A final introductory note: The 'stream' of feminist body-politics which is my chief focus in this chapter is the politics of appearance. Even though Foucault himself had little to say about this – or about women – I construct most of my examples and illustrations of Foucault's ideas from this domain, to which I view his ideas as particularly applicable. (For the same reason, I use Foucauldian terminology in describing early feminist perspectives of the body, even though that terminology was unknown to the writers themselves.) This choice of focus should not be taken as implying that I view issues concerning work, sexuality, sexual violence, parenting and reproductive rights as less illustrative of, or important to, a feminist politics of the body. It also explains my omission of any discussion of French feminism, whose contribution to feminist perspectives on the body has been significant, but which has not theorised the politics of beauty and appearance as central to the construction of femininity.

5 The Ten Points of protest listed were: 'The Degrading Mindless-Boob-Girlie Symbol'; 'Racism with Roses'; 'Miss America as Military Death Mascot'; 'The Consumer Con-Game'; 'Competition Rigged and Unrigged'; 'The Woman as Pop Culture Obsolescent Theme'; 'The Unbeatable Madonna-Whore Combination'; 'The Irrelevant Crown on the Throne of Mediocrity'; 'Miss America as Dream Equivalent to ——'; and 'Miss America as Big Sister Watching You' (in Morgan 1970: 522–4).

6 Among the 'classics': Susan Brownmiller, *Against Our Will* (1975); Mary Daly, *Gyn/Ecology* (1978); Angela Davis, *Women, Race and Class* (1983); Andrea Dworkin, *Woman-Hating* (1974); Germaine Greer, *The Female Eunuch* (1970); Susan Griffin, *Rape: The Power of Consciousness* (1979) and *Woman and Nature* (1978); Adrienne Rich, 'Compulsory heterosexuality and lesbian existence' (1980). See also the anthologies *Sisterhood is Powerful* (Robin Morgan, ed., 1970) and *Woman in Sexist Society* (Vivian Gornick and Barbara Moran, eds, 1971).

7 See Nancy Fraser (1989) and Nancy Hartsock (1990) for a very different view, which criticises Foucault's conception of power for failing to allow for the sorts of differentiations I describe here.

8 See the section on 'Discipline and the female subject' in Diamond and

Quinby (1988), especially Sandra Bartky's piece 'Foucault, femininity, and the modernisation of patriarchal power'. See also Kathryn Pauly Morgan (1991).
9 For my use of 'postmodernism', see note 3.
10 This was said by Janice Radway in an informal presentation of her work, Duke University, spring 1989.
11 For my use of 'normalisation' and 'resistance', see note 2.

BIBLIOGRAPHY

Bartky, S.L. (1988) 'Foucault, femininity and the modernization of patriarchal power', in I. Diamond and L. Quinby (eds) *Feminism and Foucault: Reflections on Resistance*, Boston: Northeastern University Press.
Baudrillard, J. (1983) *Simulations*, New York: Semiotext (e).
Bordo, S. (1980) 'Organized sex', *Cross Currents*, XXX(3): 194–8.
—— (1985) 'Anorexia nervosa: psychopathology as the crystallization of culture', *Philosophical Forum*, 17, 2: 73–103.
—— (1990a) 'Reading the slender body', in M. Jacobus, E. Fox Keller and S. Shuttleworth (eds) *Body/Politics: Women and the Discourses of Science*, New York and London: Routledge.
—— (1990b) 'Material girl: the effacements of postmodern culture', *Michigan Quarterly Review*, XXIX(4): 653–78.
—— (1991) 'Postmodern subjects, postmodern bodies: a review essay', *Feminist Studies*, 18(1): 159–76.
—— (1993) *Unbearable Weight: Feminism, Western Culture and the Body*, Berkeley: University of California Press.
Brownmiller, S. (1975) *Against Our Will*, New York: Bantam.
Butler, J. (1990) *Gender Trouble: Feminism and the Subversion of Identity*, London: Routledge.
Collins, A. (1991) 'Abreast of the bra', *Lear's*, 4(4): 76–81.
Cott, N. (1987) *The Grounding of Modern Feminism*, New Haven, CT: Yale University Press.
Daly, M. (1978) *Gyn-Ecology*, Boston: Beacon.
Davis, A. (1983) *Women, Race and Class*, New York: Vintage.
Davis, K. (1991) 'Remaking the she-devil: a critical look at feminist approaches to beauty', *Hypatia*, 6(2): 21–43.
Diamond, I. and Quinby, L. (eds) (1988) *Feminism and Foucault: Reflections on Resistance*, Boston: Northeastern University Press.
Dworkin, A. (1974) *Woman-Hating*, New York: Dutton.
Fiske, J. (1987) *Television Culture*, New York: Methuen.
Foucault, M. (1977) 'The eye of power', in C. Gordon (ed. and trans.) *Power/Knowledge*, New York: Pantheon.
—— (1979) *Discipline and Punish*, New York: Vintage.
—— (1980) *The History of Sexuality*, vol I: *An Introduction*, New York: Vintage.
—— (1983) 'The subject and power', L. Sawyer (trans.), in H.L. Dreyfus and P. Rabinow (eds) *Michel Foucault: Beyond Structuralism and Hermeneutics*, Chicago: University of Chicago Press.

—— (1989) 'How much does it cost for reason to tell the truth?', an interview with P. Pasquino in *Foucault Live*, New York: Semiotext (e).

Fraser, N. (1989) 'Foucault on modern power: empirical insights and normative confusions', in N. Fraser, *Unruly Practices: Power, Discourse and Gender in Contemporary Social Theory*, Minneapolis: University of Minnesota.

Gornick, V. and Moran, B. (eds) (1971) *Woman in Sexist Society*, New York: Mentor.

Greer, G. (1970) *The Female Eunuch*, New York: McGraw-Hill.

Griffin, S. (1978) *Woman and Nature: The Roaring Inside Her*, New York: Harper Colophon.

—— (1979) *Rape: The Power of Consciousness*, New York: Harper & Row.

Hartsock, N. (1990) 'Foucault on power: a theory for women?', in L. Nicholson (ed.) *Feminism/Postmodernism*, New York and London: Routledge.

hooks, b. (1990) *Yearning: Race and Gender and Cultural Politics*, Boston: SouthEnd Press.

Johnson, D. (1989) 'The body: which one? whose?', *The Whole Earth Review*, Summer: 4–8.

Morgan, K.P. (1991) 'Women and the knife: cosmetic surgery and the colonization of women's bodies', *Hypatia*, 6(3): 25–53.

Morgan, R. (ed.) (1970) *Sisterhood is Powerful: An Anthology of Writings from the Women's Liberation Movement*, New York: Vintage.

Omolade, B. (1983) 'Hearts of darkness', in A. Snitow, C. Stansell and S. Thompson (eds) *Powers of Desire*, New York: Monthly Review Press.

Rich, A. (1980) 'Compulsory heterosexuality and lesbian existence', *Signs*, 5(4): 631–60.

Willamette Bridge Liberation News Service (1971) 'Exercises for men', *The Radical Therapist*, December-January.

Wollstonecraft, M. (1988) 'A vindication of the rights of women', in A. Rossi (ed.) *The Feminist Papers*, Boston: Northeastern University Press.

Zerilli, L. (1991) 'Rememoration or war? French feminist narrative and the politics of self-representation', *Differences*, 3(1): 1–19.

Chapter 9

Violence, power and pleasure
A revisionist reading of Foucault from the victim perspective[1]
Dean MacCannell and
Juliet Flower MacCannell

INTRODUCTION

Foucault's relationship to feminism is a curious one, highlighted by the fact that, unlike Lacan and Lévi-Strauss, he never made the 'woman question' central to his enquiry. He invested instead in distancing *the self* from subjectivity marked and shaped by sexual identification. In an undisguised moralism which is central to his project, he argued that sexual identification should not be the foundation of the self; nor should sexual practices be the object of the exercise of authority and power, including the power to define, name and categorise. His writings are sympathetic to women, children and the 'sexually deviant' (all victims of oppressive and exclusionary exercises of power), but only to set up his argument that collective liberation requires rendering all markers of sex insignificant. In a late interview (Rabinow 1982: 340–1) Foucault specifically denied the importance of sexuality, emphasising that this was not a contradiction, but an extension and affirmation of his earlier reduction of sexuality to discourse practices. Foucault provides an alternative parade, from ancient to early modern times, of other virtual formations of the self, analysing their accommodations with (or provision of obstacles against) *pleasure* and *power*.

In this chapter we focus on these two central concerns of Foucault's – *power and pleasure* – but we relate them back to women. We critically examine these two concepts and bring them together in an analysis of women's relation to pleasure when it is 'structured' and disturbed by the free use of power upon her; that is, when woman is a 'victim'.

Throughout Foucault's work, power is distinguished from force. Power is the realm of freedom, the field of possibilities no one owns: 'power is exercised by free subjects only over free subjects and only in so far as they are free' (Foucault 1983: 221). Devoid of all taint of 'force', power is granted a neutral if not benign character: as one feminist reads him, Foucault's 'power' operates to 'structure' but not to 'force' (Sawicki 1986: 30).[2] Deeming it a pure, impartial drive to structure, Foucault wanted to demonstrate that power was open to all, even when it appears to be held by a few.[3] Similar to Weber's 'bureaucracy', power is a mode hypothetically available for multiple users. We will show, however, that Foucault's crucial assumption that power is neutral does not hold, either theoretically or empirically, for women.

Foucault, like Nietzsche, wants us to be able to supplant power-holders without falling prey to the 'slave' morality which historically accompanies reversals in power relations.[4] Since traditional, especially sex-based, identities mainly serve as excuses for regulating and controlling the individuals caught up in them, Foucault thinks these should yield eventually to a more or less orderly chaos of 'new forms' of identity under the dominance-neutral regulation of a 'critical self': power is Kantian in its outlines. He declares his intention to 'adequately represent all power relations and all possibility of power relations' (quoted in Rabinow 1982: 380), with power again defined as what holds only over 'free subjects' (Sawicki 1986: 30). By viewing historical practices of power at a 'critical distance', Foucault aspires to render them merely impotent, local 'procedures', replaceable by any number of other possible procedures.

The ascription of 'neutrality' to technologies of power is not disturbing in itself. We have, however, attempted here to look at the same systemic questions from the other side, from the perspective of the victims of power. From this viewpoint we find 'neutrality' is less an essential characteristic of power than it is a method or a mode of power. We find in 'neutrality' the main technique used by the powerful to cover or justify their use of violence. We hope to demonstrate, using a method closely derived from Foucault's own, that hiding violence behind the pretence of 'neutrality' requires substantial concrete historical, institutional, mythic and psychic supports, aggressively promoted throughout the culture and economy.

We re-approach the question of the 'self' and new forms of identity starting with the question of why violent assault attacks the 'pleasures of the self' that Foucault thought would eventually be the promise of power, not the object of its destructive drive. We are concerned, that is, that Foucault's vision may have been prematurely Utopian; that redefinition of sexual and other identities remains subject to ancient power relations and violence even, or especially, in our postmodern epoch; that if some appear to escape tyranny based on their categorisation it is because they have been allowed to escape only to serve power by masking its effectiveness; that power is not neutral, diffuse and freely available but fiercely protected by those who hold it and their agents; and finally that threats and the actual use of force and violence remain essential to the exercise of power. We will show how Foucault was himself enough of an advocate of power that he could not identify or speak in the voice of the victim of violence. When he does speak of and for these victims he does not speak from their perspective, nor does he incorporate their 'local' knowledge into under-standing local practices of power.

In this chapter, we attend closely to the words of actual victims of violence to supplement Foucault's 'discursive practices' with specific regard for woman's way to language. To this end we have utilised narratives and oral histories of women who have been victims of familial sexual abuse, especially inter-personal violence from someone of the opposite sex. We will show that the abuser is often self-identified as benignly paternal, and that his aim is to attack the woman's experience of her own pleasure.

Methodologically, we stay close to the edge of violence, between acts of violence and their subjective appropriation. Independent of what happens to the body, the most violent acts are those resulting in long-term or permanent damage to the victim's subjective functioning, extending to the subjective functioning of those who would try to love her afterwards. An assault is serious in the degree that it fragments subjectivity or constantly 'breaks in' on the inner dialogue of the victims and those who are victim-identified to the point that they can no longer conduct themselves in a way that can be termed 'normal'.[5] Victims describe the experience of their assaults as receding but never disappearing from memory. Even those who are traumatised to the point that they cannot remember exactly what happened to them carry their violation around in their memory as a 'thing' (Cardinal 1983).[6]

EVERYDAY VIOLENCE AND ITS SUBJECTIVE EFFECTS

That some are privileged to think of their power as neutral, to think of themselves and those with whom they enter into power relations as 'free', is based on the suppression of violence. This suppression is so effective and complete that in polite society (and theory) it is regarded as 'sick' to discuss the possibilities for violence that exist by virtue of the physical co-presence of humans. The most obvious is the most overlooked. Every human encounter can be an occasion for nasty looks, verbal abuse, humiliation, insult, defilement. Every human body is potentially both weapon for and subject to physical assault, ranging from being roughed up or beaten, to rape, mayhem, torture, dismemberment. Violence is another realm where we are reminded of the narrowness of the scope of 'social norms' and social theory by those whom the norms of civil order, of 'civilisation', have dramatically failed to protect: abused children, the sexually deviant, and women who are kept in their place by physical force.[7]

Some victims over-conform to the mundane requirements of daily life, making a fetish of schedules, minor details of job performance, study habits, fine points of personal appearance, asepsis in housework, etiquette, and so on, attempting to prove to themselves and others that they are psychologically 'fine' by demonstrating a capacity for total involvement in current small matters at hand. The determined investment in proving focus and commitment may be manic, or frequently interrupted by periods of dramatic incapacity in these regards.[8] The situation of the victim is not unlike that of one who secretly carries an unregistered hand gun or a gem of exceptionally high value and must move 'casually' through crowded public space. No matter how appropriately involved the victim may successfully appear to be, her 'thing' is the real centre of all her subsequent dealings and affairs.[9]

Other victims of violence are fully incapacitated when it comes to the simplest day-to-day tasks, and cannot even fake a semblance of hyper-normality. For example, the anorectic is 'surely the most startling and stark illustration of how cavalier power relations are with respect to the motivations and goals of individuals, yet how deeply they are etched on our bodies, and how well our bodies serve them' (Bordo 1988: 109). Others have disabling memory disorders, lose their voice,[10] attempt murder or suicide, have terrifying flashbacks, live in a state of perpetual fear, lose their libido and other desires, are unable minimally to care for themselves or their children, unable to enter into or maintain friendships, and so on.

The cause of *subjective damage* is not as easily established as trauma from puncture wounds, burning, gun shots, strangulation, bludgeoning and other physical tortures. There is no point-for-point correspondence between the severity of physical injury and associated subjective response to it. The emotional recovery of a woman whose skull is fractured by a mugger who pushes her down on the street and takes her purse is quicker and more complete than recovery from a rape which does not break the skin. Nor can the 'test' of subjective violence be the Anglo-American legal definition involving the perpetrator's *intent* to do harm. The case record contains numerous examples of ultra-religious incestuous fathers who tell the courts that they engage in sexual relations with their own children for the 'good of the family'. They explain, with apparent sincerity, that if their daughters can have their sexual needs met at home, they will not bring shame on themselves and their family by 'sinning' with promiscuous boys in the community. Assailants can inflict severe psychological damage while masking their violence from themselves and their victims behind a screen of 'good intentions' or high moral ideals.[11] By contrast, peasant victims of the cruellest *intentionally* inflicted political tortures do not necessarily lose focus or identity and, if they are released or escape, sometimes try to return to their destroyed fields and villages with unabated commitment to rebuilding their lives even before their physical injuries heal: the evident cruel intention of the torturer may actually become a component of the victims' ability to recover.[12]

In the realm of intra- and inter-subjective violence a word or a 'look' can do more lasting harm than physical injury. Elizabeth Stanko (1985: 23) comments: 'The father who fondles his genitals while he stares at his daughter as she undresses invades his child's feelings of security' (in Women's Research Centre 1989: 81). Intra-psychically, there is more at risk here than can be glossed by reference to the child's emotional or physical security. When a girl notices her father, or other adult male relative, staring in a way that clearly communicates to her he is thinking about her in a sexual way, and if she lacks the sophistication to interpret his act as a serious failing on his part, minimally she will begin to see herself as a curious object of misplaced desire.[13] Even if the father only looks, and never follows through with physical molestation or rape, the daughter may not eventually be able to relate to her own sexuality except as something outside of herself, alien and powerful; something she must rigorously attach to things not ordinarily thought of as 'sexual'; something she must diplomatically mute in order to maintain personal safety and domestic peace; something she will perhaps someday be able to leave behind in the house or the grave of her father.

Some victims try subjectively to assimilate their assault, even brutal assault, through the expedient of blaming themselves for having made a simple mistake that had unfortunate but predictably understandable consequences. In one case, a young woman caught the wrong bus in New York which took her to the wrong side of Central Park:

> She got out and realised her mistake. It was about five o'clock in the afternoon. She decided to walk through the park. On the way she met this gang of boys, about five or six of them, aged ten to maybe eighteen. They all successively raped her. She got raped like a few times by that gang. Then she started to run after they were done and got stopped another time by this huge guy. He raped her. And then she ran the rest of the way home. . . . It was written up in the *Spectator*. She was interviewed about a week later. She said it didn't bother her. She just realised what the situation was, and she was in the wrong. She wasn't traumatised by it at all. She said, 'I was in the wrong place at the wrong time. I made a mistake and this weird thing happened to me.' She wasn't traumatised by it. Really weird.
>
> (Reported by Wachs 1988: 118)

This account suggests the socio-geographic *location* of a violent act may have much to do with the way it insinuates itself into subjectivity. A woman who is raped 'in the security of her own home' is also robbed of the opportunity casually to blame herself. Brutalisation under 'expected circumstances' apparently allows the victim to retain a sense of her own power to choose – even to 'take back the night' on the streets. Far from excusing them, she renders her assailants ultimately powerless where it counts for her – the power to define her subjectivity and her sexuality. US Army Major Rhonda Cornum commented on her sexual abuse by Iraqi soldiers after her helicopter was shot down in the recent Gulf War:

It was irritating but not devastating. . . . I know all the feminist sensitivity groups think I'm a terrible person for not being traumatised more. . . . If you had to give me a choice between having a man's fingers in my rectum vs. having a tooth exploded out of my mouth with the spark from a car battery (something that happened to a major in the Air Force) let's be reasonable . . . which one of the things would you pick?

(*San Francisco Chronicle*, 14 August 1992: D4)

However ill-begotten such subjective accommodations might be from the standpoint of justice, apparently they are providing protection against severe subjective damage.

Location and relationship are also factors in post-assault interventions by authorities who might help the victim. If a woman is beaten or raped in her own home by a family member she may not have recourse to external authority. In a classic 'double bind', the isolation of the victim increases as her social distance from the perpetrator and the scene of the crime decreases. Weisman (1992: 100) reports:

Historically, the police have been reluctant to intervene in a scene of domestic violence, a fact partially explained by the social beliefs that a home is a 'man's castle' and interference in private family 'spats' is wrong. They have been trained to make every effort to keep the family unit together – an approach that keeps a battered woman in a very dangerous environment. . . . Boston City Hospital reports that 70 percent of the assault victims treated in its emergency rooms are women who have been attacked by a husband or lover in their homes. Richard Gelles determined that scenes of violence are most frequently enacted in the kitchen.

POWER AND VIOLENCE

The violence that re-organises the personality of the victim is neither essentially in the act itself nor in the subject. The relationship between the victim and her assailant, and the type of crime (especially sexual versus other forms of violence) produce subjective responses to violence which retain significant incongruities (even when socio-spatial *context* is taken into consideration). The paradox of violence is that sometimes the subject can be ripped into by a glance, while at other times it holds tight against relentless brutality. In searching for a solution to the riddle of subjective violence, we take clues from Foucault's separation of power from force.[14]

In his earliest writings, Foucault *did* link power to the threat and use of force. Eventually, certainly by the mid-1970s, Foucault turned away from his original approach to power as based on 'Nietzsche's hypothesis', on the capacity to wage war, on political repression. He declared he was more concerned with the triangle of 'power, right, truth' (Foucault 1980: 93). We do not disagree with his eventual equation of power and truth which he so masterfully and ironically turned against Greek, Christian and Enlightenment variants of the same equation: 'we must produce truth as we must produce wealth, indeed we must produce truth in order to produce wealth in the first place' (ibid.). We do argue, however, that the theoretical connection of 'power, right, truth' can be strengthened by renewed consideration of the relationship of power to force and violence. Power claims the right to determine ground rules for what constitutes the truth, but it does not always enforce its claim on the truth by non-violent means. Once their 'truth' is questioned, there is very little left to the powerful except to become violent.

After the Enlightenment, Foucault argued, power no longer emanated from the patriarchal or sovereign negative imperative: 'no!' 'thou shalt not'. Power became not merely prohibitive but constitutive and diffuse. In the place of a sovereign ruler and his subjects emerged a complex system of differentiated social arrangements, each individual the product of local configurations of power. The 'sovereign subject' gave way to multiple identities forged by diverse institutional mechanisms of supervision, surveillance and review, collectively conceived by Foucault as *the gaze* and implemented by new panoptic school and prison architecture and administration, psychiatric method, social science survey techniques, medical and economic record-keeping.[15] The power of *the gaze* constructs each individual identity as a unique combination of medical, driving and prison records, job and school résumés, credit reports, postal addresses, charge-card purchase records and so on. Replacing the sovereign by *the gaze* renders individual empowerment and self-definition historically 'there for the taking'. We need only follow the same historical lines of force, ridding ourselves of the last vestiges of gender, ethnic and class-based subjectivity, eventually constituting ourselves, each and every one of us in our own individuality and specificity.

Foucault's *gaze* is interested and involved or involving; it intends, or frames its object, and thus nominates itself as a model for a powerful 'desubjectification', liberating the subject from its previous class, gender and other definitions, limits and restrictions. It is exactly at this point in his theory that it is helpful to allow in a bit more dialectic than Foucault usually allowed: there is a temptation, strongest among the powerless, to identify with power – the all-powerful gaze is the post-industrial version of the all-seeing god.[16]

What is historically new is an effective mechanism for suppressing the apparent need for violence in the exercise of power. The use of force is unnecessary to the extent that individuals identify with and internalise the gaze of authority and nicely comport themselves exactly as their leaders and oppressors would want. The distinctive site of *modern* power, as opposed to traditional forms, is not an organ or arm of political, military or economic strength. It lies instead in the exigencies of exposure, constant real and imagined surveillance emanating from a generalised subjectivity that is 'power' or 'authority' in the abstract. Individuals, rendered powerless by the gaze, must identify with the very power shaping their lives if they are to seem to re-gain any power or authority for themselves. Thus, the site of modern power shifts to the micro-practices of everyday life: power is 'in' all of us, or, better, it is manifest in and through the details of our behaviour as seen or seeable by others; everyone can assume primary responsibility for shaping power relations with others.

In this theoretical scheme, *violence* occupies the same place as it does in polite social discourse. It is assumed to be manifest only at the extreme social margin, outside ordinary relationships; it is thought to have been refined out of visibly proper behaviour and centralised and institutionalised exercises of power.[17]

it seemed important to accept that the analysis . . . should not concern itself with the regulated and legitimate forms of power in their central locations, with the general mechanisms through which they operate, and the continual effects of these. On the contrary, it should be concerned with power at its extremities, in its ultimate destinations, with those points where it becomes capillary, that is, in its more regional and local forms and institutions. Its paramount concern, in fact, should be with the point where power surmounts the rules of right which organise and delimit it and extends itself beyond them, invests itself in institutions, becomes embodied in techniques, and equips itself with instruments and eventually even violent means of material intervention.

(Foucault 1980: 96)

One conclusion to be drawn here is that if power is continuous and diffuse and operates only in and through everyday acts, and is non-violent except when it exceeds the bounds of its own legitimacy, each individual can safely align herself with the central version of the truth. They can become the site of legitimate applications of power or resistance to it and, if not overturn power, at least contribute to a reversal of existing power effects based on half-truths.[18]

THE 'EVENTUALLY VIOLENT MEANS OF INTERVENTION' AND THE VICTIM PERSPECTIVE

Foucault has provided an essentially nice formulation, one intended to be liberational. But it keeps an important part of human experience (assault) at arm's distance from theory and philosophy, making the entire framework questionable from the victim's perspective. It suggests that we should be witnessing a historical decline of physical violence and ongoing redistribution of power on the local level at a time when neither is happening.[19] Victims know that localised power in all its forms and applications remains supported by threats and actual use of violence and force.[20] They cannot dismiss the linkage between power, even legitimate power, and the threat of the use of force and violence, as Foucault was apparently able to dismiss it in 1976. Foucault's discovery of 'capillary' power operating throughout the body politic is essential, but it should be accompanied by an understanding of 'capillary violence'. Power did not leave forceful threat and the actual use of violence behind as it moved to the margins. Wheresoever power is found, violence is sure to be. Wheresoever resistance to power is encountered, force will be applied. Threats, or actual application of direct, legal or administrative violence back up all power. That this goes mainly overlooked is based solely on the victim's identification with, or belief in, authority as based on 'truth', 'knowledge', 'right' and so on.

We can identify three types of force or violence on which power continues to depend:

1 *Direct violence*: verbal abuse, physical brutality, rape, murder and so on, and threats thereof.

2 *Legal and/or bureaucratic violence*: formal filing of false accusations, arbitrary firings and evictions, insertion without due process of 'black marks' into a person's record, blacklisting, and any other (ab)use of rules and regulations for the sole purpose of destroying an individual's capacity to support themselves and their dependants, maintain minimal standards of shelter and safety, protection from disease and so on.

3 *Administrative violence*: zealous and sadistic execution of office in such a way that it destroys the life chances and sometimes the lives of those who come in contact with the organisation. Locally thought of as 'progressive' or 'hard nosed', 'responsible' administration, it is not an abuse of the *rules* as in item 2 above. Rather, it is a heartless, soul-killing over-application of rules and regulations. Fathers who are overmuch concerned with being a 'father figure' administer violence in their routine execution of office. Administrative violence ranges from petty authoritarianism to torture and 'administrative massacre' (Arendt 1964: 294) or genocide – all re-conceived as 'unfortunate' byproducts of enthusiastic organisational 'can doism'. Everyone is involved in the 'process' together so no one is responsible for it. Administrative violence is typically perpetrated by those whose personalities are already re-organised around being victims themselves. They have adapted to their own victimisation by transforming themselves into an administrative ideal: 'getting with the programme', without resistance to authority, their identity is organised around currying approval from their superiors through demanding abject servility from their inferiors.

These forms of violence can still be found in every kind of social arrangement and they crucially determine the subjectivity of victims. The victim demonstrates that violence, not the gaze, conveys power to the margins of society.

The Gulf War made clear that legitimate power has not abjured violence; that the diffusion of power has not necessarily broken up concentrations of power, and may have increased centralised power by federating with it; that the concentration of power is inseparable from the uneven distribution of the means of violence; that power may appeal to its juridical right to use violent force after the fact, but *right* is not necessarily a central concern in the application of power:

US defends burying alive Iraqi troops

Washington (Newsday)   The Pentagon said yesterday that a 'gap' in the laws governing warfare made it legally permissible during the gulf war for US tanks to bury thousands of Iraqi troops in their trenches and for US warplanes to bomb the enemy retreating along the so-called Highway of Death.

(*San Francisco Chronicle*, 11 April 1992: A10)

THE VICTIM AND THE GAZE

There are two forms of relationship of the victim to the gaze: *instrumental* and *identificatory*. Both are potentially two-way, with the figure of authority turning its gaze on the victim and the victim looking back. But in the case of instrumental gaze it is the 'looking' of authority that is crucial – snooping into the victim's affairs, maintaining an information base in order to increase the effectiveness of threat and so on. In the case of identificatory gaze, the victims' 'looking up' to authority is crucial – their desire to see themselves in the eyes of authority, to identify with Margaret Thatcher's 'firm resolve' and so forth. Of course, in a perfect fascist state, both would occur simultaneously and with equal intensity.

Administrative violence relies on the identificatory gaze, on individuals internalising the point of view of controlling authority, and carrying out their own oppression as their only means of seeming to have some authority of their own. This co-operation on the part of victims maintains the fiction that the gaze is sometimes not linked to violence, that there is such a thing as 'pure' authority with which we should all identify without having to be coerced or intimidated.

The linkage of the gaze to *direct violence* is not metaphoric via identification. It is instrumental, mechanical, pragmatic. The role of the gaze in acts of direct aggression is to isolate the victim as an object of intimidation, and instrumentally render harassment, attack or torture more effective or efficient.

After Foucault, critical theory has tended to attribute power to the gaze itself. We suggest that the gaze does not have power in itself but only in association with actual violence or identification with those capable of violence. There are grounds for the concern that the proliferation of technologies for monitoring the details of the everyday life of the average citizen may constitute a threat in themselves. Currently, 'routine' surveillance includes domestic spying on politically suspect individuals, employer requirements that employees take lie and urine tests, computerised databases which monitor everything from arrest and health records to handling of credit responsibilities, widely circulated lists of reading habits, consumer tastes and so on. But unless these unsavoury procedures are backed by serious threat (such as job loss, arrest or to personal safety) the effect of all this surveillance would only be to drown the record-keepers in their own data. One recalls Abby Hoffman's famous response to the dreaded question from the House Un-American Activities Committee, 'Are you now or have you ever been a member of the Communist Party?': 'Yes I am and the days of your government are numbered.' Because Hoffman (and others) had insufficiently internalised the gaze of authority, or were not enough impressed by the threat of force backing it and called its bluff, the House Committee disbanded. Government surveillance does nothing unless it is linked to the possibility of arrest, blacklisting or capital threat.

Everyday experience structurally and psychoanalytically binds power and the gaze. Power and the gaze are always linked in the mind of the intimidated. Those who fear being denied a livelihood or a place to live if an aspect of their medical or police record is revealed, or their sexual orientation is known, dread exposure as much as they fear denial. The pragmatic response is for the intimidated to focus on the gaze, not on possible violence against them which is more troubling to contemplate. The intimidated will try to pass unnoticed, to maintain a clean record, or if they cannot, they may attempt to deflect the gaze, to hide or modify test results, hypocritically mouth accommodating rhetoric, taking great care to represent themselves and their behaviour in a way they think appears as positive to their oppressors, or otherwise compromise themselves ethically in their attempts to appear 'correct'.

Victims of ongoing assault experience, as the most salient fact of their lives, need to identify with their oppressor. Under conditions where situations and psyches are organised in such a way that there is no alternative to be other than either a master or a slave, the victim of violence necessarily derives her sense of herself from the cruelty inflicted upon her and the cruelty she might inflict on others in her turn. Her hatred for her oppressor does not necessarily preclude her becoming emotionally dependent on him and his treatment of her.

NAMING: PHILOSOPHICAL VIOLENCE AND EVERYDAY VIOLENCE

Foucault (like Derrida 1976: 112) argued that the original form of violence is social categorisation; that is, to be named or to be identified as a member of a class. The social order is set up to protect this first 'proper naming'. The philosophical reflex is to reach behind this set-up. But only rigorous empirical investigation confronts the violent effects of this 'naming' in its full expression as experienced *by the victims*. Patricia's story:

> Jack abused me every way he could. . . . I have been spit on, cursed, kicked, strapped, hit with a clothes iron and other objects, including being beat from head to toe in one awful session. . . . So I went to the shelter. . . . So then on March 21st, he asked me to come to the house and get my things. He said he would give me some money so our son and I could leave the shelter and go to my parents' home. I believed him. I went. Company came. Jack was very loving, telling everyone how happy he was that I was back home, and how sweet and loving we were going to be from then on. Everyone left. He sure tricked me! After about thirty minutes, he started to beat me! He stripped me of all my clothes in front of my four year old son and beat me more. While my son was watching, Jack threw me down on the sofa, took his three big fingers and inserted them up my vagina and dug around until I started bleeding. Then he slapped me in the face with his bloody hand and made me smell it, calling me a 'stinking bitch'.
>
> (Hintz 1985: 50)

In the progression of this narrative, naming ('stinking bitch') is not a 'first violence' but rather a dramatic endpoint. Patricia's story logically follows a reverse cultural trajectory back to the 'originary' violence of the (im)proper name. In her 'natural', unnamed state, she was no more nor less a 'stinking bitch' than a 'brilliant flower'. Philosophically, to name her *anything* is a violation: 'stinking bitch' is no different from 'brilliant flower'; both names equally separate the subject from herself and inscribe her within a system of differences, denying her unique subjective integrity in order to make her a member of a class.

Patricia has been violated not just philosophically but also empirically. She can learn very little from the philosopher because she knows from her experience that on the empirical level there is no equivalency within the violence of the proper name. Perhaps the philosopher can learn something from the victim who would be quick to ask 'Who is naming whom?' and 'What's in the name?' The function of naming, of name-calling, of re-naming, being 'called out of one's name' (Angelou 1969: 91) in social practice may be exactly the opposite to that in philosophy. The name can be a violation, and the name equally can protect against violation. A process of re-naming, advanced most passionately in certain fictions and by psychoanalysis, is the only known cure for psychic wounds inflicted by previous names and blows. Physical violence can be stopped by counter-force; the fragmentation of the victim's subjectivity can be sutured by counter-naming.

In Foucault's reading of sexual categorisation as a violence second to the first naming, what is now known as the phallic or symbolic order can be seen as the protective apparatus set up around the 'proper name'. The institutional mechanism deployed to prevent a repetition of the first violence, the 'social contract', is supposed to protect us from violence if we agree to live within its terms. If we agree to them, all the 'forces of order' (phallicised paternal authority, the police, military and so on) will be directed not against ourselves but against others, against those who refuse to go along with the rules. We are supposed to accept our place in the symbolic order in exchange for its protection and because we are terrified to re-live the trauma of our original separation from nature, the violence of first naming.

Again, victims know that none of this is true. The victim knows human life was not just traumatic in the first place, or to begin with. It continues to be traumatic and terrifying, especially for the powerless and the underclasses, but even for the privileged. The only protection privilege provides is periodic blindness to terror;

false confidence based on the height of the walls erected between oneself and others. Ask the Kennedys. A merely imaginary phallic order offers no guarantee of protection. When they are at their best, at the scene of the crime, the 'forces of order' offer excuses and condolences. In cases of 'domestic disputes' the police often return the victim to the hands of her assailant. Sometimes the police sadistically join with the assailant in continuing to abuse the victim.

Modern functionaries who believe that their primary duty is to uphold a 'symbolic order' cannot both over-valorise phallic authority *and* prevent violent assault and abuse. It is a simple contradiction. Upholding the symbolic order in the form of paternal hierarchy requires a triple affirmation: first, that law-giving figures of authority always comport themselves as 'ideal fathers' – that is, are never unfair or inequitable in distributing justice and administering the common good; secondly, that figures of authority do not have any interests, needs or desires of their own other than the efficient and peaceful functioning of the part of the system under their control; and thirdly, that forceful or abusive behaviour does not routinely occur in the administration of legitimate institutions such as marriage or education. As *symbol*, the 'father figure' is a decent general model for balancing and modulating passions and drives, leading to the smooth functioning of modern democratic institutions at all levels. But victims know that this does not work in practice. The general model of paternal neutrality, denial and modulation is often an ideological fig leaf covering the actual practices of full enjoyment under cover of abusive authority.

Victims experience how figures in authority sometimes express unspeakable desires; that they, the victims, must bear the scars of abuse and also the blame for it. They know that when they are violated by authority they will be told there was a 'good reason' for it, they 'asked' for it – they left their door open, or became intoxicated and invited trouble; they acted insubordinate, sexy, uppity, so they deserved what they got; it was just punishment for their own misconduct; they had an 'attitude problem' and had quietly engaged in a campaign of subtle harassment of their own bringing retribution on themselves.

Thus when victims appeal to authority for protection, they predictably discover that authority is set up in advance to protect their assailant, who, by definition, stands in the position of power.

A woman who discovered that her husband, 'a full gospel minister', was regularly having sex with their thirteen-year-old daughter, filed for divorce and appealed to another minister for spiritual guidance:

> I was told by my minister that 'it would not be God's will to obtain a divorce'. Submit to him. The question I asked was: 'Anything he wants we have to do?' The minister's reply, 'He would not ask anything of us that was wrong.'
>
> (Hintz 1985: 12)

Later, when the daughter went to the same minister accusing her father in writing of sexual misconduct, the wife–mother reported:

> We were all called into the pastor's office and a 'hearing' was held. Jack was declared innocent; Alice guilty of lying on him. It was horrible! I remained silent all the time. I knew it was over for her . . . Jack was placed on a higher level in the church. Alice and I were on a lower level.
>
> (Hintz 1985: 13)

Another woman being stalked by her estranged husband appealed for help from the police:

> Another time he told me by phone what I was wearing and doing in my apartment. Late that night he phoned again saying he was going to blow my brains out and described in detail how he planned to do it. So I phoned the police. I was told they don't have time to go chasing ghosts. The officer then told me, 'If he shoots you give us a call.'
>
> (Hintz 1985: 16)

A woman repeatedly assaulted by her GI husband appealed to military authority:

> I remember lights flashing as he choked me and said he would kill me if I moved one more time. Another time when he was drunk again, he hit me and threw things around the house. I phoned the military police twice before they came. When they did arrive, my spouse was trying to kick the door off the wall. Then he began swinging at the police officer. I was shocked when one officer told Luis that he could hit his wife, but not them.
>
> (Hintz 1985: 17)

When this same woman went for counselling at the base, she was labelled 'a non-adapting military wife' and accused of being a 'recluse who drove her husband to drink'. The base psychologist suggested to her,

> the problem was in some way my fault. He then asked me if I had gone out on my husband and if I MASTURBATED!!! Again, at no time did we discuss . . . my husband's violence to me and his excessive drinking. I became so sick inside that I just walked out of the office.

(Hintz 1985: 17)

Not every victim is able silently to endure, or to walk out on unsupportive authority when it sides with the assailant. Some must actively participate in transferring the blame to themselves, often copping a plea to a lesser offence. A case-worker reports the experience of a woman who, when she was nine years old, complied with her father's demand for sex to 'comfort' him on the occasion of his own father's death:

> She responded 'by doing the same thing I did when I was three', and her father rubbed his erect penis against her body. But unlike when she was younger, this time he ejaculated and told her to take care of cleaning up the bed. The woman recalled her mother discovering the still-soiled sheets the next day. 'She got angry and accused me of, I guess, initiating something sexually with my father. I don't really remember, but I do remember that she was angry. So I tried to convince her that I'd wet the bed.'

(Women's Research Centre 1989: 121)

For these victims, authority and the law do not function to balance everyone's needs and suppress violence in a fraying 'symbolic' order. For them, 'law' and 'authority' are integral to the ongoing trauma and meaninglessness of experience. From the victim's rather than the philosopher's viewpoint, the law is definitely *not* the guarantor of a symbolic universe. The law and other symbolic expressions of authority open as many wounds as they close. We are both unequal *to* the law, and unequal *in* the eyes of the law. This is what the victims have taught us. And there will be no redress until there is a close examination of the perversion of the symbolic order; namely, exposure of the cover-up of violence that is routine to institutional administration.

... AND PLEASURE

Violence that results in damage to subjective functioning attacks sites of pleasure. This is the only common feature that we could find to acts of violence which effectively disrupt the personality of the victim. If there is pleasure in eating, the victim is forced to eat vomit. If there is pleasure in absolute trust of another human being, the baby is tossed into the air and not caught. If there is pleasure in appearance, the victim's face is slashed or doused with acid. Violent rape is the prototypical violent act directed at the core of subjective functioning because it attacks sites of the most intense pleasure. It also happens at the site men are required to restrict their own access to (that is, through marriage) as a condition of their assuming social positions of authority and power. Sexual violence marshals all the resources of biology and civilisation (philosophy, history, institutional forms, psychological pre-dispositions) at its disposal as it drives to disrupt pleasure.

Violence does not attack pleasure directly, but insinuates itself into the *relationship* of the subject to her own pleasure. Unlike animals, humans live in culture: our needs are not merely animal, but also culturally given. We do not just need food in order to survive, we desire a particular cuisine and ceremonial occasions for its consumption. We do not just need sex in order to reproduce ourselves biologically; we desire a certain kind of sex that is literally 'fantastic'. In short, cultural beings are already separated from any original capacity they might have had for the simple satisfaction of their needs. Culture is not set up to satisfy needs except incidentally and in passing. Culture stakes its future on its capacity to keep desire alive. In our modern cultural set-up, the central imperative has become the command, 'ENJOY'.

Obedience to the command 'enjoy thyself', or even 'have a nice day', is not as easy or pleasant as it appears. The relationship of the subject to its own pleasure is never easy, even 'impossible' (Zizek 1991).[21] The problem of recognising and understanding one's own desires, of relating to them, dealing with them, is a primary component of intimate relationships in the modern world. Intimates are supposed to confess not merely their desires but their anxieties and dreams relative to their desires. They are supposed to remind us of our own desires when they believe we fail to see them ourselves, and to help us to satisfy our desires, or to suppress them when they are destructive. Intimate relations are framed by a dialectic of surplus and lack. The role of intimates is simultaneously to support one another's desires, and to strive for ethical and aesthetic balance in the realisation of desire within a framework where enjoyment is always excess or lack.

Achieving balance in relating to pleasure is essential to the survival of any culture, but it also goes against the specific cultural dictate to enjoy, which links the subject back to *drive* more than *desire*. Without apologising for the apparent paradox, we are suggesting that in order for our culture to survive, we must fight against the tendencies for self- annihilation which are built into it, *and with which the violent identify*.

THE ECONOMICS OF VIOLENCE AND PLEASURE

The ultimate ground of violence is late capitalist economies and supporting postmodern culture. Within these macro-structures there must never be satisfaction, only constant desire. The solution to this problem is to over-drive desire; that is, to promote a desire for excess, for more than enough, a desire that stays alive even after it has been satisfied, a desire whose satisfaction only whets its appetite for more. The other side of this solution is to promote *lack* as taken-for-granted. This lack is not the mere absence of what is required to satisfy a human need; it is less than nothing. It is a minus or a negative that would require something (love, a paying job, cessation of violence) just to arrive at a point where one could begin to imagine experiencing pleasure or satisfying a desire. Excess feeds on lack in an endless and ever-expanding circle of desires that can never be satisfied.

Desire for excess and lack of enjoyment

In this context, it is troubling that Foucault identified the Utopia of philosophy with surplus and excess, a move recently seconded by Frances Bartkowski (1988).[22] So far no one has figured out how dependably to create excess and surplus in a society that is not class-based. Enjoyment of excess always escapes the worker. The worker can experience excess only as a loss, or surplus value: from the perspective of the workers, their loss is experienced as the surplus pleasure of others.[23] This structural violence of capitalism is identical to one which produces lasting subjective damage to its victim. Purely instrumental assaults that do not use force beyond that required to carry off some other crime, no matter how violent, rarely result in long-term personality disorders. A woman who has had her arm broken as her purse is taken can believe she was just in the wrong place at the wrong time (as in the Central Park incident above). If her arm is not broken as her purse is removed, but the assailant turns back just to break her arm after he already has her purse, it becomes another matter. The first attack was directed against her property; the second attack is clearly directed against her body but also against her sense of relief for having survived the first attack – that is, it was directed against her pleasure. Any demonstration of mastery which seems to have no practical or economic purpose affirms the hyper-phallic resolution of the deepest contradictions of capitalist culture (see J. MacCannell 1991b). The assailant mimics the capitalist when he says, in effect, 'I have it all but I can still take more; I can push you beyond your physical limits to extract even more than I want, and I will never be satisfied; you thought when I took your purse and the rewards for your labour that you had given everything you had to give, but I can continue to take and reduce you to less than nothing; your arm was nothing, I can do much more than that; even if I kill you, I am not necessarily done with you.'[24] Sub-proletarian domestic brutality may be as close as some victims and their assailants ever get to full participation in the general economic and cultural modelling of their 'civilisation'.

In one form or another, the dialectical opposition of excess and lack appears in all victim narratives, not always as starkly as in the following incident. A woman tells of her husband coming home with a cousin and (uncharacteristically) with groceries. She was surprised but delighted because he ordinarily spent his earnings on whisky and beer to the point that the children were suffering from malnutrition.

> William walked in carrying one bag after another of groceries acting like a big shot. 'Look what I brought for you. Now you can . . . eat.' As soon as his cousin left I started making salami sandwiches. All of a sudden, like a raging mad man, he grabbed the meat and threw it on the floor stomping on it . . . . He hollered, 'I did not bring this home for you. I'd rather give it to the dog.' We just stood there frozen in our tracks.
>
> (Hintz 1985: 10)

At all levels of society, rather than balancing needs (for example, the needs within a family), the play of excess and lack can become a ferocious will to pleasure directed against the possibility of pleasure of specific others. In domestic violence, childhood incest, rape and other hate crimes, the assailant may be motivated to commit the crime *for no other reason* than to affirm his will to pleasure, to 'have it all' while reducing his victims to less than nothing, clumsily occupying the subject position of a classic capitalist.

Violence and the fragmentation of the victim's access to pleasure

Inter-and intra-subjective violence always involves a double fragmentation or separation. *First*, it breaks the relationship of the victim-subject to her own pleasure. This appears to be the precise aim (even it is unconscious) of violent crimes involving exposure and humiliation, degradation, oral, anal and vaginal penetration, food torture, sleep deprivation and so on.

> Jack would shake the bed in the night and wake me up. Then when I was awake he would tell me he did not shake the bed! I couldn't sleep because of my rapid pulse and nerves.
>
> (Hintz 1985: 12)

> We hardly had any food in our house. When we had meat in the house 'the man of the house' ate the steak because 'he was the breadwinner'. [He] would cut off the fat and douse it with Tabasco sauce and make my children eat it without any water.
>
> (Hintz 1985: 10)

> I do not like my husband's treatment of our children. He will feed the boys hot peppers. He knows both boys' faces break out red and they cry because it hurts. He laughs.
>
> (Hintz 1985: 30)

> [He came home drunk and] vomited in several rooms in the house and all over the new carpet. . . . [T]hen he sat me in the vomit and laughed because I was screaming. . . . Our nine year old daughter got out of bed and tried to make him let go of me. He yelled at me how much he hated me because I was too smart, clean and neat, and did not like his friends. Then he picked up a handful of vomit and tried to make me eat it. He asked, 'What is the matter you f . . . bitch, is it too good for you?' . . . I fainted.
>
> (Hintz 1985: 18)

Once assaulted in one or several of these ways, it is difficult for the
victim to restore the affected body part or function, or region of
subjectivity, to its former role in the satisfaction of desire without
carrying forward the stain of the assault. There is often a
compulsion to repeat aspects of the assault.[25]

Fragmentation of the victim's relationship to her own pleasure
inevitably extends to anyone who would attempt to love her after
her assault. Frantz Fanon (1963: 249-316) describes the case of an
Algerian revolutionary whose wife was raped by French
authorities because she refused to tell them his whereabouts. She
apparently recovered from her ordeal, but the husband was
unable to continue to love her physically or mentally. *Because* she had
protected him, he could only relate to her via his guilt, never again
via desire. An assault that goes to the level of subjective functioning always leads to a break or a hitch in the discourse of pleasure
and desire; that is, the assault is always there, if only as what is
being overcome. The victim cannot entertain a relationship to her
own pleasure and desires, nor can her future intimates enter
relationship with their desires for her without perplexity. Some
victims become trapped in a circular bind in which they must heal
both physically and mentally before they can even think of their
own pleasure again, but they cannot heal without experiencing
pleasure. Alternatively, the victim relates to her own pleasure
defensively and subversively always 'just around the corner' from
her thoughts about her assault(s) and her assailant(s).

Individuals with a history of childhood physical and sexual
abuse remark that even though they hate the violence and know
it is 'wrong', they nevertheless continue to associate sexual
pleasure and love with violent abuse to the point that they miss the
violence and have difficulty experiencing intense pleasure
without it. After freeing herself from her assailants, a woman who
was physically and sexually abused as a child and as an adult
comments:

> as weird as it may seem, I sometimes miss being beaten! If
> someone is good to me and doesn't abuse me, I get moody. I'm
> learning to analyse this emotion and am usually able to pull
> myself out of it. It is something I have to battle all the time. I do
> get depressed.
>
> (Hintz 1985: 57)

One of Bass and Davis's (1988: 261-2) respondents relates:

When I was little, my mother would start yelling and screaming and throwing things . . . and what that usually meant was that I could count on my father being in my room later. So there was a connection established between violent scenes and sex. And that's been repetitive in my adult life. It's the 'break up to make up' syndrome. Sex is always better after a fight. . . . I know when I was beat up by my last lover, one of the things that really frightened me was that when I was on the floor and she was kicking me, I flashed back on my mother. I had no idea who was hitting me. My lover pulled me up by the hair, and I knew at that very moment that it could only end in two ways. One was me taking the door to the right, which was outside. Or I could take the door to the left, which was to the bedroom.

Bass and Davis (1988: 262) remark:

Many survivors can feel sexual arousal or have orgasms only if sex incorporates some aspect of abuse. One woman could climax only if she imagined her father's face. Another only if she imagined being bound or raped. Another only if she was stimulated in the way her neighbour stimulated her as a child. Another only if she fantasised being the abuser herself. Many masturbate while reading incest literature. 'For weeks on end I compulsively read about incest – *If I should Die Before I Wake* in one hand and my vibrator in the other.'

Others who manage to escape from someone they love who is also harming them (an abusive father or husband) may never escape a *fear of desire itself*, feeling that they must break off any growing intimacies even, or especially, safe ones, of which they have the least experience and where they tend to feel most vulnerable.

Thus the first aim of violence is to block the victim from any relationship to her own pleasure not mediated by the violence. This is not the same as blocking pleasure itself. A few victims report that their capacity for pleasure has been destroyed either temporarily or permanently. But it is more common for pleasure to become localised, specifically associated with or contained within the assault, owned by the assailant, or alternatively defined by the assault as occupying an unattainable libidinal terrain at a great remove from the assault. Some victims report achieving orgasm only with difficulty and by shutting out the immediate situation of intercourse by concentrating on a neutral image such as rowing a boat, looking at a waterfall or a ball of pink fuzz, and so forth.

The second aim of violence is to separate and isolate the victim from intimate relationships with all others except her past, present and future assailants and perhaps those whom she herself might wittingly and unwittingly abuse. One of Bass and Davis's (1988: 256) respondents expresses great but perhaps groundless expectation for future intimate relations:

> it's going to be difficult. . . . [W]hen I imagine having a lover, I'm making love to him and everything is going along beautifully until he takes out his penis. And then I vomit all over the floor. . . . So whoever I'm with is going to have to have an understanding of that and a secure enough sense of his own maleness that he isn't going to take it personally.

Intimacy can only be built from mutual involvement or complicity in the other's relationship to her and his own pleasure. Violence with lasting subjective impact on the victim abolishes the victim's relationship to her own pleasure by placing it under the control of her assailant. Once the victim can no longer freely relate to her own pleasure, she has also lost the basis for intimate ties with others. Another of Bass and Davis's respondents reports:

> Sex is the act of being out of control. It is wonderful, but it terrifies me to give up control. It's the approach that stops me. I have to stop and think, 'Do I want this to be happening? Or is it because someone is approaching me and I am letting it happen?' If I initiate it's much easier. Then I'm the one feeling sexual, I *know* I'm feeling sexual, and I am pretty sure I'm not being molested.
>
> (Bass and Davis 1988: 258)

As occurs in the other narratives and accounts, what would be a fleeting moment of doubt for a person without a history of abuse becomes an impossible reality for the victim. She clearly expresses a desire to repeat her rapist's act of taking total control of the situation. She believes she does this in order to reassure herself she is 'feeling sexual'. But she cannot '*know*' this with any certainty. Her emphasis on '*know*' is a form of denial. She may be 'feeling sexual', or she may want desperately to believe she is 'feeling sexual' to cover her identification with her assailant, her repetition of her assault, this time with her in the position of the assailant, or at least 'in control'.

Intimacy and the subjectively damaged victim

One-dimensional (therapeutic and other) quasi-intimate relationships can form between victims and non-victims, provided that the non-victim party is willing to subordinate interest to the victim's impossible reality; namely, her way of accommodating herself, or not, to her own pleasure. Thus the non-victim partner to quasi-intimate relations with a victim may discover that he or she must always be on guard to avoid certain behaviours, practices or topics, or be constantly prepared eventually to find out that innocent gestures were, in fact, unwanted, threatening, or otherwise meaningful in ways that could not be anticipated. Alternatively, if the subjective damage to the victim is great, the non-victim party may discover there is only one real topic of every conversation or non-verbal encounter, no matter how varied the ostensible issues.

The victim is separated one-by-one from her family and friends, who cannot understand what it means to lose touch with one's own pleasures and desires. Once she has been isolated, even or especially in memory, by her assailant to the point that he is her last 'friend', or the only person she can appeal to for relief from his brutality, he can exploit every interaction as an opportunity to remind her of her utter exclusion from humanity. One of the most characteristic features of victim narratives is the recollection of the repetition of a specific violent act in spite of pathetic pleading to stop. Whether it is the brutal thrusting or blows of a rapist, throwing a child against a ceiling or a wall, what stays in the mind of the victims is that they pleaded for it to stop and still 'he did it again, and again, and again'.

> When my son Donald was six weeks old, he woke up crying for his 2:00 a.m. bottle. That made my husband mad because he was woke up. He grabbed that poor innocent baby like a mad man and threw and bounced him real hard from the bed to the ceiling about ten times. William turned blue and lost his breath screaming at him.
>
> (Hintz 1985: 10)

There is no clearer demonstration of complete exclusion from humanity than to be reduced to something less than human, even less than animal: one who is unworthy of sympathy or pity. It is striking that half of humanity is routinely subject to this exclusion.

Grafting the assault experience on to the victim's relationship to her own pleasure does more than merely block it. It demands, insidiously, that all future intimates find her pleasure *only* through her assault, leaving them 'on their own' with respect to her: that is, she cannot help them find their way to her pleasure because she cannot know the way there herself. She may experience pleasure, but only clouded in mystery, as a lucky accident, or by rigorously excluding others from the process.

GUILT AND THE LIMITS OF PLEASURE IN FOUCAULT

Impeding the victim's relationship essentially takes the form of *guilt*. It is here that we find Foucault potentially most instructive for the troubled subjectivity of the victim trying to re-connect with her own pleasure. Throughout Foucault's work he challenges the 'deep division that lies between innocence and guilt' (Bouchard 1977: 227).[26] The original division of guilt and innocence was, for him, the imposition of sexual division by 'culture' (that is, language);[27] sexual division is, structurally, the first guilt; going beyond it promises innocence, but at a price: 'culture' as we know it.[28] Only the absolute guilt of 'the Christian world of fallen bodies' (ibid.: 30) had come close, for Foucault, to representing adequately an

> inability to divide continuous forms of desire, of rapture, of penetration, of ecstasy, of that outpouring which leaves us spent . . . [these] lead us right to the heart of a divine love of which they were both the outpouring and the source of returning upon itself.
>
> (Bouchard 1977: 30)

Foucault joined Bataille in celebrating Sade as reviving the possibility of happiness in evil (Bouchard 1977: 49), with both divorced from moral contexts and diverted to the aims of pure self-fashioning.

The call is radical. Foucault's challenge, no less than Sade's, is issued to man – after God died – to retrieve the power to shape the self. Self-fashioning is to be undertaken without any of the customary pre-constraints. Thus Foucault's support for the 'criminal', the 'insane', the women and children is less a classical 'liberal' posture than a demand for liberation from all restrictions on pleasure and power.[29]

We have argued that Foucault shows a premature Utopianism on the issue of power. Can we now say he is more successful on the issue of pleasure, especially feminine pleasure? The promise of a pleasure beyond guilt, of mutuality and of reciprocity were also heralded by Sade, who proclaimed a philosophy in the bedroom that advanced Kant's sexual egalitarianism by extending the right to enjoyment: 'I have the right to enjoy your body, and you have the right to enjoy mine.'[30]

But, despite his undeniable authenticity of feeling for it, we find Foucault disappointing on the question of pleasure taken to the limit. His goal of a non-sexed, generic *jouissance* is debatable in the light of the everyday experience of women. More disheartening theoretically, he fails to address the enforced division of 'woman' from the signifier – the structural grounding for the abusive behaviours described here.

Some feminists have none the less identified with Foucault's dream of self-sovereignty beyond the subject; that is, of deriving power from neutering, finding a path through Foucault to pleasure for women – especially in the lesbian sado-masochist theatre of 'woman as victim'.[31] Even if a new, positive, theatrical space of pleasure can be opened by Foucault for the female victim cured by perversion, pure horror can result when 'neutral' power and 'egalitarian' pleasure meet on the body of the woman. Recall that the logic of Foucault's quest for innocence in sexual sin eventually led him to participate in a movement to decriminalise rape.[32]

CONCLUSION

Foucault called for an unlimited series of new forms of self constituted by localised power relations among free subjects. His writing is, however, remarkably free of any specification of such 'new' forms, making few concrete proposals, and his Utopianism remains rooted in the present.[33] Unfortunately, in the case materials we reviewed we *did* find a nightmare version of Foucault's dream already inhabiting certain details of everyday life. With the exception of homosexuality and sado-masochism, Foucault chose not to provide a glimpse of concrete future liberations from subjectivity and sexuality. His real desire – for a Utopian present where 'deviants' could live free and undisturbed – remained unsung. Specifying future Utopias has often proved embarrassing to men of good will in the past and we do not wish to rebuke Foucault for any circumspection on this point: he felt he was opening the way for multiplicities.

We can, however, assess his effort to revive subjugated discourses by bringing them all back to the singular question of power. As an inherently neutral machine, Foucault is indifferent to who gets to start power up, to operate it, and for how long: it becomes the great Equaliser.[34] By characterising all subjects of *subjugated* knowledge as 'local' he unwittingly undercuts them for being minoritarian not simply in relation to specific oppressors, but in general, in relation to an idealised power. His 'victims' must yield their specific 'local' qualities if they are to assume its reins.

'Woman' thus remains unresolved. Though Foucault dreamed of joining the 'full', unlimited enjoyment of the lawless 'woman' beyond-the-phallus with the power and privilege of the masculine into a single form he had no real model of feminine pleasure. Nor did he ever address the specific ways in which woman takes 'power' over her self, fashioning her own relation to *jouissance* (which, unlimited, would be as unbearable for her as for any man). He overlooked women, inadvertently leaving them as they are, unprotected, subjected to being restricted by others.

Despite this, feminists respond warmly to Foucault's Utopian valorisation of the de-sexualisation of sex and corresponding theoretical neutrality. Those writing about Foucault grant him praise for 'suspending traditional assumptions', for his 'politics of uncertainty', his 'steering between the Scylla of a moralistic dogmatism and the Charybdis of a libertarian pluralism in which anything goes'.[35] It troubles us that the feminist appreciation of his liberatory and creative stance on 'new life forms' – rendered possible only by critique – is everywhere counter-balanced by feminist praise for his middle-ground strategy, his restraint on choosing sides, his checking of 'anything goes'. It is less that Foucault pulled back from the brink of the total revaluation of all values, than that he went very far indeed, but was unable to make the necessary leap into the truly imaginary, remaining bound to those well-established radical variants our culture has specifically devised as its own safety valves – homosexuality and sado-masochism. Ultimately Foucault did not explore the dark possibilities of new subjective forms being created every day by a violence that takes off the mask of power: the contemporary cult of the gang, the Gulf War. . . . As such, we have to question whether, indeed, Foucault ever really went 'beyond' Oedipal sexual identification and its effects.

In the end, we think it is the comforting assertion of sexual equalisation that seduces feminist critics, especially those who are relatively undamaged subjectively, who can identify with the sexually deviant because they are not. Despite Sade's statement, you and I are not just alike. To pretend that inequality based on sexual difference does not exist, just because it should not, perpetuates the inequality. Among other things, in western culture, all women are sexually deviant when examined from the phallic standard. Women's 'natural' and 'socially constructed' sexuality keeps company of oppression with the homosexual's 'unnatural' and 'socially condemned' sexual identity in that both have been violently put on the outside of power and its institutions. But, so long as the role of violence goes unrecognised and accounted, this familiarity is a trap, and a confusion: if the resistance to ownership of power is located in local discourses whose 'subjugated *knowledges*' can be learned of, it is clear that the power to define and name the subjugated, sexually deviant/ socially constructed 'natural woman' and 'unnatural man' has not been disturbed or subverted enough by Foucault's critique.

NOTES

1 The authors wish to acknowledge their gratitude to Dora Epstein for her assistance in gathering the case materials for this project and her exhaustive and insightful comments; to Tracy McNulty for her research; and the Organized Research Initiative in Women and the Image at UC Irvine for financial support.
2 Being 'structured' has far more potential for psychological damage than being forced: it touches the root form, not only the expression of the will.
3 Kittler (1991) brings Foucault's terms to bear on concrete technological entities with specific semiotic regard for women's status. See also Poster (1984: 159ff) for an appraisal of Foucault's discovery of power as a multi-centred network to be the truth of technological being and radically re-configuring 'the' will to power.
4 Like Nietzsche, Foucault dethroned the pseudo-sovereign individual of humanism – to him, a slave 'subjected' to omnipresent prohibitions in civilisation. Equal participation in power would vitiate class, economic and familial divisions which ultimately stem from sexual division. His deep source is Sade's dream of equal participation in pleasure by overthrowing the contradiction of division by sex. See notes 30 and 31.

5 We do not use the feminine form of the third person in this paper out of consideration for 'political correctness', but because men cannot be victimized in the ways described in this chapter in so far as they are estranged from their own pleasure by their cultural position as males. Most of the case examples of violence cited below involve men doing to women what they imagine their culture has already done to them.

   We read the brutal assaults described below as attempts on the part of men to interrupt or fragment the woman's relationship to her own pleasure so that she is incapacitated by their assault on her in the same way as they are incapacitated by their cultural position. The men who commit these crimes of violence on some level feel they are not benefiting from their 'deal' with culture – specifically, that they are not deriving sufficient return on their 'castration'. They justify assault, in turn, as 'saving' women from an overwhelming *jouissance* (a mythic pleasure always imagined to exist elsewhere).

6 An articulate victim of childhood sexual abuse comments:

   > What one does with incest, is to compress it, to make it tiny, make it small; to fit it into the smallest space possible, after eliminating the details. Incest victims, like victims of anything, are without detail. Years of the unspeakable remain unspoken, and I am no exception.
   >
   > (Lee 1982: 166)

7 Politically, our analysis counters the current approach to the same phenomenon: namely, promoting social division, separation and segregation; living in gated communities; blaming the victims; arming oneself. Until violence, its effects, its ubiquity and its relationship to power are better understood, such regressive responses will only increase, not decrease, the political problem.

8 The unpredictability and internally contradictory nature of victims' responses can lead to 'destructive behaviours' (McNaron and Morgan 1982: 159).

9 This sentence is part of a complex named 're-victimisation' which infamously occurs at rape trials where the victim is compelled to give details of her sexual history and to re-live her rape while her assailant 'gets off' (again). By describing lasting effects of violation as damage to the subject, we risk appearing to provide support for discrimination against victims. We think this is a necessary risk that has to be taken in the course of work toward cure and prevention of intra-subjective violence.

10 See Maya Angelou's moving account (1969: 65–82) of how, after she was raped as an eight-year-old, she lost her power of speech for over a year.

11 See illustrations of the abuse of 'religious authority' in Women's Resource Centre (1989: 39ff) and 'Women and religion stories' (Hintz 1985: 10ff); also discussions of aggressors who claim they are doing it for the good of their victims, in Butler (1978: 91ff).

12 For first-hand accounts of casual bravery in the face of viciousness, see Mirante (1989).

13 Butler (1978: 66–7) reports: 'One young woman, whose father was 'only' an exhibitionist and never touched her, still is besieged with nightmares and is unable to have satisfying sexual relationships with men her own age.' Butler means to say this father never touched his daughter 'sexually'. Actually his technically non-sexual touches figure prominently in the daughter's subsequent emotional problems. No matter how severe his daughter's psychological reaction to his behaviour, under current penal codes this father did not commit a crime.

14 We can also draw on the work of Arendt, Lacan and Frantz Fanon who worked with the subject as we know it, and studied the way in which violence – force, not power – 'structures' personality under normal, fascist and colonial conditions.

15 The best ethnographic account is still Goffman's discussion of 'surveillance' and 'free space' in *Asylums*(1961). This work can be extended beyond the asylum wall into other institutions (the family, the ethnically mixed neighbourhood, the military, class and sexual relations) opening enquiry into everyday violence.

16 Foucault's 'gaze' is a variation on the Protestant gaze historically analysed by Weber, though as Fraser comments (1989: 32): 'Foucault writes as though he were oblivious to the existence of the whole body of Weberian social theory with its careful distinctions between such notions as authority, force, violence, domination and legitimation.'

17 Foucault's gaze ultimately *exculpates*: it affirms the Cartesian dream of total visibility wherein no dark or unconscious 'spot' marks it. Total guilt equals total innocence. This contrasts with Lacan, for whom the (Cartesian) gaze structurally stains the subject with their own unknowable, unbearable *jouissance*. See Copjec (1989) for a structural analysis; J. MacCannell (1991a) and D. MacCannell (1989) for complications in the structure of the gaze and enjoyment.

18 Total inculpation/exculpation obviates the need for *legitimacy*, grounding power in visual appeal, opinion and 'approval'. Wolin (1988: 180) argues that legitimacy has yielded to 'approval ratings' and 'admiration' as determining who holds power.

19 Even those who are not its victims are constantly reminded of the ubiquity of violence and subjective responses to it. The cultural apparatus of popular entertainment is, increasingly, an organised representation of violence under conditions of relative safety for the viewer. Such situations can be experienced as 'intimate' and/or 'thrilling' because of the presumption that they would ordinarily be dangerous; they are 'exciting' in proportion to their participants associating exposure, vulnerability and the gaze with the possibility of violence, even 'damnation'. Exhibitionism is the obverse of fear of real violence; it has become the virtual field for deep intimacy in modern society: our 'fifteen minutes of fame'.

20 Atwood's *Handmaid's Tale*(1968) features the 'eye-ocracy' of Gilead as a Foucauldian dystopia of the gaze for women. See J. MacCannell, forthcoming.

21 Zizek's work on enjoyment as a political factor (1991) is indispensable.

22 Foucault sympathised with figures of *lack* (the psychiatric patient, the hysteric, the incarcerated, the housewife, the poor) excluded from normal social intercourse. But his positive love is for philosophy, which flourishes where there is economic surplus – historically dependent on confining woman to the home. See also Bartkowski (1988: 56–7). Foucault would willingly open philosophy to all different peoples, not just men, though this could only be Utopian, not responsive to current conditions of unequal distribution.

23 Pierre Naveau (1984) presents a most comprehensive analysis of capitalism's relation to surplus enjoyment.

24 Recent news reports and films on cannibal acts indicate a current struggle to 'work through' this structure of supplementary assault. See D. MacCannell (1992: ch.1).

25 We ask: 'What does she want from her assailant?' 'Why does she return to the scene of the crime against her and re-enact it?' The answer is in part linguistic: she is willing to sacrifice her own body and subjectivity so that language can convey a *truth*. When her assailant *says*, 'I'm sorry, I won't hurt you again,' she wants to believe him. When he calls her a 'stinking bitch' she worries that the statement is *true*. As Willy Apollon (1992) remarks in another context, 'she is looking for a word' from her assailant, but she has already abandoned the feminine position *vis-à-vis* language: she does not approach these utterances as conveying a *meaning* that might possibly rebound upon their speaker. She looks not for meaning, but the truth; hence the words of her assailant cannot awaken her to the chance that they have a different aim, that he might be trying to put her off guard. Unlike Foucault's dream in 'Truth and power', victims cannot turn the tables on their assailants by taking over the distribution of truth. They just get beaten senseless for being 'little miss uppity'. It is time to develop an applied semiotic of 'empowerment' that addresses the processes of ceding the 'truth' to the powerful and violent while creating territories of meaning in the meeting ground between assailants and their victims, and that keeps these grounds demilitarised.

26 Foucault admired Bataille's description of pleasure as 'so close to ruinous waste that we refer to the moment of climax as "a little death"' (Bouchard 1977: 47).

27 The division of the sexes by language (Lacan) produced by the division of signifier from signified, saw the signifier (phallic) as what could never attain the signified (non-phallic), but one whose function nevertheless wholly depended on the projection of a non-phallic/uncastrated Other. Foucault, by contrast, strove to eliminate this elementary dialectical contradiction, replacing it with a unification bringing 'us closer to the possibility of a non-dialectical language' (Bouchard 1977: 41): 'Modern thought is advancing towards that region where man's Other must become the same as himself' (Foucault 1970: 328). Foucault hopes that 'rigorous language' which 'arises from sexuality' will exceed it to the point where finally 'it will say [man] exists without God'.

28 Foucault attacked the humanist 'culture' of Judaeo-Christian religion

and psychoanalysis, founded on taboo, inhibition, prohibition. He hailed a future 'desubjectification' ('self-mastery') which suppressed 'taboos and the limitations and divisions imposed upon the sexes'. To this end he called for 'the setting up of communes; the loosening of inhibitions with regard to drugs; the breaking of all prohibitions that form and guide the development of the normal individual' (in Bouchard 1977: 221–2).

29 Foucault was more traumatised by the death of God than he imagined: desiring absolution from sin is impossible in a world without a God who could grant it, unbearable without a superego who might not punish.

30 Lacan (1989) analyses Sade's enunciation of equality in detail, but re-affirmed the insolubility of the division by sex: the path of the signifier is phallic, but it is the human path. By detailing the ways 'woman' can work through the signifier, the Lacanians fill in a gap which seems critical in the light of our research on violence: the gap of pleasure, now seen from two sides of a phallic divide.

31 Lesbian sado-masochist feminism adopted Foucault. As Adams (1989: 264) points out, though, it attempts to pervert Oedipalism, not re-configure feminine *jouissance*. Adams' account of lesbian sado-masochism could serve as an account of victim subjectivity: neither moves beyond the phallus. But the lesbian sado-masochist at least can disavow it, *à la* Foucault: 'The lesbian sadomasochist has separated sexuality from gender and is able to enact differences in the theatre where roles freely circulate' (ibid.: 264).

32 For a thorough discussion sensitive to the very complex issues here, see Winifred Woodhull (1988).

33 His friends Deleuze and Guattari (1977) can help us fill in the blanks in Foucault with their 'desiring machines', 'lines of flight' and so on, though they empower a somewhat different cadre from Foucault's and their emphasis is on a *resistance* to established powers that Foucault downplays.

34 Attacked by de Certeau (1984: 48–50) for his failure to stress resistance, Foucault responded with his 'specific intellectual' who facilitates the uncovering of 'a particular, local, regional knowledge, a differential knowledge' (1980: 82), and opposes global commitments and characterization: such knowledges and practices are, unlike the larger form 'power', 'incapable of unanimity' (ibid.).

35 Unlike us, Teresa de Lauretis emphasises 'the techniques and discursive strategies by which gender is constructed and hence . . . violence is en-gendered' (1989: 245). In contrast, we see violence as a technique for producing a particular gender-effect out of the material of sexual division.

BIBLIOGRAPHY

Adams, P. (1989) 'Of female bondage', in Teresa Brennan (ed.) *Between Feminism and Psychoanalysis*, London and New York: Routledge.
Angelou, M. (1969) *I Know Why the Caged Bird Sings*, New York: Random House.
Apollon, W. (1992) 'Four seasons in femininity', Unpublished paper presented to the Organized Research Initiative in Women and the Image, UC Irvine (April).
Arendt, H. (1964) *Eichmann in Jerusalem: A Report on the Banality of Evil*, Harmondsworth: Penguin.
Atwood, M. (1968) *Handmaid's Tale*, New York: Fawcett.
Bartkowski, F. (1988) 'Epistemic drift in Foucault', in I. Diamond and L. Quinby (eds) *Feminism and Foucault: Reflections on Resistance*, Boston: Northeastern University Press.
Bass, E. and Davis, L. (1988) *The Courage to Heal: A Guide For Women Survivors of Child Sexual Abuse*, New York: Harper & Row.
Bordo, S. (1988) 'Anorexia nervosa: psychopathology as crystallization of culture', in I. Diamond and L. Quinby (eds) *Feminism and Foucault: Reflections on Resistance*, Boston: Northeastern University Press.
Bouchard, D.F. (ed.) (1977) *Language, Counter-Memory, Practice: Selected Essays and Interviews by Michel Foucault*, Ithaca, NY: Cornell University Press.
Butler, S. (1978) *Conspiracy of Silence: The Trauma of Incest*, San Francisco: New Glide Publications.
Cardinal, M. (1983) *The Words to Say It*, P. Goodheart (trans.), Cambridge, MA: Van Vactor and Goodheart.
de Certeau, M. (1984) *The Practice of Everyday Life*, Berkeley and Los Angeles: University of California Press.
Copjec, J. (1989) 'The orthopsychic subject', *October*, 49.
Deleuze, G. and Guattari, F. (1977) *Anti-Oedipus: Capitalism and Schizophrenia*, New York: Viking.
Derrida, J. (1976) *Of Grammatology*, G.C. Spivak (trans.), Baltimore and London: The Johns Hopkins University Press.
Diamond, I. and Quinby L. (eds) (1988) *Feminism and Foucault: Reflections on Resistance*, Boston: Northeastern University Press.
Fanon, F. (1963) *The Wretched of the Earth*, New York: Grove Weidenfeld.
Foucault, M. (1970) *The Order of Things: An Archaeology of the Human Sciences*, New York: Random House.
—— (1980) 'Two lectures', in C. Gordon (ed.) *Power/Knowledge: Selected Interviews and Other Writings 1972-1977: Michel Foucault*, London: Harvester Wheatsheaf.
—— (1983) 'The subject and power', L. Sawyer (trans.), in H.L. Dreyfus and P. Rabinow (eds) *Michel Foucault: Beyond Structuralism and Hermeneutics*, Chicago: University of Chicago Press.
Fraser, N. (1989) *Unruly Practices: Power, Discourse and Gender in Contemporary Social Theory*, Minneapolis: University of Minnesota Press.
Goffman, E. (1961) *Asylums: Essays on the Social Situation of Mental Patients and Other Inmates*, Garden City, NY: Doubleday.

Hintz, J. (1985) *Victim Survivor: Women of Domestic Violence*, Tiffin, Ohio: Sayger Printing.

Kittler, F. (1991) *Discourse Networks*, Palo Alto, CA: Stanford University Press.

Lacan, J. (1989) 'Kant with Sade', ('Kant avec Sade', *Ecrits*, Paris: Editions du Seuil, 1966) J.B. Swenson (trans.), *October*, 51: 55-104.

de Lauretis, T. (1989) 'The violence of rhetoric', in N. Armstrong and L. Tennenhouse (eds), *The Violence of Representation: Literature and the History of Violence*, London and New York: Routledge.

Lee, A. (1982) 'Untitled incest piece', in T.A.H. McNaron and Y. Morgan, *Voices in the Night: Women Speaking about Incest*, Pittsburgh: Cleis Press.

MacCannell, D. (1989) 'Faking it: on face play in the pornographic frame', *American Journal of Semiotics*, 6, 4: 153-74.

—— (1992) *Empty Meeting Grounds: The Tourist Papers*, New York and London: Routledge.

MacCannell, J. (1991a) 'Sex symbols', *Text Performance Quarterly*, 11: 217-32.

—— (1991b) *The Regime of the Brother: After the Patriarchy*, London and New York: Routledge.

—— (forthcoming) 'History and hysteria in *The Handmaid's Tale*', *Newsletter of the Freudian Field*.

McNaron, T.A.H. and Morgan, Y. (1982) *Voices in the Night: Women Speaking about Incest*, Pittsburgh: Cleis Press.

Mirante, E. (1989) 'The victim zone: recent accounts of Burmese military human rights abuses in the Shan state', *Contemporary Crises*, 13, 3: 211–66.

Naveau, P. (1984) 'Marx et le symptome', in *Perspectives psychoanalytiques sur la politique*, Paris: Navarin Éditeur.

Poster, M. (1984) *Foucault, Marxism, and History*, Cambridge: Polity Press.

Rabinow, P. (ed.) (1982) 'Interview', *The Foucault Reader*, New York: Pantheon Books.

Sawicki, J. (1986) 'Foucault and feminism: towards a politics of difference', in *Hypatia*, I (2): 23-36.

Stanko, E.A. (1985) *Intimate Intrusions: Women's Experience of Male Violence*, London: Routledge & Kegan Paul.

Wachs, E. (1988) *Crime Victims' Stories: New York City's Urban Folklore*, Bloomington: Indiana University Press.

Weisman, L.K. (1992) *Discrimination by Design: A Feminist Critique of the Man Made Environment*, Urbana: University of Illinois Press.

Wolin, S. (1988) 'On the theory and practice of power', in J. Arac (ed.) *After Foucault*, New Brunswick, NJ: Rutgers University Press.

Women's Research Centre (1989) *Recollecting Our Lives: Women's Experience of Childhood Sexual Abuse*, Vancouver, BC: Press Gang Publishers.

Woodhull, W. (1988) 'Sexuality, power, and the question of rape', in I. Diamond and L. Quinby (eds) *Feminism and Foucault: Reflections on Resistance*, Boston: Northeastern University Press.

Zizek, S. (1991) *They Know Not What They Do: Enjoyment as a Political Factor*, London and New York: Routledge.

Chapter 10

Women's sexuality and men's appropriation of desire

Caroline Ramazanoğlu and Janet Holland

Foucault has offered a serious challenge to feminist analyses of western sexuality, particularly through his conceptions of the nature of the body and the nature of power.[1] His work can be perplexing for feminists, partly because of the difficulty of grasping the different statements he makes about power, and what these might mean for women's lives, and partly because feminism's political strategies are based on conceptions of power and the body which are not wholly compatible with Foucault's theory. They start from women's experiences of being subordinated. Meaghan Morris argued some years ago that Foucault cannot be put to work *for* women because his writing is profoundly androcentric (Morris 1979: 152). This male-centredness in his thinking has been well documented in more recent feminist analyses of his work (Fraser 1989; Braidotti 1991; Sawicki 1991), but nevertheless these and other feminists have found his work useful in bringing out problems in the way we think about the complexities of power.

Feminist interest in the transformation of power relations has produced persistent problems in thinking about the nature of power. There are particular problems in thinking simultaneously about transforming women's relationships with men and also attending to the numerous social divisions that divide women and divide men. Foucault undermines feminist politics because his view that power is widely diffused through networks of social relations appears to dissolve feminist claims that through some relatively stable sex/gender or patriarchal system, men possess power which they hold over women (and subordinate men and children). In feminist theory, women, in spite of the social divisions between them, are seen as very generally dominated by men.

More specifically, feminists have taken the body to be a site of sexual politics and, in particular, of struggles over the control of women's bodies (Gatens 1988). If women want to gain control of their own bodies – for example, with reference to contraception, reproduction or sexual pleasure – then they must struggle to empower themselves by transforming specific and local relationships which shore up men's power. (It is not, though, always noted that these struggles over sexuality can also be differentiated by other power relationships such as those of racism and class.)

Feminist notions of heterosexual relations have tended to conceive power in terms of the possibility of women resisting men's sexual domination, and so empowering themselves. These notions imply a subject with agency, however, which has no place in most of Foucault's thought.

Foucault did not necessarily deny that in recent western history men *have* generally exercised power over women (although he had little apparent interest in the topic). He acknowledged that there can be 'massive binary divisions' and 'great radical ruptures' in 'society' (1984: 96), but his interest in power increasingly shifted away from such divisions. He accepted that power relations can produce 'wide-ranging effects of cleavage that run through the social body as a whole', leading to 'major dominations' (1984: 94), but his originality lay in pointing to social cleavages that 'shift about, fracturing unities and effecting regroupings, furrowing across individuals themselves, cutting them up and remolding them, marking off irreducible regions in them, in their bodies and minds' (Foucault 1984: 96). He clearly denied that power can be a possession which one group or category can 'hold' over another (ibid.: 93–4). Women cannot then empower themselves in relation to men, because men (or 'classes' or 'races') as a block do not 'have' power. Foucault did not see this as a problem, since he thought that women, or other subordinates, could destabilise power by seeking shifting, local and specific points of resistance. He did not, however, speak from women's experiences of having power exercised over them, or from women's anger and pain, and he did not see it as his role to specify political actions for those who might resist.

Radical feminism, in contrast, has offered women very forceful analyses of sexuality and the body which identify 'normal' heterosexual practices and relationships not just as social rather than natural, but as constructed in men's interests to control women's bodies and subordinate women. Although these analyses were not necessarily strong in terms of their philosophical foundations, internal coherence or sensitivity to social divisions between women, they were political dynamite in valuing and articulating women's experience of sexuality. New-wave feminism was born with few inhibitions about telling other women exactly what to do (and consequently attracted severe criticisms), but this new feminism can be said to have empowered women to see their personal experiences in terms of sexual politics.

This does not mean that women's experiences can simply be taken as given, factual or neutral. Feminism remains divided on how to validate women's accounts of their experience. We take the view that the processes through which experience becomes knowledge are both at some level grounded in what is 'real', and at the same time always shaped by the ways in which we can think about these 'realities'. The tension between conceptualising experience as 'true' and 'factual', and experience as constructed, formulated and made meaningful by thought, is as confused and contested in feminism as it is in most other areas of social theory.

Feminism has been effective, however, in providing new ideas that made women's experience intrude into thought in new ways. Diana Fuss (1989: 118) has commented: 'While experience can never be a reliable guide to the real, this is not to preclude any role at all for experience in the realm of knowledge production.' It was, in part, women's experiences of subordination and marginalisation by feminists themselves which helped to produce more general knowledge of the ways in which other social divisions interact with gender. Rape crisis centres and changes in policing, refuges and safe houses for 'victims' of domestic violence, the coming out of lesbians, struggles over contraception, abortion and control of women's bodies during childbirth, are evidence of the political consequences of interpreting women's experience through the theory that men in general 'hold' power over women and that women can identify this power and collectively resist it. If we want to keep this sense of men's possession of power, and women's agency in challenging their varied experiences of subordination, we need clear responses to Foucault's conception of power.

THE MIDDLE GROUND OF POWER RELATIONS

In this chapter we want to consider some of the problems of thinking about empowerment and resistance in relation to women's bodies which arise from feminist appraisals of Foucault, and from interpretations of women's experience. Both Foucault and feminism have greatly illuminated the detailed processes through which power is exercised at the level of relations between people. But neither Foucault nor feminism has adequately specified what we might loosely term the 'middle ground' of power, where complex links need to be traced between the micro-politics of the exercise of power at the level of relations between people, and some conception of the entrenchment of male power more generally, in ways which systematically privilege men over women.

Foucault's theory that bodies are effects of power, produced in social relations by discourses of sexuality, medicine, education and so on, has been a productive influence on feminist work, as other contributions to this volume indicate.[2] His claim that power is not possessed by any group, and so cannot be properly understood in terms of a dualism of oppressors and oppressed (Foucault 1984), is more problematic. There is an explanatory gap between his conception of power as coming from everywhere and spreading through society from below with a capillary action, and his intermittent acknowledgement of the cleavages between concentrations of power that can result (ibid.).

He speaks of the 'network of power relations' as 'forming a dense web that passes through apparatuses and institutions, without being exactly localised in them' (Foucault 1984: 96). Jana Sawicki (1991: 24) comments that, 'by utilising this ascending analysis, Foucault shows how mechanisms of power at the microlevel of society have become part of dominant networks of power relations'. The leap between the micro-physics of power, and investigation of men's dominance in networks of power relations, is, however, both one of theoretical agility (since we have to conceptualise power at every level) and also one of political dexterity (since women need diverse but effective strategies of resistance).

Men's grip on women may be fragile, shifting, rooted in vulnerability, easily fractured, but this grip has a temporal and geographical ubiquity and tenacity which constitutes men's power as sturdy and persistent relations of domination and sub-ordination on which women's resistance has made little impact. This concentration of power is interwoven with other social divisions but reproduces discourses and institutional arrangements in favour of men. In feminism, conceiving men's power in terms of some system of patriarchy has proved extremely problematic, but it is this solidification of multiple power relations which has attracted feminist concern and which was not of primary interest to Foucault.[3]

The differences between the approaches of Foucault and feminism are brought out by Nancy Hartsock's view that power is an essentially contested concept (Hartsock 1990: 158). She argues that different theories of power rest on different assumptions about both the content of existence and how we come to know it. Theories of power which come *from* the experience of domination are challenged by the political aim of women's empowerment. The experience of subordination can give us insights into power relations which are missing from 'top-down' theories of power, but, as criticisms of feminism have shown, speaking from experi-ence can also limit our visions of power and ignore the political differences between women.

In empirical studies carried out with colleagues in the Women, Risk and AIDS Project and the Men, Risk and AIDS Project, we have needed some theory of the operation of male power in sexual relationships, and some notion of women's empowerment and agency, in order to interpret accounts that young women and young men have given of their sexuality.[4] For the purposes of this chapter we have drawn upon both feminism and Foucault in trying to explore the intermediate area between what feminists have called patriarchy (dismissed by implication by Foucault as monolithic, totalising, modern theory) and the micro-politics of power exercised at the level of sexual encounters; the everyday processes of the construction of self, identity and sexuality. In this chapter we have concentrated on issues of gender and power in sexual relations between young women and their male partners. We have found that differences of age, class and 'race'/ethnicity make little consistent difference to the ways in which men exercise power in sexual relations (Holland 1992).[5]

Foucault's work can be illuminating for feminist studies of sexuality, and our interpretations of our data provide support for his contention that the body is a site where the large-scale organisation of power is connected to the most minute and local practices (Holland *et al.* 1992c). But Foucault does not provide feminism with a means of specifying the links between men's exercise of power in particular sexual encounters, and male power more generally.

Foucault raises for feminism an acute problem of how we can think about men's exercise of power, and how women can interpret their own experiences of powerlessness and resistance. If men demand sexual intercourse but refuse to wear condoms; if young women fake orgasms to keep their man happy and so ensure a continued relationship; if women silence their own desires by defining 'sex' as his penetration, his orgasm, his satisfaction, explanations are needed of how power is being exercised, how men get and keep control, and what, if anything, should be resisted. These questions raise further problems about the validity of women's experience of sexuality, the extent of men's vulnerability in sexual relationships and whether the feminist conception of empowerment is rendered unnecessary by Foucault's conception of resistance. In this chapter we explore some of the possibilities and limitations of thinking about this middle ground of power in relation to young people's accounts of their sexuality.

FEMINISM AND SEXUAL TRUTH

Foucault's work has had the effect of disturbing the truths of the dominant discourses of western sexuality; that is, the ways in which the 'truths' of sexuality are currently allowed to be defined in, for example, medicine, sex education, employment, marriage counselling, psychiatry. In particular, he set out to trace the history of the links between the regulation of what is sexually permissible (sexual interdictions) and social pressures on people to 'tell the truth' about themselves (Foucault 1988b: 17). His work is useful to feminists because, while feminism has charted a separate course largely ignored by Foucault, it has also been upsetting the truths produced by the discourses of western sexuality.

Feminist arguments are far from uniform but a strong case has emerged, in spite of internal contradictions (Bell 1991), that feminism has fundamentally disrupted western sexual truths by identifying men as a gender, documenting the extent and nature of men's domination of women and challenging the legitimacy of men's power (Jaggar 1983; Vance 1992). Considerable effort has gone into the analysis of sexual violence against women, identifying the complex links between socially constructed sexuality, violence and power (rhodes and McNeill 1985; Stanko 1985; Hanmer and Maynard 1987; Kelly 1988). Conventional sexual 'truths' such as that the autonomous, desiring, sexually active woman either wishes a 'real' man to dominate her, or constitutes a threat to his masculinity: an abnormal or rapacious woman, a slut or slag, are exposed as carrying hidden power relations. Conventional sexuality then expresses male desires and silences female desire (Coveney *et al.* 1984; Wilton 1991; Holland *et al.* 1992a).

This identification of the 'missing discourse of desire' (Fine 1988) identifies both heterosexual men as an immediate political problem for heterosexual women, and also the existence of heterosexuality as a social system of male domination. These views effectively dispute the idea of women's natural femininity, by claiming that femininity and masculinity are socially constructed rather than corollaries of being female or male (Sayers 1982). Feminist analyses constitute an attack on the dominant view that women's natural femininity complements and services men's natural sexual needs so that women find their sexual pleasure in servicing men. But feminism has never been entirely clear on what is then the 'truth' of sexuality.

This strong sense of sexuality as socially constructed runs counter to the thread of biological determinism or essentialism which can also be found in feminism.[6] While there is no consensus on what natural sexuality or femininity might be, this thread implies the view that while men's domination of women is not legitimate, there are essential differences between men and women. This thinking does clearly distinguish feminist explanation of gender differences from Foucault's position on sexuality as social rather than natural.

Some feminist intellectuals have responded to Foucault's ideas on sexuality, by treating the new wave of western feminism from the 1960s as contaminated by essentialist beliefs. By embracing Foucault's anti-essentialism, they can not only take sexuality and sexual relationships, but also bodies, to be socially constructed – the effects of discourses, and so effects of power. In this embrace there is the danger that any creative potential for thinking, along with Foucault's possibly radical impulse, may be inappropriately simplified or rigidified (Bordo 1990: 665; Lather 1991: 125; Sawicki 1991: 122).

Some radical feminists have distinguished sex as biological from gender as social, or have taken other essentialist positions. But the force of the political logic of radical feminism has been to challenge essentialism in dominant ideas of sexuality. Essentialism has been much more implicit or ambiguous in radical feminism than consistently explicit; a consequence of trying to construct a universal theory of oppression, rather than its starting point. Feminism, as a result, has been deeply divided over how to take account of both the natural differences which evidently exist between men and women, and the social construction of sexuality. Many feminists have had to struggle against being labelled 'essentialist'.

The editors of *Trouble and Strife*, a British radical feminist journal, for example, claim that they have 'always argued against a biologically determinist analysis of women's oppression' – *Trouble and Strife*, 14: 42 (Dworkin 1988). The journal reprinted an emotional article by Andrea Dworkin (1988), in which she describes the hostility she has experienced in speaking to audiences of women convinced that men are a distinct and inferior species. She stresses her own rejection of this kind of biological determinism with its related claims of female superiority. 'It is shamefully easy for us to enjoy our own fantasies of biological omnipotence while despising men for enjoying the reality of theirs' (ibid.: 45). Her analysis of women's sexual oppression, however, unlike Foucault's, is based on the claim that men *do have* power. Her account of intercourse (Dworkin 1987) is a long documentation of women's sexual experiences from the perspective of women, in terms of invasion, occupation, pain, destruction of freedom and the will to freedom, and male domination generally. But she does not claim that heterosexual intercourse *has* to be a system of male domination, nor that the forms it takes arise from men's biological needs.

The editors of a collection of conference papers on male violence against women from the early 1980s published by Onlywomen, a radical feminist, lesbian press, specifically deny that the message of these numerous papers is essentialist, 'It is not nature that has constructed this effective system for the subordination of women. The system is constructed by men, in men's interests, for the benefit of all men' (rhodes and McNeill 1985: 7).

The problem posed by analyses of the 'truths' of sexuality in radical feminism is not that it is always assumed that sexuality is necessarily simply imbued with essentialism, deriving from men and women having different physical and emotional needs, but that radical feminism took off without a clear enough theory of power. Where men's access to power comes from, how to take account of material bodies, and why men have been so successfully powerful and women so unsuccessful, remains a fuzzy area. Theories of patriarchy have not been able to explain in sufficient depth *why* men so generally have power over women, even when men can be frightened, vulnerable, emotionally dependent, anxious to give pleasure and oppressed themselves by masculinity. Our data include a number of accounts of relationships and sexual encounters in which men are able to dominate women, even when they appear not to wish or intend to. Foucault's work can be illuminating here through his claim that 'One doesn't have here a power which is wholly in the hands of one person who can exercise it alone and totally over others. It's a machine in which everyone is caught, those who exercise power just as much as those over whom it is exercised' (Foucault 1980c: 156).

A further point of confusion is that feminism has given relatively little attention to women's efforts to support and enable men's power over them; efforts which are strikingly evident in young women's accounts of their sexual experiences (Holland *et al.* 1992a). Feminism has concentrated on documenting in immense detail and from every part of the world and every area of social life that men *do* dominate women, and *how* they do this. Much less attention has been given to connecting to the diversity of experience what we mean by men having power, or power having a source in producing docile bodies.

The problem of how to understand sexuality in radical feminism seems to be part of a more general problem of understanding what part material, physical 'pre-discursive' bodies play in the complex social interactions of sexuality.[7] Foucault's attempts to present bodies as constituted by discourses in power relationships exposed this problem to a new light, but without resolving it.

Wendy Hollway (1984: 68) illustrates the tensions between feminists' grounded sense of sexualised bodies and Foucault's conception of sexuality as a product of discourses. She argues that 'Feminism should not reproduce the assumption that men's power – in or out of sex – is monolithic'. This is because she takes heterosexual sex to be contradictory, and so a site of politics. She argues with Foucault that women can produce their own accounts of sexuality which 'do not collaborate in the sexist assumptions that the power of the penis is uncontestable. It is not. The power of the penis is a "knowledge" produced by sexist discourses' (ibid.). The feminist grounding of sexuality in women's experience, however, raises some problems for Hollway's version of Foucault's analysis. First, there is the question of how far the power of the penis is also a material power, a gendered difference in embodiment which leaves women at physical risk regardless of what discourses they produce – that is, whether the fact that we live out our social lives in physical bodies, and so are differently 'embodied' as male or female, has any bearing on the exercise of power. Secondly, it is not clear how women's accounts of sexuality can be forms of resistance which do anything to subvert the entrenchment of 'penis power' in every area of social life.

We are left with the problem of what social construction means for those trying to deconstruct sexuality in practice; *why* bodies and sexuality become endowed with some meanings rather than others, and how far sexuality might be a bodily as well as a social phenomenon. The differences which have arisen between feminism and Foucault cannot adequately be explained by essentialism in feminism being opposed to anti-essentialism in the work of Foucault, or a feminist focus on men's power being opposed to Foucault's focus on the multiplicity of power relations.

From Foucault's perspective on the possibilities of resistance to power, it is a weakness of feminist accounts of sexuality that feminist theorists have not made an adequate case for power as a male possession. Neither has feminism resolved the problem of how to take account of biology in thinking about power. It is in the complexity of the interaction between the material and the social that explanation of the systematic and persistent male dominance of women in sexual violence, sexual submission to men, unintended pregnancy, faked orgasms, acceptance of unwanted intercourse, and so on, can be sought (Holland *et al.* 1992b).

While it is fair to say that feminism has not resolved these problems in any final way, the extensive debates within feminism have served to show that, from the perspective of women's diverse experiences, Foucault's theory of power is also problematic. Foucault did not recognise that his supposedly neutral analysis of truth, power and sexuality, constituted in discourses, comes from a gendered perspective; feminism's sense of gender as experience is missing from his analysis. In the next two sections we consider the implications of arguing that Foucault's theory of power is itself gendered.

DOCILE BODIES AS GENDERED BODIES [8]

Foucault's approach to sexuality, power and the body encourages feminists to emphasise multiplicity and the shifting of discourses over time. In his view, the body has no essential existence of its own which gives us a 'true' identity as 'essentially' male, 'really' female, 'truly' lesbian, 'genuinely' bisexual. Obviously physical bodies exist and experience pain and pleasure. But Foucault does not see bodies as sexual in any simple way; rather, he links sex to power (or rather the discourses on sex to historical relationships of power).

It is this diffusion of power throughout society which produces the docile bodies of western cultures. Foucault saw bodies as disciplined by many techniques of power, including those we exercise over our own bodies (for example, in deportment, diet, ornamentation and hygiene). It is this plurality of networks of power relations and techniques of power which has seemed politically attractive to academic feminists struggling with the problem of how to grasp and respond to the many social differences between women. By seeing resistance to power as everywhere, local and diverse, there is, apparently, no need for women to unite across their differences, and so no need for a general theory of male oppression. This has meant a departure from earlier feminist ideas of liberation which depended on an Enlightenment conception of an essential self which could be freed from a repressive system of male power.

Hekman (1990) takes the view that the transformation of thought required by Foucault means that feminism must abandon its conception of universal political interests (women against patriarchy) and transform its politics into a Foucauldian conception that power, being everywhere, must be opposed everywhere, without the need to appeal to 'universal values of human dignity, autonomy, freedom. In many instances of

oppression these western humanist values are irrelevant'
(Hekman 1990: 185). In Foucault's terms, specific instances of the
exercise of power produce specific resistances, and resistance
produces new discourses and so new power. Feminism, in
Hekman's argument, is helped by postmodernism to see itself as
a counter discourse that resists 'the hegemony of male domination' and utilises 'the contradictions in these hegemonic
discourses in order to effect their transformation' (ibid.: 190).

But critics of Foucault have pointed out that, while feminism
cannot remain unchanged by encounters with Foucault, it cannot
simply merge into the preoccupations of poststructuralism
(Braidotti 1991). Rosi Braidotti argues that poststructuralists have
undermined feminism by ignoring feminist work and
desexualising and disembodying theoretical practice. The
political strategies for struggles around bodies and pleasures
which feminists can draw from Foucault are constrained by his
theory of power resting on a masculine model of 'man'.

The problems with Foucault's approach to sexuality from the
perspective of feminism are neatly summarised by Sandra Lee
Bartky (1990: 65):

Foucault's account in *Discipline and Punish* of the disciplinary
practices that produce the 'docile bodies' of modernity is a ge-
nuine *tour de force*, incorporating a rich theoretical account of
the ways in which instrumental reason takes hold of the body
with a mass of historical detail. But Foucault treats the body
throughout as if it were one, as if the bodily experiences of men
and women did not differ and as if men and women bore the
same relationship to the characteristic institutions of modern
life. Where is the account of the disciplinary practices that engender the 'docile bodies' of women, more docile than the
bodies of men? Women, like men are subject to many of the
disciplinary practices Foucault describes. But he is blind to
those disciplines which produce a modality of embodiment
which is peculiarly feminine. To overlook the forms of subjection that engender the feminine body is to perpetuate the
silence and powerlessness of those upon whom these disciplines
have been imposed. Hence even though a liberatory note is
sounded in Foucault's critique of power, his analysis as a whole
reproduces that sexism which is endemic throughout Western
political theory.

Harding (1992: 252) also argues that while Foucault has shown us that humans are embodied creatures, female embodiment is different from male embodiment. These bodily differences are produced at the level of discourse and so, as effects of power in public policies. Women are then in the difficult position of arguing against anatomy being destiny, while also arguing for gender-specific policies relating to their bodies around such issues as childbirth, abortion and contraception. As Foucault has pointed out (1988d: 115), women did resist the medical discourses from the eighteenth century which reduced them to their sex, and their sex to 'man's sickness', but their resistance came through embracing their female specificity.

Foucault does not pursue the political implications of such resistance in terms of the limited possibilities for change which follow for women. Judith Walkowitz (1985: 175), however, argues that 'brilliant organising drives' by nineteenth-century feminists against male sexual abuse of women were often self-defeating. Their aims of protecting and empowering women produced a new discourse of sexuality, but their efforts were soon subverted and controlled by men. First, they lacked the necessary 'cultural and political power to reshape the world according to their own image' (ibid.: 187), but they also defined women's sexuality in essentialist terms as quiescent, domestic and pure, which placed a contradiction at the heart of their campaigns and made the production of an active, female sexual agency impossible.

Elizabeth Grosz (1990: 71–2) concludes that feminists *can* use Foucault's conception of the body to articulate women's lived experiences and potential for autonomy, but she cites Monica Gatens (1983) to argue that masculinity and femininity mean different things according to whether they are lived in male or female bodies: 'what is mapped on to the body is not unaffected by the body on to which it is projected' (Grosz 1990: 72). For feminists the problem is that, while sex may not be simply essential, bodies have to be understood as more than effects of power. In both young women's and young men's experience, material, physical bodies intrude into sexuality in painful, pleasurable or messy ways which are not only produced by discourses.

In making sense of young people's accounts of their sexuality we have found it useful to conceive relations of power as lying between two poles: first, a grounded and intensely material basis of power in sexual relations, both in the body and in physical control over it, in which the penis is more than 'knowledge'; secondly, in Foucault's terms, in discourses of sexuality. The evident power which is constituted in discourses of sexuality cannot, however, be wholly abstracted from material bodies. The material basis of power is illustrated by one young woman who described months of having sexual intercourse every night because her boyfriend was violent to her:

A: There was no night went by without it, because that's the way he wanted it. If I didn't have it he was a total shit.

Q: Were you able to say what you wanted, that you didn't want to have sex?

A: If I didn't want to have sex there would have been violence.

This young woman was not totally physically trapped in violence as, after many months, she did manage to escape from this relationship. Sexual relationships cannot then be explained purely at the level of material bodies. Sexual behaviour is also constituted as discourses of heterosexuality which construct female sexuality as subordinate to male needs, expectations and desires. Women then discipline their bodies, not to take care of them but to express their femininity in meeting men's needs. Another young woman commented:

A: I saw friends, people I know, go out with older blokes and being frightened to say no or to suggest things – because the bloke would be older. And they didn't feel fully in control of their own bodies – feelings like what was an orgasm? Most women didn't know what they should feel. It was very much on the receiving side, doing something to please someone else. Not pleasure for themselves.

Young women's accounts of docile bodies being made feminine are clearly accounts of socially gendered bodies. They illustrate something of the problems of interpretation and political strategy that we have encountered, since they raise questions about what forms of resistance to relations of power are possible and effective.

Seeing docile bodies as gendered can enable us to clarify the multiple and contradictory pressures on young people to be sexual in various ways, and can help account for the extent of unsafe sexual practice. In our data, we find that young women give accounts of experiencing contradictory pressures in different ways: as personal and embedded in the ways they think about and live their own sexuality; as social, coming from the institutions and groups in which they are located; and as coming directly from men. These distinctions are merely our devices for clarification, since each set of pressures is entwined with the others and can be seen as contributing to the social construction of sexuality. They can be usefully seen as aspects of the deployment of sexuality. The critical point around which these experiences are articulated is the young women's expectations of men, and the meaning and importance they attach to men's sexual needs and behaviour. Here their gendered embodiment, the kind of docility produced in the female body, differentiates their experiences of power and resistance from those of men.

Young women gave many accounts of their own complicity in defining sexual encounters as men's penetration of their bodies, and the satisfaction of men's pleasures. For example:

A: It was like as soon as he got an erection that was all right no matter how I was feeling. Whether I was aroused or not, you had to do things because that was the point when things happened – when he was aroused, not when I was aroused.

They also, however, as in this excerpt, gave accounts of reflecting on their experiences (particularly when they had been influenced by feminist ideas), and there was a general awareness of a double standard in sexual behaviour, with men and women deriving very different reputations from the same sexual practices. This process of reflection on sexual relationships did help open up possibilities of leaving relationships, negotiating changes or, in rare cases, deliberately educating male partners into activities that were pleasurable and safer for both partners. The young woman cited immediately above was, at the time of the interview, with a new partner with whom she had discussed her pleasures as well as his, and with whom penetrative sex formed only a small part of their sexual activities. This change in power relations at the personal level, though, is not necessarily connected to any wider social change which could be predictably sustained in subsequent sexual experiences.

In some respects feminist theory and practice provide the conditions of, and strategies for, resistance, and indeed a counter discourse to that of heterosexuality. Feminism can propose that these reflective young women have the possibility of empowerment in the sense of being able to redefine their sexuality. Through this redefinition they can assert their own pleasures, making their bodies less docile in relation to men's. But this is arguing more than that they have developed a counter discourse. Foucault's notion of resistance is very different from feminist notions of women's empowerment because his definition of power underestimates the intransigence of the powerful in defending their privilege, and so does not enquire sufficiently into what resistance to entrenched male power might entail.

FROM POWER TO EMPOWERMENT

In explaining the nature of sexual power, Foucault makes a distinction between 'sex' and the 'deployment of sexuality' (Foucault 1984: 157). This distinction is developed through his attack in *The History of Sexuality* on the idea that each of us has a true sexual self which needs to be liberated from sexual repression. It is not its essential nature, but the ways in which sexuality is deployed which makes sex seem so desirable, and 'it is this desirability which makes us think that we are affirming the rights of our sex against all power' (Foucault 1984). It is, he says, our being fastened to the deployment of sexuality which makes us think we have a true sexual self – seeing ourselves reflected in the 'dark shimmer of sex' (ibid.: 157). Far from being an essence, Foucault sees sexuality as a real historical formation which gives rise to the notion of sex, and creates sex in different ways. He draws attention to the way the exercise of power works through sexuality, and regards this, rather than what we think sex 'really is', as the key to understanding the links between sex and power: 'sex is the most speculative, most ideal, and most internal element in a deployment of sexuality organised by power in its grip on bodies and their materiality, their forces, energies, sensations and pleasures' (Foucault 1984: 155). In this view, the power exercised in sexual relations does not have any specific origin or source. Power cannot be a possession, since it comes from everywhere, is everywhere, without an original source. Power over women can be exercised *by* men but cannot come *from* men. Our sexual identities are products of particular discourses, or sets of rules which develop and change historically as ways of defining what is permitted to be true. Femininity and masculinity are produced by prevailing social conceptions, laws, dominant medical views, psychoanalytic practices, which lay down and regulate what and how sexuality, and so sexual desires, practices and relationships, can be, and can be thought about; what is normal and what is perverse.

Foucault's conception of sexual truths as social constructions does seem, at first, to get us out of some of the limitations and inadequacies of existing theories of power and the body. We can certainly see femininity as an effect of power produced in discourses, so that women have to struggle to become feminine just as men struggle to become masculine (Smith 1988). But Foucault's concerns were not those of women, and so some issues which are critical in sexual politics, especially the need to transform the relations between women and men, tend to disappear.

What Foucault does not ask is why these historical discourses are so systematically produced by men and in men's interests. He says in *The History of Sexuality* that 'we must not think that by saying yes to sex one says no to power' (1984: 157). By this he means that we must not think in terms of freeing ourselves from sexual repression by embracing our 'true' sexual selves:

> on the contrary one tracks along the course laid out by the general deployment of sexuality. It is the agency of sex that we must break away from, if we aim – through a tactical reversal of the various mechanisms of sexuality – to counter the grips of power with the claims of bodies, pleasures and knowledges, in their multiplicity and their possibility of resistance. The rallying point for the counterattack against the deployment of sexuality ought not to be sex-desire, but bodies and pleasures.
>
> (Foucault 1984: 157)

Whatever sexuality we practise will be a product of the discourses of power or resistance. In Foucault's view, sexual power, like other forms of power, is always productive, rather than repressive, so sexual power will always allow for resistance. Young people in his view are caught in the general deployment of sexuality, they cannot say no to power, but they can break out by asserting their own pleasures.

The practical obstacles confronting young women struggling to wield their bodies and pleasures in counter-attack, however, seem to be seriously under-estimated (Holland *et al.* 1992a). When young women say yes to sex, they say yes to power differently from their male sexual partners. Both are caught in the general deployment of heterosexuality, but they are situated differently within it. The feminist theory of empowerment, and the political strategy of promoting women's agency, is not apparently compatible with Foucault's position.

Foucault's theory of power does not allow us to ask where men's sexual power comes from, nor why it is so powerfully consolidated, institutionalised and reproduced. But feminism has focused, clearly, intensively and in great detail, on precisely *how* men exercise power over women, and has brought into prominence women's accounts of their experiences of this power and their own lack of power in what is now a very extensive literature. The question of *why* men have power over women cannot be entirely reduced to analyses of discourse, since the links between individual relationships and the institutionalised power of heterosexuality and masculinity cannot then clearly be traced.

Feminists have greatly extended the meaning of power to show the struggles in sexual politics, but Nancy Fraser (1989: 31–2) has argued that Foucault's conception of power is such a 'catch-all' category that it leaves him unable to distinguish between the exercise of different kinds of power, and so unable to judge between the morality of different kinds of constraints.

Foucault did, however, make some distinction between types of power, although the shifts in emphasis between his earlier and later work make these somewhat unclear. These distinctions do sketch in the boundaries of Foucault's conception of power. In a lecture, Foucault clarified his distinction between power (which always allows for resistance) and force (which cannot be resisted) in a way which indicates a key restriction in his notion of power:

Power is only a certain type of relation between individuals. . . . The characteristic feature of power is that some men can more or less entirely determine other men's conduct – but never exhaustively or coercively. A man who is chained up and beaten is subject to force being exerted over him. Not power. But if he can be induced to speak, when his ultimate recourse could have been to hold his tongue, preferring death, then he has been caused to behave in a certain way. His freedom has been subjected to power. He has been submitted to government. If an individual can remain free, however little his freedom may be, power can subject him to government. There is no power without potential refusal or revolt.

(Foucault 1988c: 83–4)

Foucault's distinction between power and force here offers his (male) victim a rather bleak choice between death and a little freedom. It allows Foucault to limit the definition of power to what is productive rather than repressive, but cuts out many situations which feminism would treat as the exercise of oppressive power relations. (Some implications of this distinction are more fully developed by Dean MacCannell and Juliet Flower MacCannell in their contribution to this book.) In Foucault's intellectual distinction between power and force, he loses the moral ground from which men's power over women can be judged. Foucault has no sense of the radical feminist's judgement of the coercion used by men against women, and the possession and invasion of women's bodies in medicine, domestic and sexual violence, as violent, immoral and needing to be changed. His nuances of freedom seem largely irrelevant to women's lives.

Foucault defined power as always allowing for resistance, but never developed an analysis of power from the *perspective* of resistance. He explains:

I am not positing a substance of resistance versus a substance of power. I am just saying as soon as there is a power relation, there is a possibility of resistance. We can never be ensnared by power: we can always modify its grip in determinate conditions and according to a precise strategy.

(Foucault 1988d: 123)

His claim (1984: 96) that power comes as a package with the possibility of resistance is not then grounded in experience, nor an inference from history; it is a condition of the way he conceptualises power. Because of this condition, he can only conceive women's liberation as a reversal of the mechanisms of sexuality through the assertion of bodies and pleasures; that is, in the form of new discourses (Foucault 1980b: 219–20).

Foucault did not see it as his responsibility to ask where precise strategies of resistance to relations of power might come from, nor how far modifying the grip of a power relation could lead to any real change in social conditions for those in the grip. He suggests that there is no particular direction to resistance: 'I believe in the freedom of people. To the same situation, people react in very different ways' (Foucault 1988a: 14). Although he conceived people as able to resist dominant discourses, he did not seem concerned about the difference between resisting and winning. Feminism has preserved a more active conception of resistance linked to empowerment with which to challenge dominant discourses of sexuality, but little has changed in women's experiences of sexual power because the consolidation of men's power more generally has not been transformed.

There is a further conception of power in Foucault's work, where he makes a distinction between the power relations that produce resistance, where all is fluid and power is unstable, and a notion of domination which conceives power as much more settled and persistent. Foucault's idea of domination, in contrast to power, is of some kind of solidification of power relations that can become relatively fixed in asymmetrical forms which cannot simply be resisted. He distinguishes power from a general system of domination exerted by one group over another: 'the over-all unity of a domination is not given at the start but is one of the terminal forms which power takes' (1984: 92). Best and Kellner (1991: 65) argue, however, that in his later work Foucault's 'emphasis on technologies of the self decentres the prior emphasis on power and domination'. Whereas feminism has sustained a political interest in opposing domination, Foucault's interest moved towards concern with how individuals shaped their own identities and constructed themselves as subjects. Best and Kellner (1991: 68) comment that Foucault's refusal to take a moral stand on power 'forces him into vague formulations, as when it prevents him from clarifying what our freedom should be from and for'.

This vagueness is noticeable in the concept of apparatus with which Foucault indicated connections between bodies, discourses and more stable forms of power. He uses apparatuses to recognise forms of power from the level of physical punishment to the level of institutions (Foucault 1980a). It is perhaps significant, though, that when he tries to clarify this term, he is in some difficulty. In a discussion (Foucault 1980b) he used the term 'apparatus' to indicate a 'heterogeneous ensemble' of elements which include discourses and also non-discursive elements. But when he was pressed by a questioner to clarify what such non-discursive elements could be, how apparatuses get 'beyond discourse' (ibid.: 197), Foucault falls back on a conceptual vocabulary rather different from his own. He talks in terms of 'institution' and the 'function' of a 'system of social constraint' (ibid.: 197–8). He then cuts off his questioner by stating that this distinction between discursive and non-discursive elements is not very important.

In the term 'apparatus' he appears to want to link up diverse aspects of forms of power, including those which are more established and institutional than the shifting programmes of discourses. But he is more interested in what an apparatus produces than why it takes the form that it does. He sees apparatuses as emerging in response to an 'urgent need' such as the need to control populations (ibid.: 195), but this does not explain why men's urgent need to defend their privilege is so much more successful than women's urgent need to defend their bodies.

In *Discipline and Punish* Foucault did characterise the prison system as well-defended power: 'rooted as it was in mechanisms and strategies of power, it could meet any attempt to transform it with a great force of inertia' (Foucault 1991: 305). But he did not see changing the specificity of the prison system over time as particularly difficult. If he had thought in terms of abolishing this entire system of control, he would perhaps have been closer to feminists' political dilemma in confronting men's power.

Foucault leaves feminists with a somewhat shadowy notion of consolidated male power in place, men's exercise of force unacknowledged, and women's freedom reduced to unstable local resistances which may change little.

CONCLUSION: MEN'S APPROPRIATION OF DESIRE

The question of whether we can find, conceptualise and oppose the middle ground of male power remains both as a problem of explanation and as one of political strategy. As Nancy Hartsock comments: 'To create a world that expresses our own various and diverse images, we need to understand how it works' (1990: 171–2).

One point which still nags both at feminism and at Foucault is that of how material life might structure, constrain or interact with social life; how far docile bodies are materially embodied. Young women's accounts of their sexuality can be interpreted as supporting the view that men have appropriated desire, and that sexuality is, in variable ways, both socially and materially embodied. There is a complex interaction between grounded embodiment, the discourses of sexuality and institutionalised power. Understanding this interaction is critical for targeting political struggles, but it remains an elusive area.

Although a few young women had reflected very critically upon their experience and set out to change their relationships with men and men's control over them, such reflection was difficult to achieve and very difficult to practise consistently. Young women can assert their pleasures in particular relationships, but can still be raped, lack skills in the market place, be paid less than men and be perceived as sexual objects. The reasons why women give way sexually to men are complex and contradictory; but our interpretations of our data do not support the view that they are explicable wholly in terms of discourses of sexuality or power situated *in* the intimate relationships of sexual encounters. Women's sexuality is contradictory in both contesting men's power, and contributing to its continued success, through women constituting themselves as acceptably feminine.

Foucault's work cannot resolve feminism's dilemma of what power is morally acceptable, nor how power *should* be exercised. He accepts that societies must have restrictions, but insists that individuals should be able to alter them (Foucault 1988e: 295). He says that there can be freedom of sexual choice but not freedom of sexual acts: 'because there are sexual acts like rape which should not be permitted whether they involve a man and a woman or two men' (ibid.: 289). This leaves us with an uncertain prospect for young women since we have found that not just rape and sexual abuse, but a whole range of sexual practice is socially produced in the interests of men. Women's bodies and pleasures can emerge, but only as unstable and in repeated struggles.

Foucault does not take seriously the entrenchment of men's power in every area of social life as a problem for women (and so for men too). The political experience of women daily subordinated by men, by masculinity, by the social construction of their bodies, makes resistance and change much more complex and problematic than Foucault seems to allow. Foucault enables us to find young women working hard at silencing their own desires, and supporting masculine domination of sexuality, through their careful constructions of feminine selves. But he leaves us unable to deal with the immensity of the consolidation of men's power.

NOTES

1 Foucault has a historical focus on aspects of European sexuality. Once sexuality is seen as historically produced, and historically variable, it cannot be assumed to be general across times and cultures without investigation.

2 By 'discourses', Foucault meant sets of rules at any given period which define what can be said – for example, about the truth of sexuality – and the limits of what can be said (see Chapter 1).

3 Feminist research on the micro-physics of body politics differs from Foucault's genealogical method in the way in which it is grounded in women's bodily experiences (see Martin 1989; Prendergast 1989; Thompson 1990; Waldby *et al.* 1991).

4 The Women, Risk and AIDS Project (WRAP) was staffed by the authors and Sue Scott, now at the University of Stirling; Sue Sharpe, free-lance writer and researcher; and Rachel Thomson, now at the Sex Education Forum of the UK National Children's Bureau, working collectively. It was financed by grants from the ESRC, Department of Health and Goldsmiths' College. WRAP used a purposive sample to interview 150 young women in London and Manchester in depth between 1988 and 1990. The Men, Risk and AIDS Project was a comparative study of forty-seven young men interviewed in London 1990–91. The study was financed by the Leverhulme Trust and Goldsmiths' College. Tim Rhodes, now at the Centre for Research on Drugs and Health Behaviour, was a team member on this project. Results are available as WRAP Papers from the Tufnell Press, 47 Dalmeny Rd, London N7 0DY, UK.

5 This does not mean that we consider that such differences are not socially significant, but that we have focused here on common experiences of the exercise of male power within sexual relations.

6 Essentialism implies some version of the belief that not only physical differences between women and men, but also the social differences between them, can be explained by biological dissimilarity. Diana Fuss (1989) usefully discusses the complexity of trying to distinguish what is essential from what is socially constructed, and argues that social constructionists 'do not definitively escape the pull of essentialism' (Fuss 1989: 5).

7 Some of the wider issues are brought up in Benton 1991, 1992; and Sharp 1992. Benton argues that if we are to abandon the body/mind dualism, we need to look again at conventional divisions of explanation between social and biological sciences.

8 By 'docile bodies' Foucault meant that in modern societies people did not generally have to be ruled by force from above. Individuals are produced as docile bodies through various forms and techniques of discipline, including those they exert over themselves (Foucault 1977).

BIBLIOGRAPHY

Bartky, S.L. (1990) *Femininity and Domination: Studies in the Phenomenology of Oppression*, London: Routledge.

Bell, V. (1991) 'Beyond the "thorny question": feminism, Foucault and the desexualisation of rape', *International Journal of the Sociology of Law*, 19: 83–100.

Benton, T. (1991) 'Biology and social science: why the return of the repressed should be given a (cautious) welcome', *Sociology*, 25(1): 1–30.

—— (1992) 'Why the welcome needs to be cautious: a reply to Keith Sharp', *Sociology*, 26(2): 225–32.

Best, S. and Kellner, D. (1991) *Postmodern Theory: Critical Interrogations*, Basingstoke and London: Macmillan.

Bordo, S. (1990) 'Material girl: the effacements of postmodern culture', *Michigan Quarterly Review*, Fall: 653–76.

Braidotti, R. (1991) *Patterns of Dissonance: A Study of Women in Contemporary Philosophy*, E. Guild (trans.),Cambridge: Polity Press.

Coveney, L., Jackson, M., Jeffreys, S., Kaye, L. and Mahony, P. (1984) *The Sexuality Papers: Male Sexuality and the Control of Women*, London: Hutchinson.

Dworkin, A. (1987) *Intercourse*, London: Arrow Books.

—— (1988) 'Dangerous and deadly', *Trouble and Strife*, 14: 42–5.

Fine, M. (1988) 'Sexuality, schooling, and adolescent females: the missing discourse of desire', *Harvard Educational Review*, 58(1): 29–53.

Foucault, M. (1977) *Discipline and Punish: The Birth of the Prison*, A. Sheridan (trans.), London: Penguin.

—— (1980a) 'Two lectures', in C. Gordon (ed.) *Michel Foucault: Power/Knowledge*, London: Harvester Wheatsheaf.

—— (1980b) 'The confession of the flesh', in C. Gordon (ed.) *Michel Foucault: Power/Knowledge*, London: Harvester Wheatsheaf.

—— (1980c) 'The eye of power', in C. Gordon (ed.) *Michel Foucault: Power/Knowledge*, London: Harvester Wheatsheaf.

—— (1984) *The History of Sexuality*, vol. I: *An Introduction*, London: Penguin.

—— (1988a) 'Truth, power, self: an interview with Michel Foucault', in L. Martin, H. Gutman and P. Hutton (eds) *Technologies of the Self: A Seminar with Michel Foucault*, London: Tavistock.

—— (1988b) 'Technologies of the self', in L. Martin, H. Gutman and P. Hutton (eds) *Technologies of the Self: A Seminar with Michel Foucault*, London: Tavistock.

—— (1988c) 'Politics and reason', in L. Kritzman (ed.) *Michel Foucault: Politics, Philosophy, Culture: Interviews and Other Writings 1977–1984*, A. Sheridan *et al.* (trans.), London: Routledge.

—— (1988d) 'Power and sex', in L. Kritzman (ed.) *Michel Foucault: Politics, Philosophy, Culture: Interviews and Other Writings 1977–1984*, A. Sheridan *et al.*, (trans.), London: Routledge.

—— (1988e) 'Sexual choice, sexual act: Foucault and homosexuality', in L. Kritzman (ed.) *Michel Foucault: Politics, Philosophy, Culture: Interviews and Other Writings 1977–1984*, A. Sheridan *et al.* (trans.), London: Routledge.

—— (1991) *Discipline and Punish: The Birth of the Prison*, London: Penguin.

Fraser, N. (1989) *Unruly Practices: Power, Discourse and Gender in Contemporary Social Theory*, Cambridge: Polity Press.

Fuss, D. (1989) *Essentially Speaking: Feminism, Nature and Difference*, London: Routledge.

Gatens, M. (1983) 'A critique of the sex/gender distinction', in J. Allen and P. Patten (eds) *Beyond Marx? Interventions after Marx*, Sydney: Intervention.

—— (1988) 'Towards a feminist philosophy of the body', in B. Caine, E.A. Grosz and M. de Lepervanche (eds) *Crossing Boundaries: Feminisms and the Critique of Knowledge*, Sydney: Allen & Unwin.

Gordon, C. (ed.) (1980) *Michel Foucault: Power/Knowledge: Selected Interviews and Other Writings 1972–77 by Michel Foucault*, London: Harvester Wheatsheaf.

Grosz, E. (1990) 'Inscriptions and body-maps: representation and the corporeal', in T. Threadgold and A. Cranny-Francis (eds) *Feminine, Masculine and Representation*, London: Allen & Unwin.

Hanmer, J. and Maynard, M. (1987) *Women, Violence and Social Control*, London: Macmillan.

Harding, S. (1992) 'The instability of the analytical categories of feminist theory', in H. Crowley and S. Himmelweit (eds) *Knowing Women: Feminism and Knowledge*, Cambridge: Polity Press in association with the Open University.

Hartsock, N. (1990) 'Foucault on power: a theory for women?', in L. Nicholson (ed.) *Feminism/Postmodernism*, London: Routledge.

Hekman, S. (1990) *Gender and Knowledge: Elements of a Postmodern Feminism*, Cambridge: Polity Press.

Holland, J. (1992) *Sexuality and Ethnicity: Variations in Young Women's Sexual Knowledge and Practice*, WRAP Paper No. 8, London: Tufnell Press.

Holland, J., Ramazanoğlu, C., Scott, S., Sharpe, S. and Thomson, R. (1992a) 'Pressure, resistance, empowerment: young women and the negotiation of safer sex', in P. Aggleton, P. Davies and G. Hart (eds) *AIDS Rights, Risk and Reason*, London: Falmer.

Holland, J., Ramazanoğlu, C., Sharpe, S. and Thomson, R. (1992b) 'Pleasure, pressure and power: some contradictions of gendered sexuality', *Sociological Review*, 40 (4): 645–74.

—— (1992c) 'Power and desire: the embodiment of female sexuality', Paper given at the *First International Conference on Girls and Girlhood*, Amsterdam.

Hollway, W. (1984) 'Women's power in heterosexual sex', *Women's Studies International Forum*, 7(1): 63–8.

Jaggar, A. (1983) *Feminist Politics and Human Nature*, Brighton: Harvester.

Lather, P. (1991) *Getting Smart: Feminist Research and Pedagogy with/in the Postmodern*, London: Routledge.

Kelly, L. (1988) *Surviving Sexual Violence*, Cambridge: Polity Press.

Kritzman, L. (ed.) (1988) *Michel Foucault: Politics, Philosophy, Culture: Interviews and Other Writings 1977–1984*, A. Sheridan *et al.* (trans), London: Routledge.

Martin, E. (1989) *The Woman in the Body*, Milton Keynes: Open University Press.

Martin, L., Gutman, H. and Hutton, P. (eds) (1988) *Technologies of the Self: A Seminar with Michel Foucault*, London: Tavistock.

Morris, M. (1979) 'The pirate's fiancée', in M. Morris and P. Patton (eds) *Michel Foucault: Power, Truth, Strategy*, Sydney: Feral Publications.

Prendergast, Shirley (1989) 'Girl's experience of menstruation in schools', in L. Holly (ed.) *Girls and Sexuality Teaching and Learning*, Milton Keynes: Open University Press.

rhodes, d. and McNeill, S. (1985) *Women against Violence against Women*, London: Onlywomen Press.

Sawicki, J. (1991) *Disciplining Foucault: Feminism, Power and the Body*, London: Routledge.

Sayers, J. (1982) *Biological Politics: Feminist and Anti-feminist Perspectives*, London: Tavistock.

Sharp, K. (1992) 'Biology and social science: a reply to Ted Benton', *Sociology*, 26 (2): 225–32.

Smith, D. (1988) 'Femininity as discourse', in L.G. Roman and L.K. Christian-Smith with E. Ellsworth, *Becoming Feminine*, London: Falmer.

Stanko, E.A. (1985) *Intimate Intrusions: Women's Experience of Male Violence*, London: Routledge & Kegan Paul.

Thompson, S. (1990) 'Putting a big thing into a little hole: teenage girls' accounts of sexual initiation', *The Journal of Sex Research*, 27(3): 341–61.

Vance, C. (1992) 'Social construction theory: problems in the history of sexuality', in H. Crowley and S. Himmelweit (eds) *Knowing Women: Feminism and Knowledge*, Cambridge: Polity Press in association with the Open University.

Waldby, C., Kippax, S. and Crawford, J. (1991) 'Equality and eroticism: AIDS and the active/passive distinction', *Social Semiotics*, 1(2).

Walkowitz, J. (1985) 'Male vice and feminist virtue: feminism and the politics of prostitution in nineteenth-century Britain', in V. Beechey and J. Donald (eds) *Subjectivity and Social Relations*, Milton Keynes: Polity Press.

Wilton, T. (1991) 'Feminism and the erotics of health promotion', Paper given at the *Fifth Conference on the Social Aspects of AIDS*, London.

Name index

Adams, P. 236
Allen, H. 93
Althusser, L. 159
Angelou, M. 233
Apollon, W. 235
Arendt, H. 213

Balbus, I. 75, 80
Barret-Klegel, B. 86
Bartkowski, F. 48, 222
Bartky, S. 53, 60, 67, 104, 155, 156–7, 250
Bass, E. 225–6, 227
Baudrillard, J. 195
Bell, V. 244
Best, S. 258
Bhaskar, R. 89
Bland, L. 151
Bordo, S. 31–2, 53, 67, 141, 142, 206
Bouchard, D.F. 229
Braidotti, R. 139, 140, 239, 250
Brownmiller, S. 106
Butler, J. 31, 100, 116, 151, 158, 194, 234

Cain, M. 83, 88, 94
Campbell, K. 159, 162, 167
Cardinal, M. 205
Castel, R. 81
Chernin, K. 101
Chodorow, N. 120
Collins, A. 187
Cornum, R. 208
Coveney, L. 245

Daly, M. 57, 106, 120
Davis, K. 188
Davis, L. 225–6, 227
Dews, P. 49, 55
Diamond, I. 31
Dollimore, J. 33
Dreyfus, H. 79, 92, 172
Dworkin, A. 57, 183–4, 185, 246

Eagleton, T. 37, 49, 64, 65–6, 69
Eaton, M. 93
Eichenbaum, L. 152, 153
Elshtain, J. 99
Ernst, S. 152, 153

Fanon, F. 225, 234
Fine, M. 245
Fiske, J. 193–4
Flax, J. 127
Fraser, N. 55, 239, 256
Fuss, D. 241, 261

Gatens, M. 240, 251
Gilligan, C. 120, 141, 145
Gramsci, A. 88, 163
Greer, G. 181
Griffin, S. 142, 143
Grosz, E. 251

Habermas, J. 29
Haraway, D.J. 100
Harding, S. 74, 88, 251
Hartsock, N. 88, 127, 133, 160, 161, 163, 243, 259
Hekman, S.J. 128, 135, 155, 163,

Subject index